IMAGES
of America

PORTAL OF THE CHIRICAHUAS

On the Cover: Taken by coauthor Deborah Galloway in 2014, this photograph of Cave Creek Canyon shows Cathedral Rock towering at left, facing the Pinnacles with the shaded creek winding between. In winter, white sycamore trunks and evergreens have stark beauty; while the cliffs, veiled in mists, glowing rose and gold, or crowned with thunderheads, are always sublime. (Deborah Galloway.)

IMAGES
of America

PORTAL OF THE CHIRICAHUAS

Deborah Galloway and Jeanne Williams

ARCADIA
PUBLISHING

ISBN 978-1-4671-1514-8

Published by Arcadia Publishing
Charleston, South Carolina

Printed in the United States of America

Library of Congress Control Number: 2016930460

For all general information, please contact Arcadia Publishing:
Telephone 843-853-2070
Fax 843-853-0044
E-mail sales@arcadiapublishing.com
For customer service and orders:
Toll-Free 1-888-313-2665

Visit us on the Internet at www.arcadiapublishing.com

To Sally Spofford, who released birds and spirits to the sky, and to Alden Hayes. He had stories for every trail and loved to share them.

Contents

ACKNOWLEDGMENTS

I fell in love with the Chiricahuas on a 1975 backpacking trip with Bill Broyles's Tucson group, but I never dreamed I would live here among friends and neighbors who have helped create this book. Deby and I hope they will feel it is their book, a legacy from earlier times.

Roy "Bud" Hiatt cleaned and annotated photographs saved by his uncle, Jim Frank Cox. Pamela Hulme shared the story and photographs of Willie Mae Sanders, her grandmother. Barbara Miller supplied Maryan and Blackie Stidham's photographs and her own images. Zola Stoltz loaned Maloney/Sanders albums and recounted their heritage. R.W. Morrow's letters were augmented by his son, Michael Morrow, who sent photographs and answered questions about his family. Carson Morrow's Bull Sheet evokes the mid-1950s. Izzy Escobar located Gomez family photographs that capture Rodeo. Mary Winkler's photographs, encouragement, and information have heartened me. Myrtle Bagwell Young reminisced about the Pugsleys and gave photographs. Mel Moe, Mary Willy, Joy and Ray Mendez, and Bill Cavaliere were generous with photographs and knowledge, as was Reed Peters, who also proofread. Thanks for photographs go to Howard Topoff, Helen Snyder, Kim Gee, Shane Burchfield, Barbara Roth, Sally Richards, Frances Grill, Barry Fagan, Sherry Nelson, Phyllis Morreale de la Garza, Tim Lawson, Kim Murphy, Jonathan Patt, Zac Ribbing (Coronado National Forest), Don Wadsworth, Tom Davidson and Karen Tweedy-Holmes. Thanks also go to the National Archives and the Coronado National Forest for images.

Dr. Nancy and Dick Reddy of the Duffner History Project sent us a trove of early Paradise photographs. Bill Gillespie, Coronado National Forest archaeologist, advised and gave information. Debb Johnson helped with problems and took specific photographs. Tamara Winkler, Bonnie Catanzaro, Delane Blondeau, Joan Jensen, Vicki Beno, and Candace Beumler Pardee made pertinent comments, as did Gerry Hernbrode and Orchid Davis, who read text and cheered me on. Laura Zeuner, at all hours, tamed my computer. I especially thank Karen and Eric Hayes for photographs and access to Alden's files.

Henry Clougherty has guided us through this endeavor with unfailing patience, useful advice, and judicious urging. I have worked with many people in publishing; he is the best.

INTRODUCTION

Southeastern Arizona, where the Chiricahua Mountains, under various names, stretch for 150 miles to the Mexican border, was not part of the United States until the Gadsden Purchase was ratified in 1854. The United States paid Mexico $10 million for land below the Gila River, from the Rio Grande to the Colorado River. A railroad route through this region to California was considered the best option, but one senator joked, "Now we should pay Mexico ten million to take it back." Still, some forty-niners headed for the Gold Rush noticed forested gashes in distant cliffs as would California Column volunteers marching to repel Confederate forces. Early in 1861, Cochise, a leader of the Chiricahuas, was unjustly arrested, but escaped. Some of his relatives were hanged and he retaliated. The Civil War loomed. Troops were ordered east, and the Butterfield Stage stopped running. Cochise and other Apaches raided encroaching miners and settlers even after soldiers returned. He was weary of battle, however, and in October, 1872, his friend Tom Jeffords helped negotiate a peace that gave Cochise's band a reservation covering most of their traditional territory, with Jeffords as agent. Cochise died in 1874; Jeffords retired; and in 1876, the new agent ordered the Chiricahuas to San Carlos, already inhabited by incompatible bands. The Chiricahuas, used to roaming free, repeatedly escaped the reservation for Mexico, killing any whites they met. They still raided through what had been their country. Soldiers were sent to quell the raiders. In 1886, Geronimo made his final surrender. All the Chiricahuas who could be found, including scouts who had tracked them down, were shipped by train to Florida.

Apaches, though they loved their homeland, were comparative newcomers. Over 10,000 years before, big-game hunters wandered into the valleys surrounding the mountains. As the climate grew hotter and dryer, they were followed by people more dependent on wild plants and, eventually, on farming. Mogollon Culture villages thrived in the canyons by AD 1200 but these were abandoned by 1400 because of searing drought. Apaches may have reached the mountains before the gold-seeking Spaniards of 1540 passed by. Traces of a Spanish mine have been found at the mouth of Whitetail Canyon, but there were no settlements in the Chiricahuas though the tireless Jesuit missionary Padre Kino followed the San Pedro River north to where it joined the Gila. He established 24 missions and chapels between 1687 and his death in 1711, including San Xavier, still in use near Tucson. Spain's small frontier garrisons could not defend settlers, mines, and ranches, nor could Mexico after winning independence in 1820. The raiding plunder was an important part of Apache economy; they left enough livestock to produce a new crop for their next visit.

Even before the Apaches were marched to San Carlos, prospectors were venturing into the mountains. In 1879, Stephen Reed built his cabin, now the research station director's home, where the North Fork of Cave Creek joins the main creek. Brannick Riggs chose land near the present Chiricahua National Monument, and the mining camp of Galeyville mushroomed in 1881. It was frequented by so-called cowboys who rustled cattle from Arizona to sell in Mexico and vice versa. Supplying beef to reservation Indians and military posts was profitable, and small ranches increased. The Southern Pacific Railroad reached San Simon in 1880, giving men like Reed a market only 35 miles away for his farm products and a shipping point for his cattle. In the mid-1880s, James Parramore and Claiborne Merchant brought in thousands of Texas cattle and organized the San Simon Cattle and Canal Company, which dominated the valley until it was dissolved around 1920.

In early November 1885, a Chiricahua named Ulzana crossed from Mexico into New Mexico and, with only 10 men, terrified the whole region, eluding troops while losing only one warrior. Gus Chenowth was on his way home December 27 with a load of salvage from deserted, short-lived Galeyville when he saw mounted Apaches ahead. He stood up and brandished his rifle. The horsemen angled away. At Turkey Creek, Ulzana's band killed two men, the last of the 38 killed on their 1,200-mile circuit. Four troops of Fort Bowie cavalry lost Ulzana's trail in a blizzard, and the warriors vanished into Mexico. Nine months later, most the Chiricahuas were on a train to Florida. Hundreds evaded capture and lived on in the Sierra Madre. A few, like Masai, escaped from the train and made their way back to the mountains. Burt Lancaster stars in the 1972 film *Ulzana's Raid*, based on that chief's exploits, escape, and return to the mountains.

Those mountains and the valleys below needed protection years before 1902, when Theodore Roosevelt's proclamation set aside 16,900 acres as the Chiricahua Forest Reserve. Much of the best timber had already been logged for mines—especially Bisbee's Copper Queen—as well as for construction and fuel. The earliest sawmills of 1879 sold lumber to Fort Bowie and filled orders from as far away as Tucson. The forest reserve required logging permits, and in 1907, when the reserve became the Chiricahua National Forest, cattle no longer wandered freely along the creek but were limited by grazing permits calculated on the land's carrying capacity. Large corporations had recklessly overstocked the range. It never recovered from the ravages of the 1892–1893 drought, but ranchers, like those of the Malpais Borderlands Group, have done much to control grazing and improve wildlife habitat. Commercial agriculture is no longer viable, though many people cherish fruit trees and gardens.

Dreams of mining wealth, a spur railroad, and Portal as a premier city vanished when Paradise's Chiricahua Mine closed in 1908. Hilltop operated from 1915 until the 1930s but was never a bonanza. The real treasure of the mountains is their wild beauty, birds, and animals. This was acknowledged by the founding of the American Museum of Natural History's Southwestern Research Station in 1956. Of the thousands of scientists and students who have worked there, a number bought property here and retired to it. Some nature-loving visitors come every year, and they often succumb and make homes here.

One poignant mark of a community's decline, as in the case of both Paradise and Hilltop, is the loss of its school. Portal School expanded with children from sister towns but lost its own identity in 1974, though its buildings and grounds are the heart of the village: library, bookstore, historical society, post office, and venue for St. Patrick's Day parade, Christmas caroling, and Oktoberfest. Amazingly, on the road to Skeleton Canyon, Apache Elementary endures after 100 years.

Unencumbered by officialdom, and not much missing it, residents appreciate Frances Grill's clinic and Portal Rescue's EMTs and firefighters. Sky Village has brought new blood, vitality, and an inspiration to look upward, as well as around us. Ironically, the frontier of dark, unpolluted skies is increasingly under attack. That stars should dim is in its celestial way as devastating as the fires, floods, and earthquakes the canyon has endured.

Just so but with much dread, Apaches have viewed railroads, plowed land, mines, and the engulfing tide of foreigners. The Apaches have come back, honored guests during a Cochise College historical trip into Mexico, and some took part in the 1986 centennial reenactment of the cessation of hostilities celebrated in Fort Bowie where Mountain Spirits danced.

Always found where they once lived are rocks like small stone islands sculpted with hollows where women chatted, grinding seeds and roots, while babies watched from cradleboards and older children played.

One

Moccasin, Hoof, and Wagon Tracks

Apaches from the far north must have reached the grasslands beneath the towering Chiricahua Mountains after the land recovered from the drought that drove the Mogollon people to abandon farming villages in the canyons by 1400 and ten thousand years after hunters speared mammoths and giant bison. There were four bands of Chiricahuas; the ones most important in this book, the Chokonen, Red Cliff People, will be referred to simply as Chiricahuas or Apaches. They roamed the mountains of that name and valleys on both sides.

Spanish expeditions—probably including Coronado in 1540—traveled up the San Simon Valley to the Gila River. Even though they found no golden cities, the Spanish Crown offered huge land grants to populate its frontier, and a few forts and missions were established. Settlements and ranches were enthusiastically raided by Apaches and Jocomes, who may have descended from Mogollons. They looted livestock, corn, clothing, and other good things.

Trying to persuade the Indians to settle peacefully near forts or missions in return for rations did not work, nor did the governor of Chihuahua's bounty of 100 pesos for each Apache scalp. Mexico won independence in 1820 but lost its war for Texas in 1836. Ten years later, a costly war with the United States ended with Mexico ceding all territory north of the Gila River and Rio Grande in February 1848. Only eight days before the Treaty of Guadalupe Hidalgo, gold was discovered in California.

The rush was on. Thousands swarmed west, most taking a route in sight of the Chiricahua Mountains, land still part of Mexico. Need for a transcontinental railroad led to the Gadsden Purchase in 1853. The United States paid $10 million for the region from the Gila River to the yet-to-be determined border, though Kit Carson declared the region "so desolated, desert and God-forsaken that a wolf could not make a living on it."

The Apaches could not have welcomed the flood of forty-niners, but it is said that Cochise's band furnished the Butterfield Overland Mail station in Apache Pass with firewood. In 1861, the chief was mistakenly accused of a kidnapping. He escaped, but soldiers hanged some of his relatives. Cochise's feud with whites coincided with the Civil War. The Butterfield stage stopped running, troops were called east, and it might have seemed the intruders were gone.

After the war, in 1872, Cochise's friend Tom Jeffords induced the chief to make peace on condition that the Apaches could remain on a reservation that covered most of their customary range. Cochise died two years later. In 1876, the reservation was closed and the band sent to San Carlos.

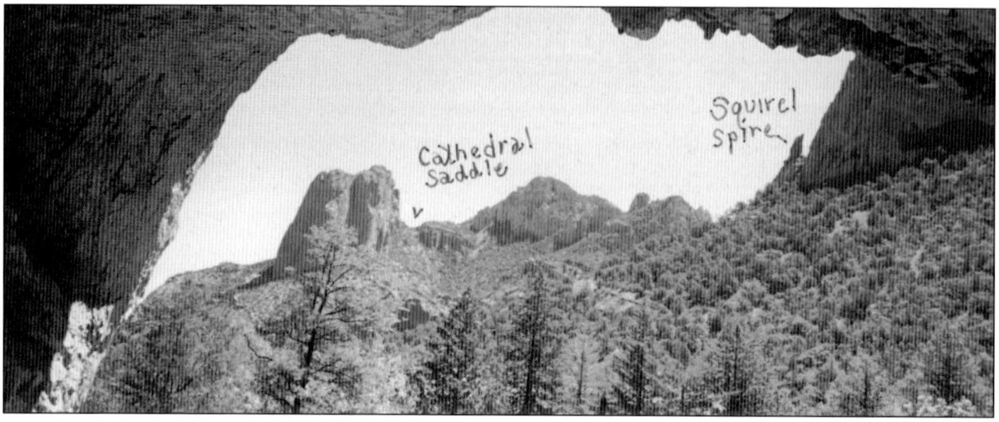

The above photograph gives an unusual view of Cathedral Rock towering above the mouth of Cave Creek Canyon, named for its many caverns. The interiors of most larger caves are blackened by centuries of fires that have warmed humans since they first wandered into this region after the Ice Age. The photograph below is of a Clovis Culture amulet, skillfully crafted of flint, which was probably worn for success in hunting. Could the man who wore it have gazed from this opening to the opposite cliffs 12,000 years ago? Mammoth bones have not yet been found on the east side of the Chiricahuas, but they have been uncovered to the west. (Above, Kim Murphy; below, Mel Moe.)

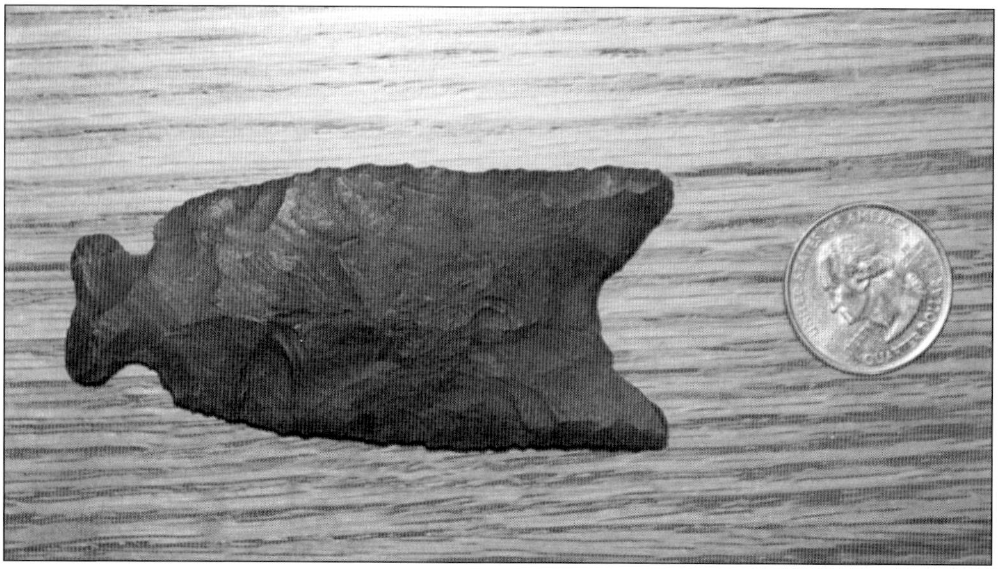

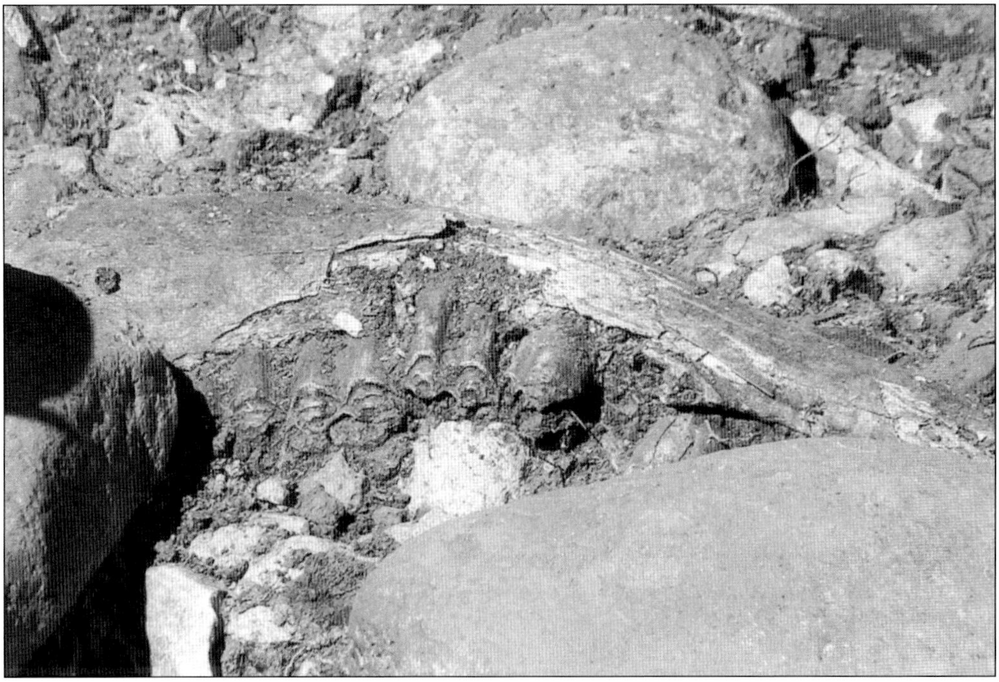

Giant bison once roamed the grasslands between mountain ranges. This photograph is of a jawbone from one of them, exposed in a recent archaeological excavation at the Cave Creek Cienega. The bone dates back to the hunter-gatherer Cochise Culture. The beast may have been killed by projectile points like the one in the photograph below. As bison and mammoths became extinct, either from overhunting and/or an increasingly hotter climate that diminished grazing, humans relied greatly on wild foods like seeds, berries, nuts, roots, and roasted agave hearts. Instead of the long spears of Clovis big-game hunters, they used wooden throwing sticks to send light spears streaking toward deer, antelope, and other quarry. (Both, Mel Moe.)

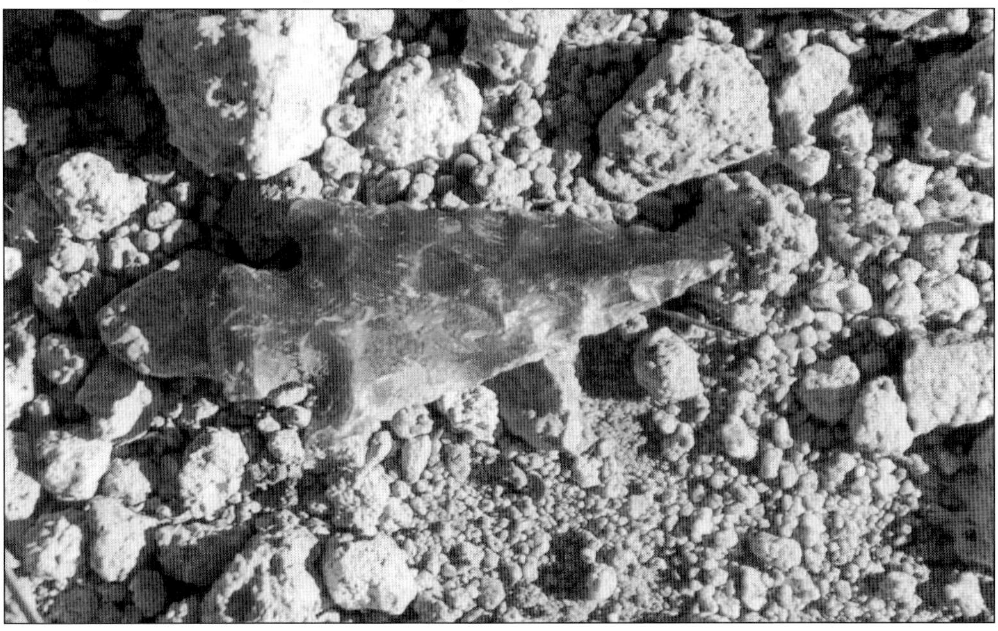

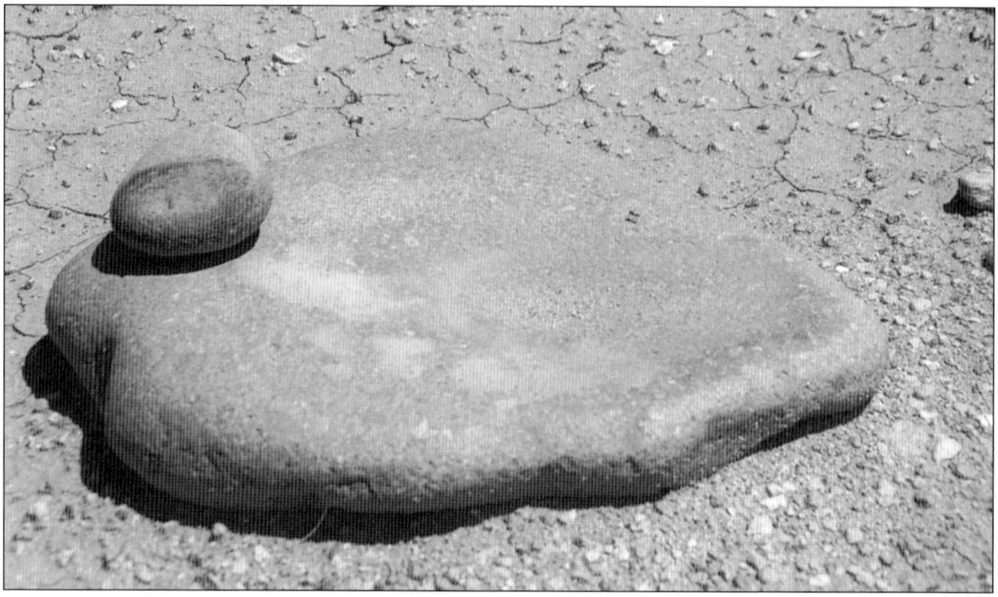

Hunting was still important after big game was extinct, but wild foods were even more depended upon, and people moved according to the seasons when these ripened, living in caves or temporary shelters. Metates and manos like those in above photograph were used in the Cochise Culture to grind seeds and roots and more and better corn when the Mogollon Culture began around AD 100 to 200. Trade with Mexico introduced pottery, squash, beans, and bows and arrows. These fed growing populations that settled where they could tend their crops. Villages thrived by about 1200 in the mouth of every suitable canyon. Scorching drought drove the Mogollons northward by 1400. The photograph below is of one of the Mogollon granaries where they stored corn and other food. The Apaches made similar caches. (Both, Mel Moe.)

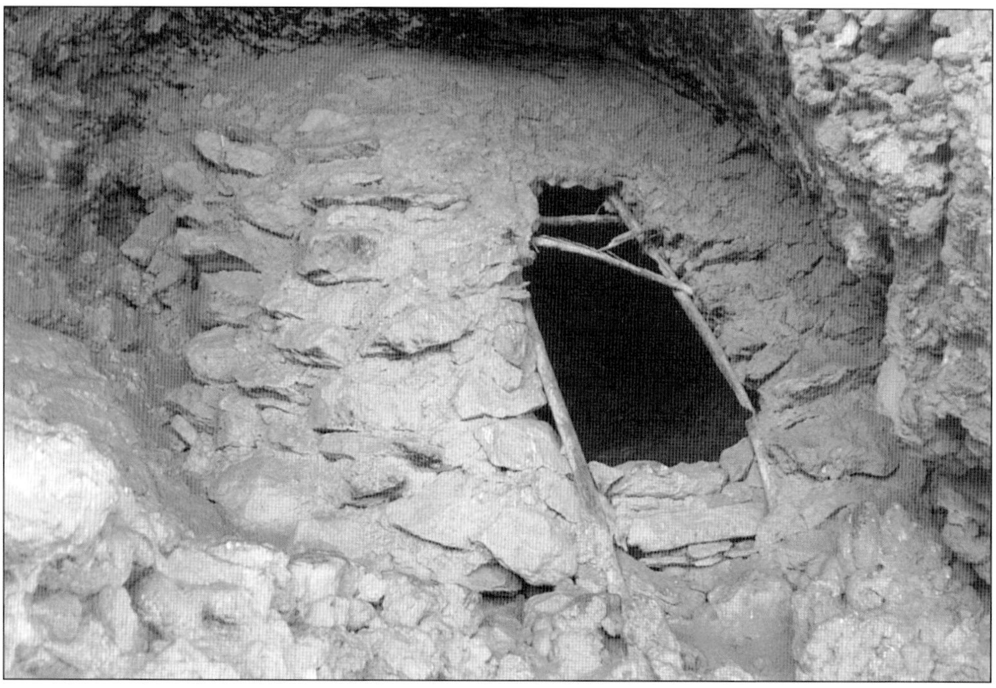

An Apache bride wears her beautiful clothing and jewelry in the 1886 photograph at right. Girls and boys played together until they were five or six but became shy of each other as they grew older. A marriageable girl might ask a boy she fancied to help her with some heavy task, or she could choose him as a dance partner. When he wrapped his blanket around her, it proclaimed their affection. If she accepted the bride gift given by the young man to her family, she rode to his camp. When she expected a baby, she was not coddled, but neither was she allowed to do hard work. As she knelt, gripping a stake, the most skilled midwife delivered the baby and performed the birth ceremony. The photograph below shows the cradleboard into which the infant was strapped snugly and where it would spend most of the time until able to crawl. (Both, Ben Wittick, National Archives.)

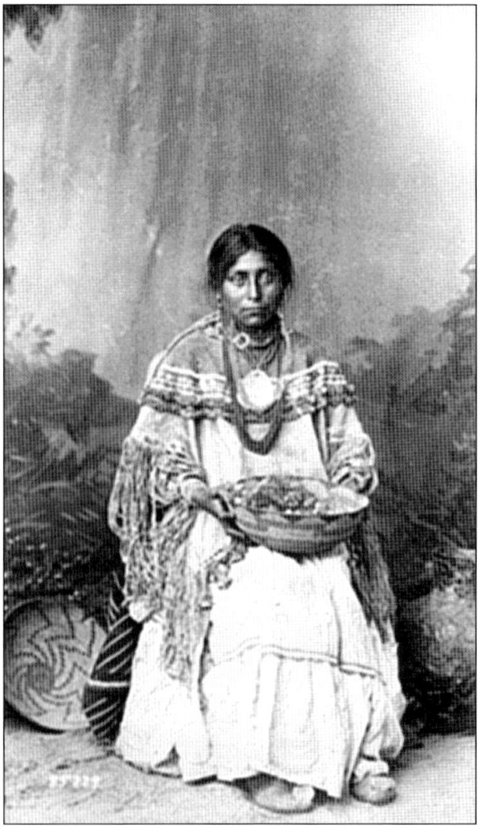

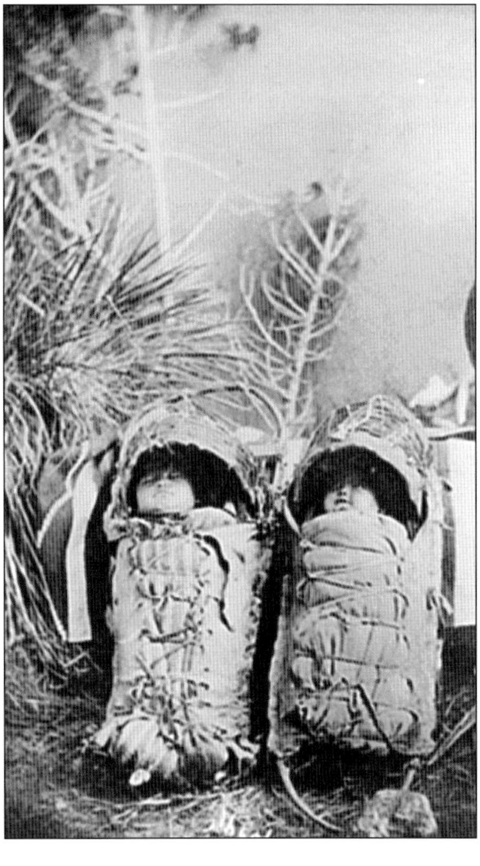

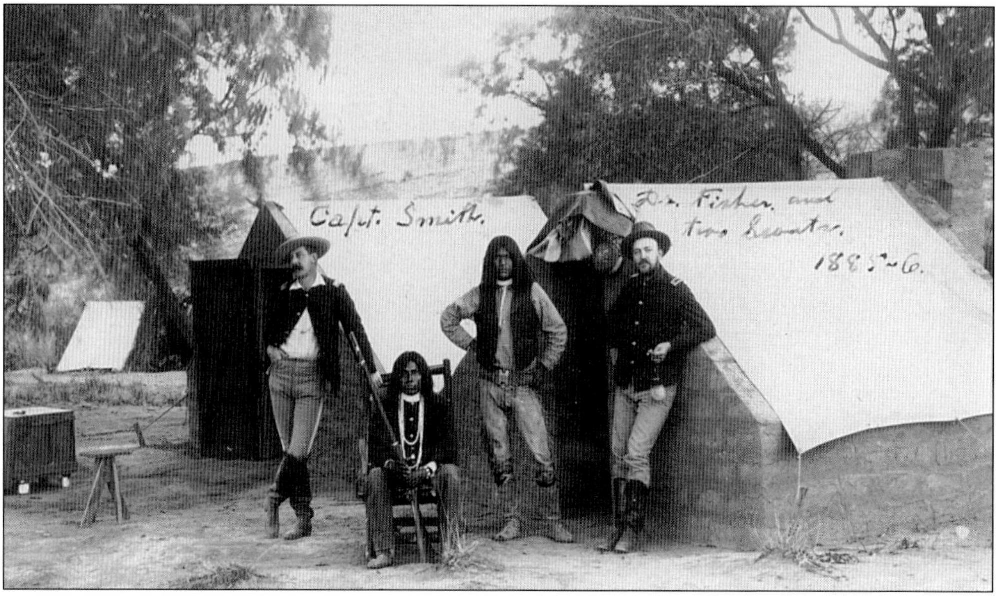

Two officers and two scouts rest at the Mud Springs outpost. Small detachments were often deployed to watch for raiders at watering places in this thirsty land. Gen. George Crook recruited scouts to track down Apaches who had fled the reservation. This was not treachery in that the various bands fought each other and allegiance was to individual groups and leaders. (Coronado National Forest.)

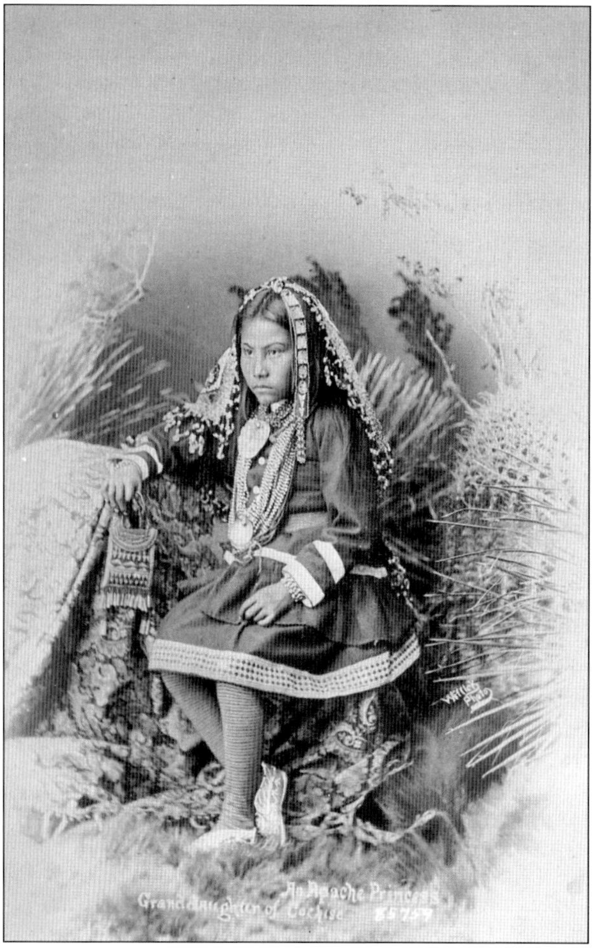

Despite her finery, the girl in this photograph looks pensive. The granddaughter of Cochise, she is probably the child of Naiche, chief of the Chokonen Chiricahuas after the death of Cochise, and his eldest son, Taza. Naiche and Geronimo surrendered in Skeleton Canyon east of the Chiricahua Mountains in early September 1886. (Ben Wittick, National Archives.)

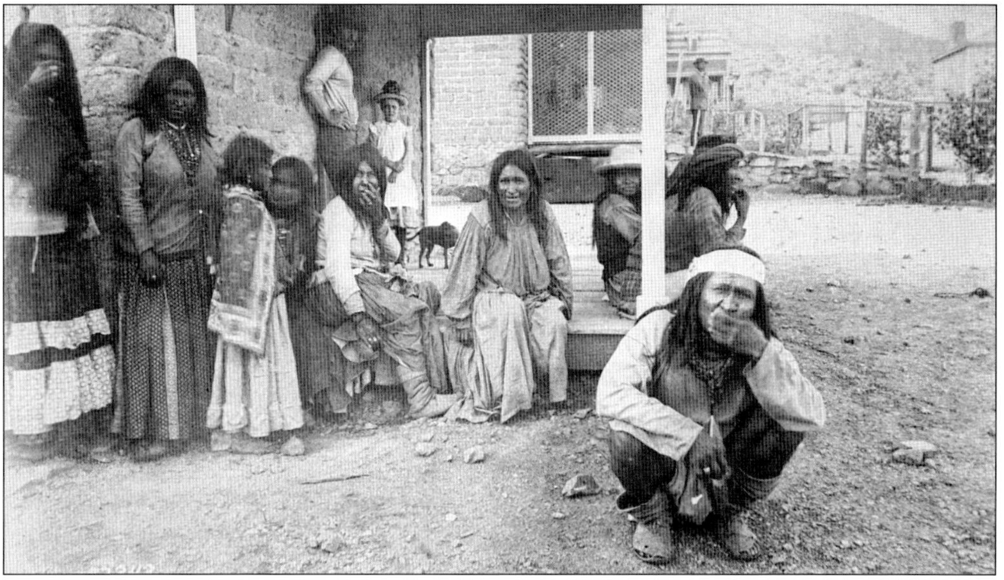

Like the Indians in this 1886 photograph, all the Chiricahuas who could be found, including Army scouts who had helped track the others down, were gathered at Fort Bowie as prisoners of war. On September 8, taken in wagons the 11 miles to Bowie Station, they were put on a train to Florida, never to see their home mountains and valleys again. (Ben Wittick, National Archives.)

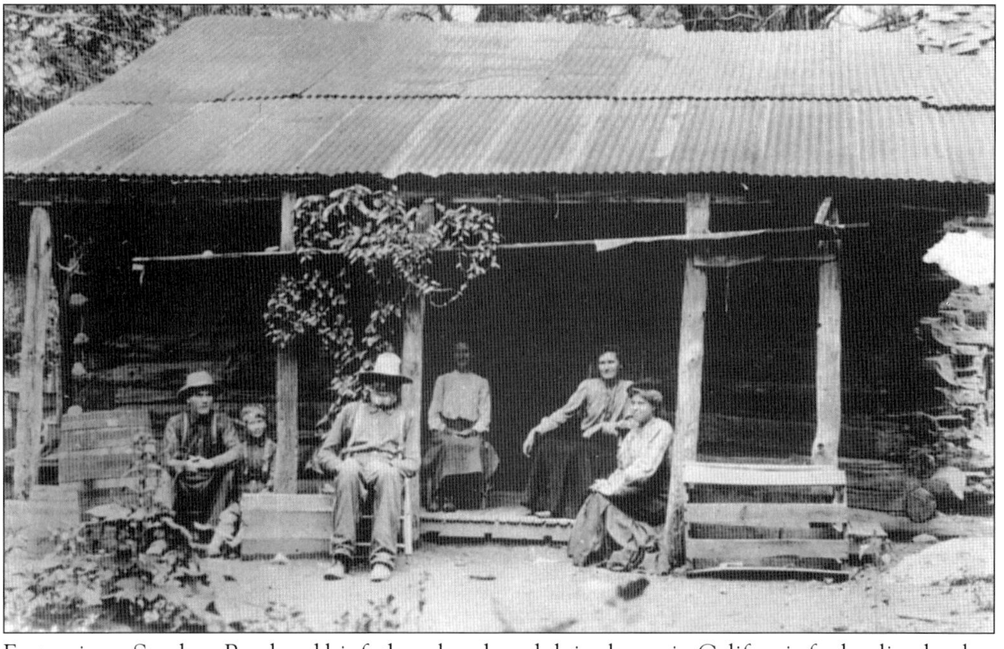

Forty-niners Stephen Reed and his father abandoned sluice boxes in California for hauling lumber to growing towns. Reed married, started farming, and fathered a son. When his wife died, he married a widow with an infant daughter. In 1875, the family moved to the Gila River, where Reed's second wife died. He had never forgotten a green canyon he had glimpsed in the mountains on his way west 30 years ago. Hearing in 1876 that the Chiricahua Reservation was open, he took his son and stepdaughter south. In 1879, four densely wooded miles from the mouth of Cave Creek Canyon, they built the cabin in this 1890s photograph. (Alden Hayes.)

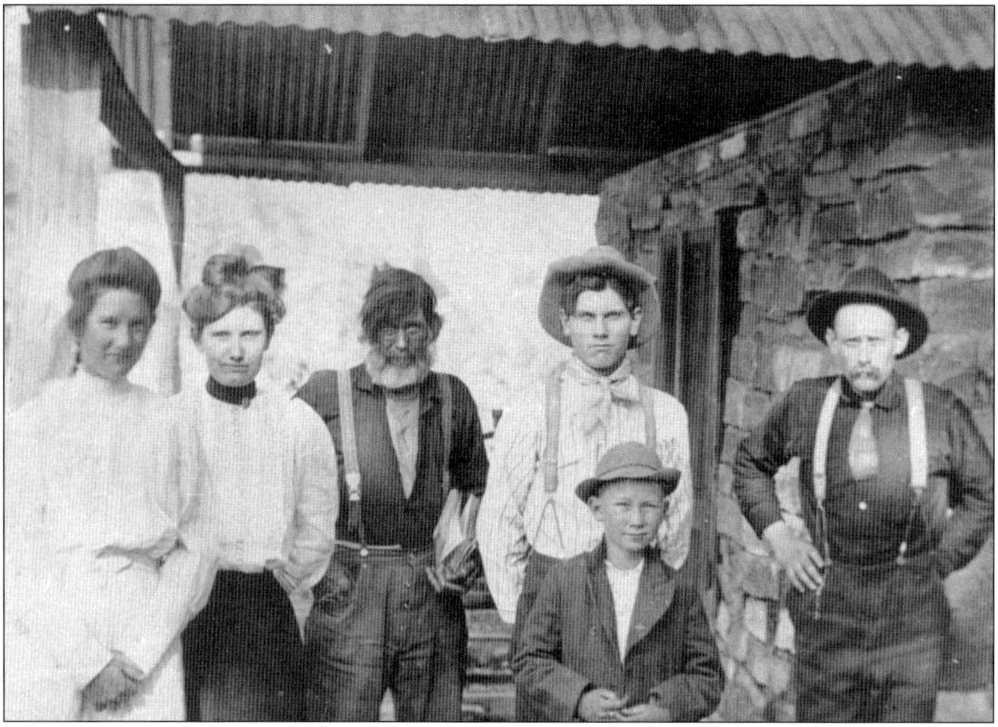

The Reed cabin stood near a warm spring where the forks of Cave Creek join. In time, the family ate well from a garden, grains, chickens, cows, hogs, and a famed orchard. Reed married his 15-year-old stepdaughter Isabelle in 1882. They had five children before she died in 1898. In this 1907 photograph, Reed (center) is shown with, from left to right, Alice, Claudie, Walter, Bill (seated), and John Hands. Most of the Reeds are buried on a slope above the cabin; Wesley, Stephen's eldest son, was there only shortly before he was joined by young Alfred Hands from Scotland. With his older brothers, Frank and John, Alfred built a cabin at the Cave Creek Cienega. While they prospected, he tended the goats. He was killed by a small band of Apaches in late March 1886. (Above, Alden Hayes; below, Bill Cavaliere.)

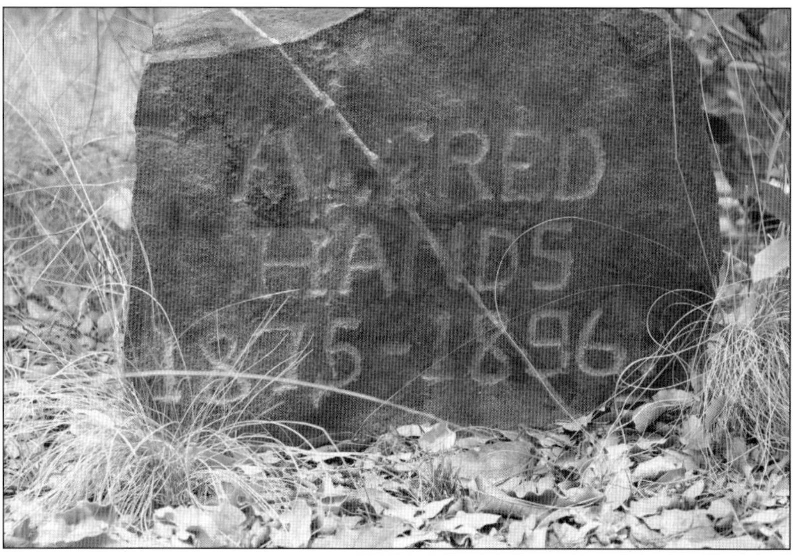

In 1882, Chief of Scouts Al Sieber recruited Ski-be-nan-ted, who served well on General Crook's 1883 Sierra Madre expedition. Ski-be-nan-ted rose to sergeant, and when a fracas broke out at San Carlos, Sieber trusted the scout to calm matters. Finding his father killed, the sergeant killed the murderer as was Apache custom. An enraged Sieber arrested Ski-be-nan-ted; he got away but turned himself in. Sentenced to prison, he escaped for good. Shown in this 1889 photograph, Ski-be-nan-ted terrorized southeastern Arizona and was called the "Apache Kid." (National Archives.)

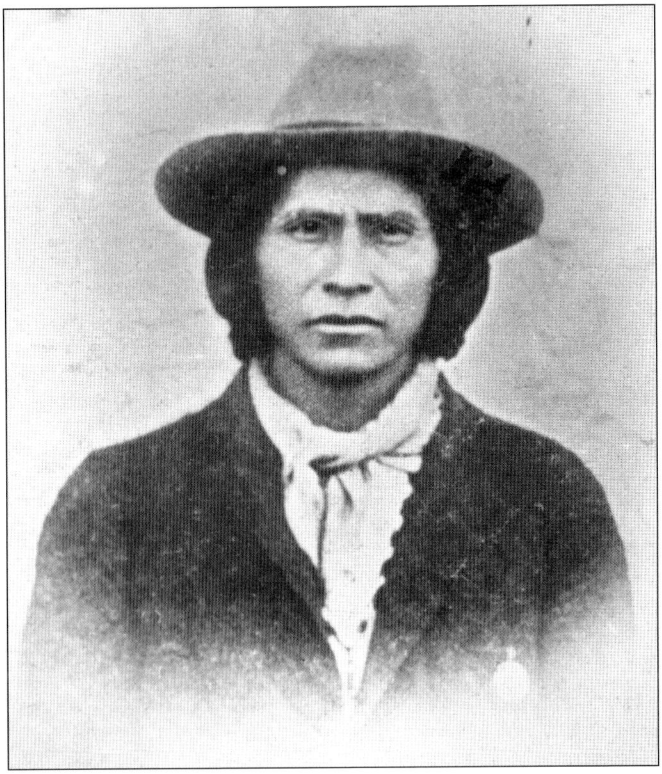

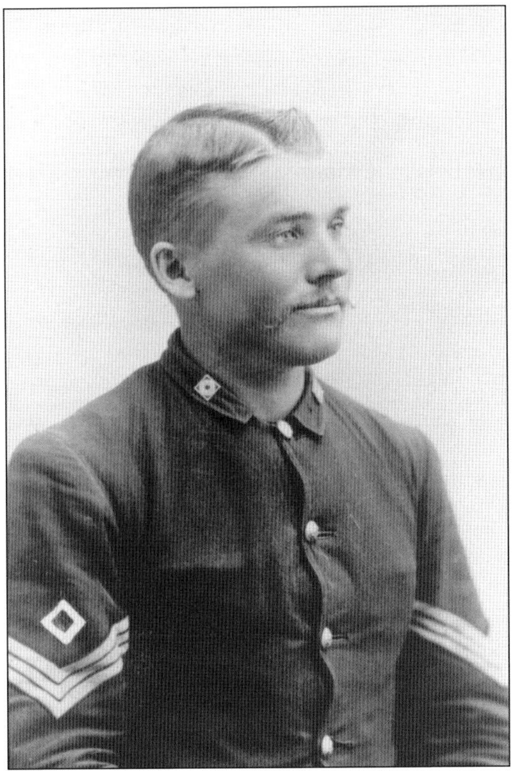

Neil Erickson was 22 in 1878 when he enlisted in the Army, partly to avenge the Sioux's killing of his father. Shown in this 1883 photograph, Erickson volunteered for southwest duty with the 4th Cavalry. After service in Texas and New Mexico, the sergeant was ordered to Fort Huachuca in 1884 and assigned to drive the wagon of an officer's Swedish housekeeper, Emma Peterson, to Fort Bowie. They married in 1887. (National Park Service.)

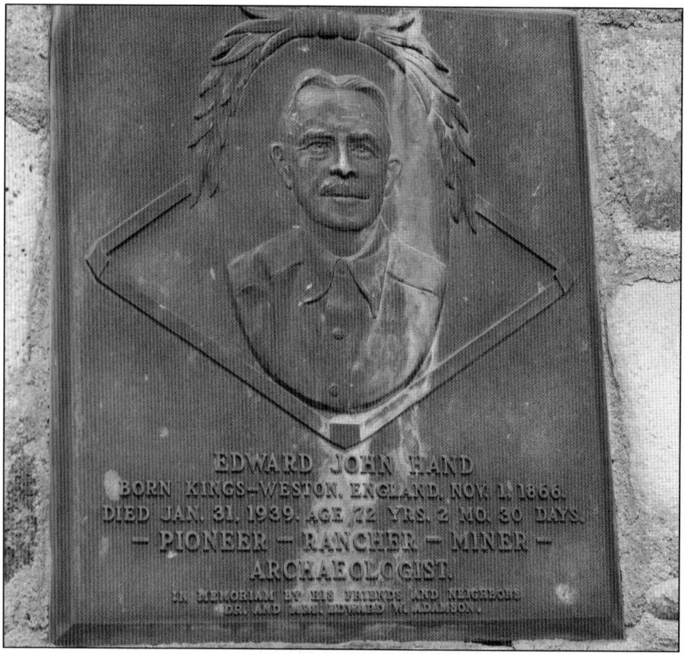

The murder of Alfred Hands in 1896 is often blamed on the Apache Kid, but it could have been any of the bands who raided their old homeland from the Sierra Madre where many fled to avoid exile. John Hands would never speak of his brother's death. He and his brothers kept working their claim, and in 1915, Chicago investors paid $120,000 for it. Hands's monument (pictured) faces the museum where he, an amateur archaeologist, stored his findings. (Bill Cavaliere.)

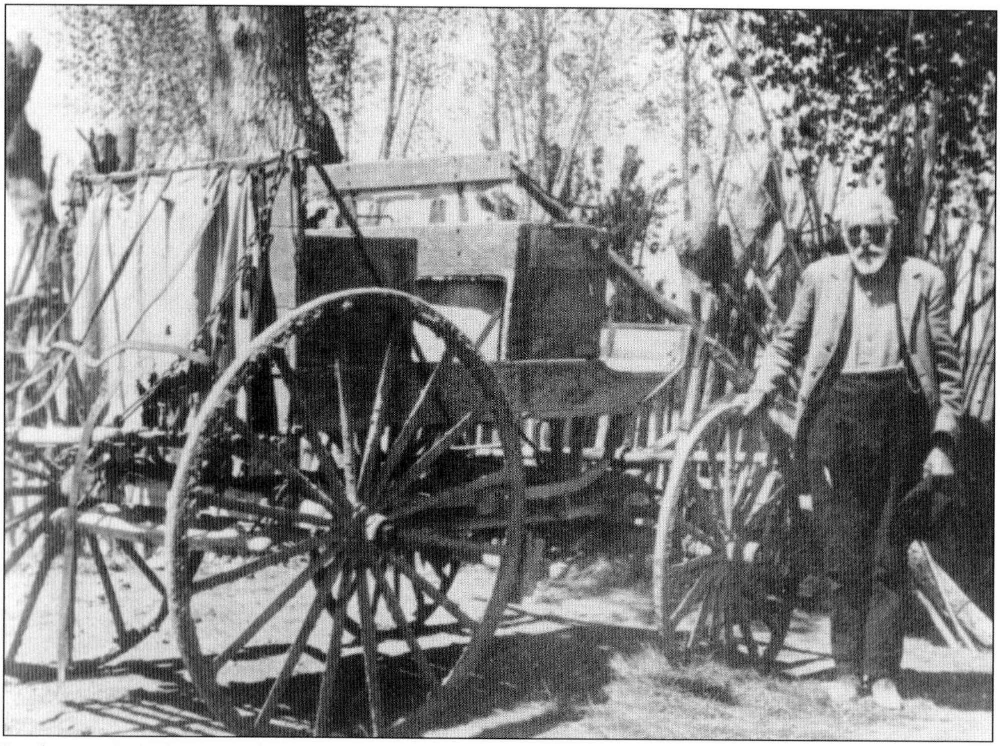

In this c. 1910 photograph, Augustus "Gus" Chenowth stands by the coach he bought when the California District Stage Line closed. A founder of Phoenix, when the Southern Pacific Railroad threatened his freighting business, Chenowth took his teams south to supply forts and mines. He was as quick with guns and fists as with his Bible. Offered a hut at the San Simon Cienega, he moved his family there and combined freighting with ranching and making whiskey. (Alden Hayes.)

Two

HUSTLERS AND RUSTLERS

When Ed Schieffelin struck the silver ore that birthed Tombstone in 1878, mining claims were feverishly staked all over the Chiricahuas. John Galey's Texas Mine, near future Paradise, had a smelter and employed about 50 miners by 1881. But Galeyville's seven saloons attracted scores of "cowboys," whose lucrative business was rustling cattle in Arizona and New Mexico to sell in Mexico and stealing Mexican stock to supply Arizona miners and military. Men too wild for Tombstone were said to haunt Galeyville. Cochise County deputy sheriff William Breakenridge rode in to invite the notorious Curly Bill Brocius to help him collect taxes owed for cattle stashed in canyons before delivery. Brocius, delighted by the sheriff's nerve, took him around to the hideaways and saw that the taxes were paid. Galeyville boomed, bloomed, and then withered when the Texas Mine closed in January 1882. Eighteen years later, what lumber was left of hotels, stores, and saloons was hauled to the new camp of Paradise.

Until the Chiricahua Apaches' reservation was closed and they were marched to San Carlos in 1876, few whites risked living there. Now, miners swarmed in. Military posts increased to defend the mining camps while woodcutters, loggers, and those at the sawmills strove to supply the demand for fuel and lumber. The whole population, including reservation Indians, had voracious appetites for beef, more than could be produced or rustled by small ranchers operating in the vast grasslands of the San Simon Valley.

These small operations were bought out in the early 1880s by Texans. Several Pennsylvania companies began giant outfits in the Sulphur Springs Valley. East of the Peloncillos, Michael Gray bought out Curly Bill Brocious, founding a ranch that, under various owners, has endured as the Animas Foundation, which works with the Nature Conservancy to practice sustainable livestock grazing while protecting a habitat that nurtures a rich variety of plants and wildlife, including birds.

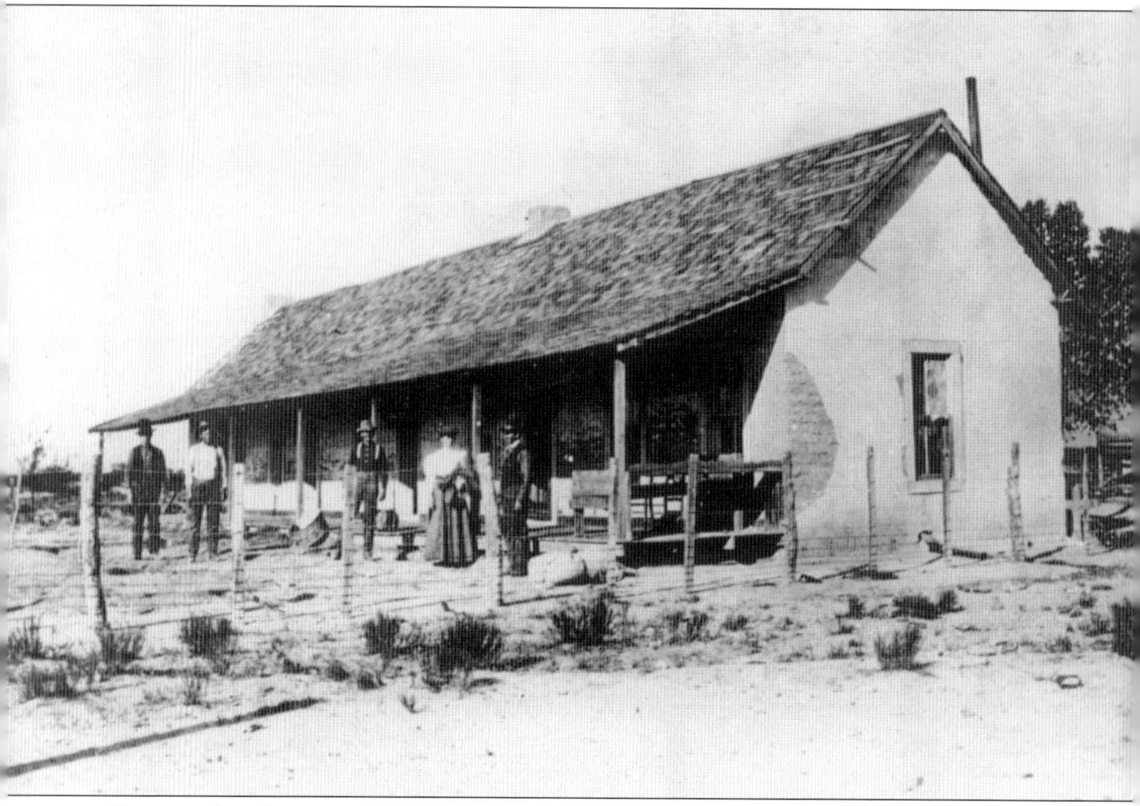

Texas ranchers James H. Parramore and Claiborne W. Merchant bought most of the small outfits in the San Simon Valley, forming the San Simon Cattle and Canal Company, called the H's because the 12,000 longhorns shipped to San Simon in 1883 were branded 7 Lazy HH. This brand was on most cattle roaming from San Simon's over 60 unfenced miles south to Parramore Crater, dividing the H's range from John Slaughter's San Bernardino Valley. A 1775 Spanish fort and 1820 land grant had long been abandoned because of Apache raids. Renowned former sheriff John Slaughter ran thousands of cattle there. Demand for stock cars made thousands of cattle wait for weeks at the holding grounds of San Simon. To water them, a 17-mile-long ditch was dug from the H's cienega headquarters to the railroad, paralleling the often dry San Simon River. In 1902, rails created the shipping point of Rodeo, New Mexico. The H's headquarters, shown in this 1920 photograph, moved near there. Even big outfits only kept a dozen or so men year-round. Cowboys trailed in herds and were paid off. Some became independent cattlemen or rustlers. Samuel "Jack" Maloney said six heifers he began with had twins, who also had twins and passed on this trait. The railroad profoundly changed the region. Men flocking to the Paradise boom got off the train at Rodeo, and freighters hauled supplies 15 miles rather than 35. (Jim Frank Cox.)

Shown at his SD ranch in the photograph at right, Benjamin Franklin "Frank" Sanford came from Sweetwater, Texas, in 1892. He was working for a ranch near Clifton when he sickened. Fellow cowboy August English took him home to his sister Nancy Isabelle English to be nursed through smallpox. Frank recovered, but Nancy contracted the disease. He took care of her but drifted off to cowboy and mine until he was lured to the Paradise boom in 1902. He was freighting between the camp and Rodeo when he found Nancy cooking at a hotel. Their wedding was celebrated February 15, 1903. Nancy continued to cook while Frank worked for the H's until they saved enough to start their own ranch east of Portal Peak in 1909, where they raised three children and lived most of the 52 years of their marriage. (Both, Jim Frank Cox.)

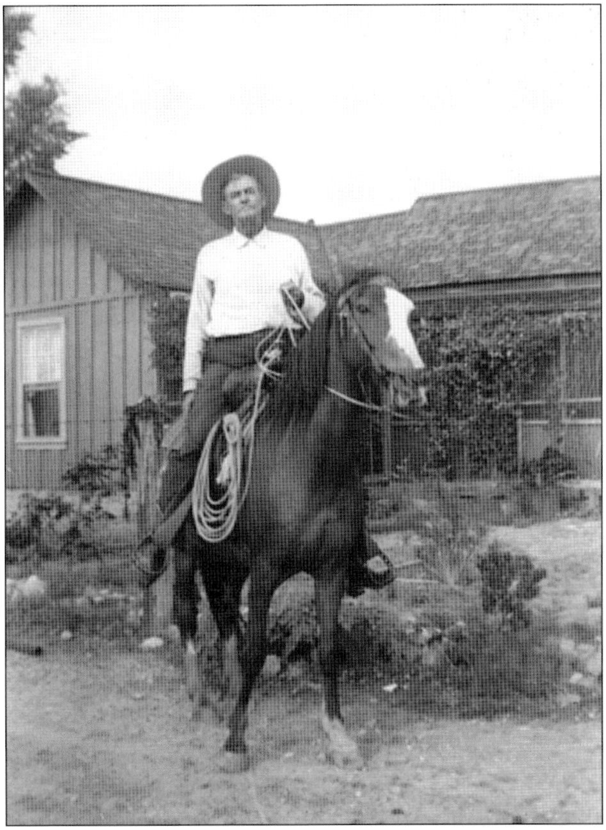

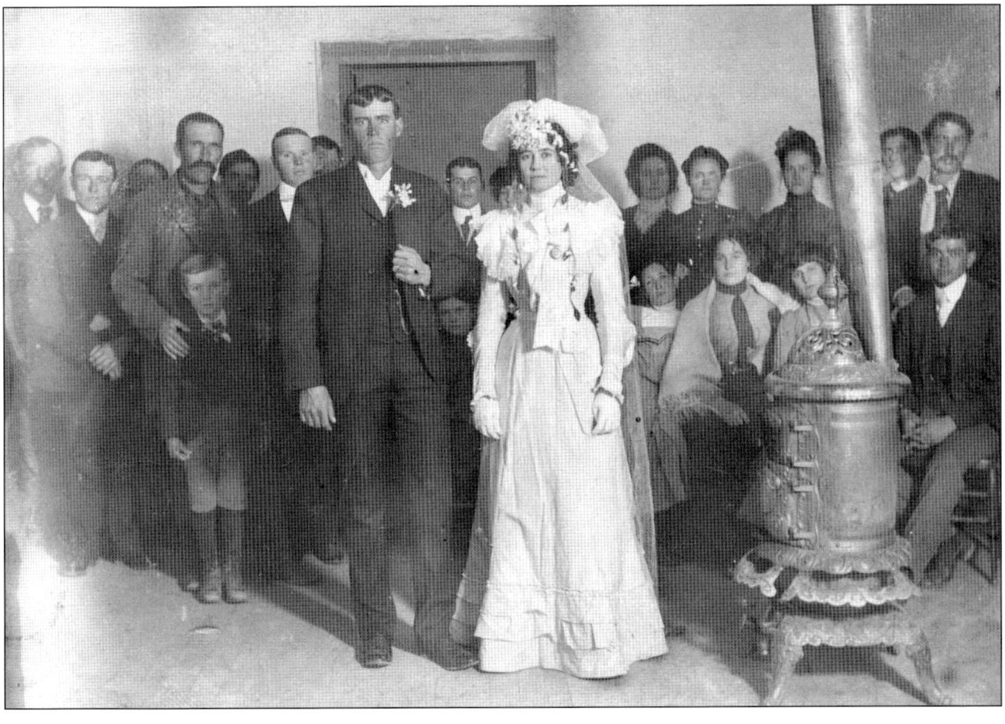

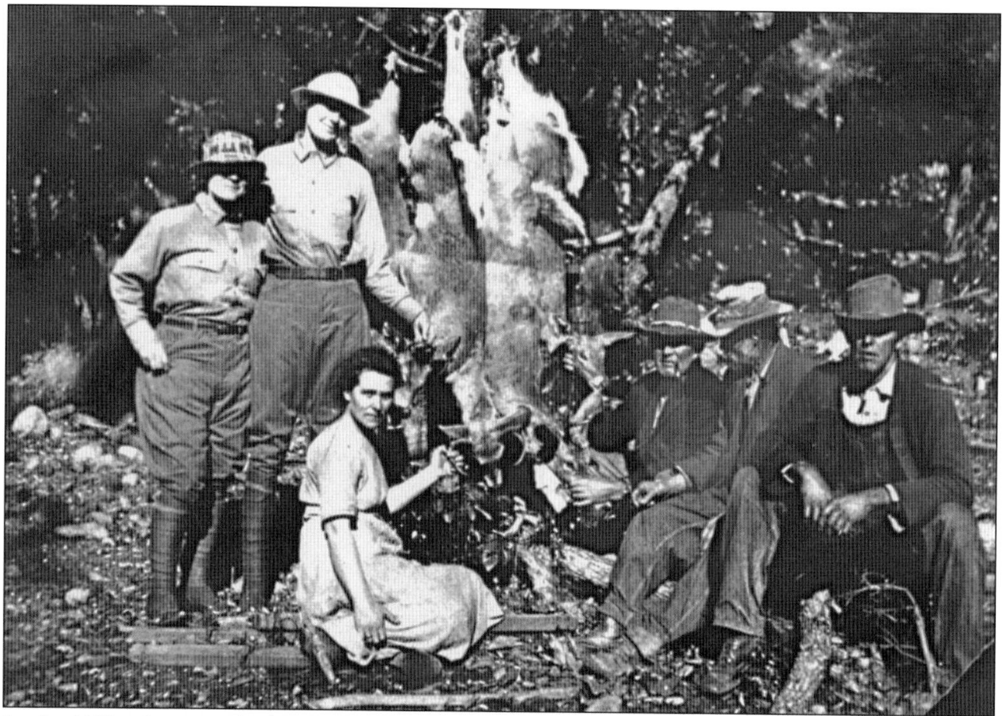

In the 1920s photograph above, several people pose beside four whitetail bucks. From left to right are two unidentified dudes, Emma Sanders Maloney, William King Morrow, Joe Sanders, and Jack Maloney. Jack Maloney guided hunters and sometimes cooked for them. Emma, Joe Sanders's daughter, married Maloney at Christmas in 1907. Friends came from all around. After dinner, the entire wedding party rode 15 miles to a dance in Rodeo. The couple lived in a tent on Sanders's place. A cabin given to Maloney for hauling it off the Chiricahua Forest Reserve burned down, and he built the home in the photograph below, shown with Emma and her flowers. Emma's father would come inside to eat and visit but persistently slept in his bedroll or dugout. She did all she could for him, even rendering out his trapped skunks to make harness oil. (Both, Zola Stoltz.)

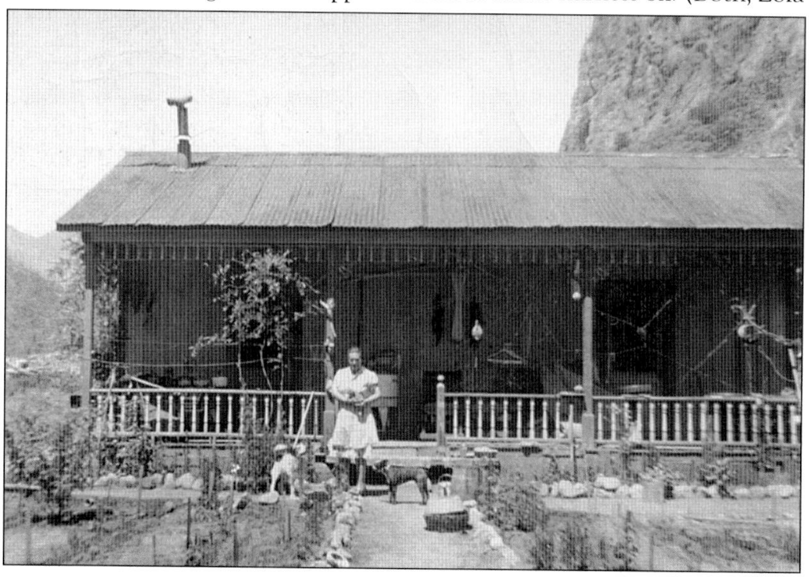

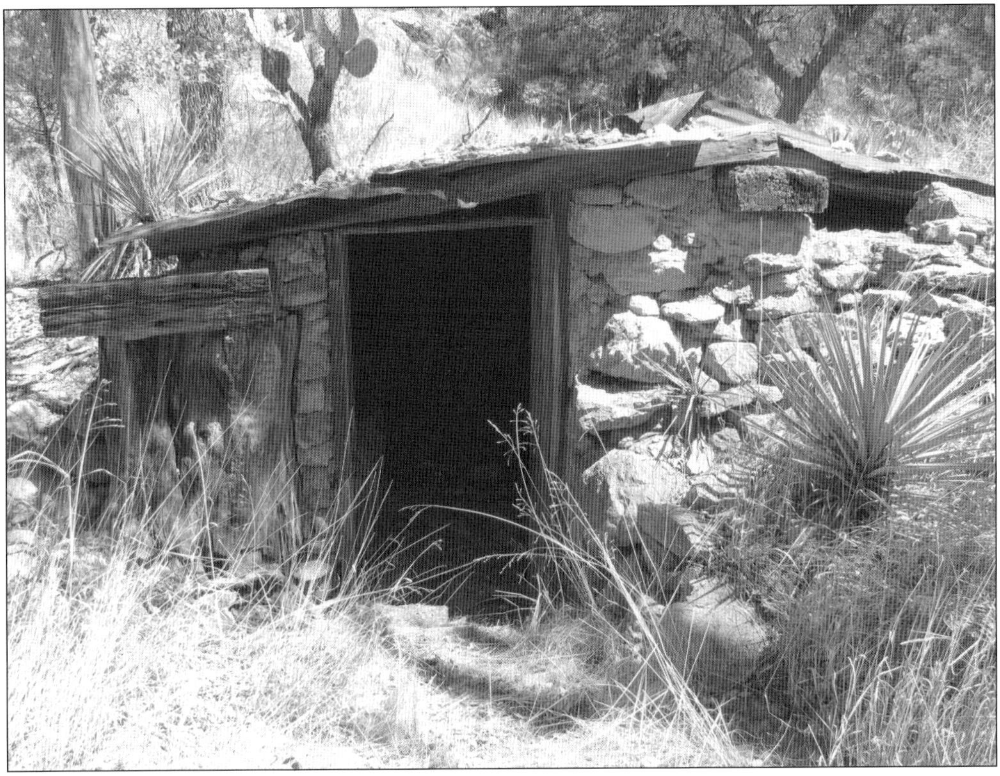

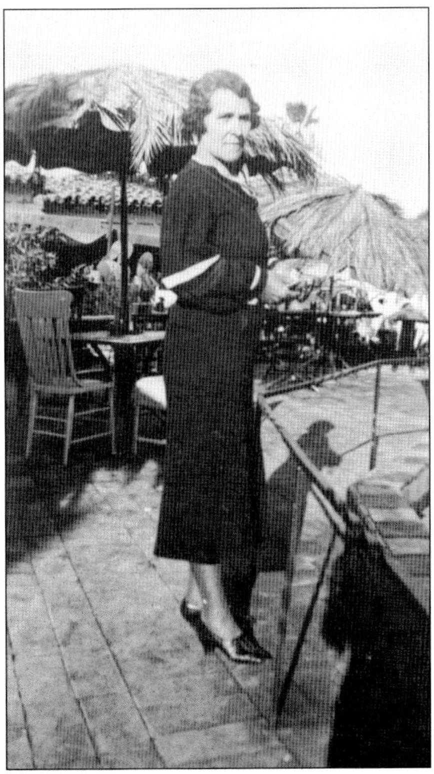

The Maloneys built this cellar, and Emma kept it stocked with jars of vegetables, fruit, jellies, and jams. Hams and bacon hung in there, and bins probably held potatoes, onions, and other root vegetables. The redoubtable Maloneys were well matched. Tired of carrying water from the creek, Jack dug a well in the house. Once, when he had been off playing cards, he cautiously threw his new Stetson inside the house. Emma thrust it into the stove. She said he was the only man who ever laughed at her and got away with it, as he did on their first encounter when she was milking a recalcitrant cow that had caught its front legs between the corral bars. Emma is fashionably dressed in the late-1940s photograph at right, enjoying a rare vacation at California's Catalina Island. (Both, Zola Stoltz.)

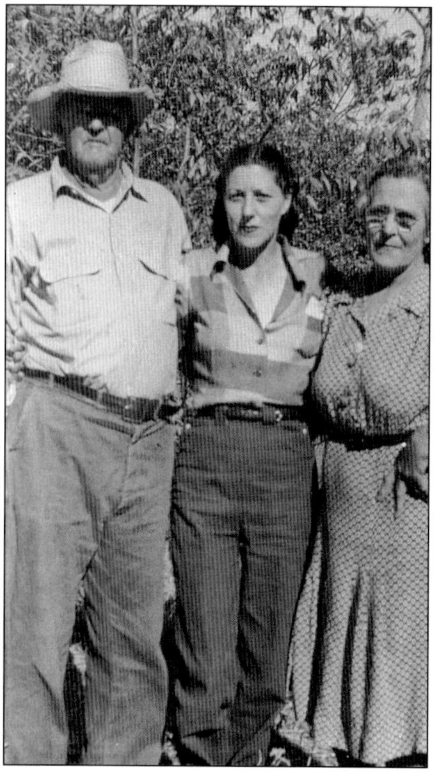

The aging Maloneys stand on either side of their only daughter, Lelia Maloney Stoltz, in this photograph. By 1953, failing health compelled their move to Douglas, where the old cowboy passed away in 1965. Jack Maloney's favorite song, "Empty Saddles on the Old Corral," was played at his funeral. Emma found comfort in designing and hooking beautiful rugs, which she had done since childhood. One with a rattlesnake motif was so realistic, it frightened a visitor into calling for rescue. Lelia Stoltz's son George "Pat" Stoltz inherited the place, still in the family. (Zola Stoltz.)

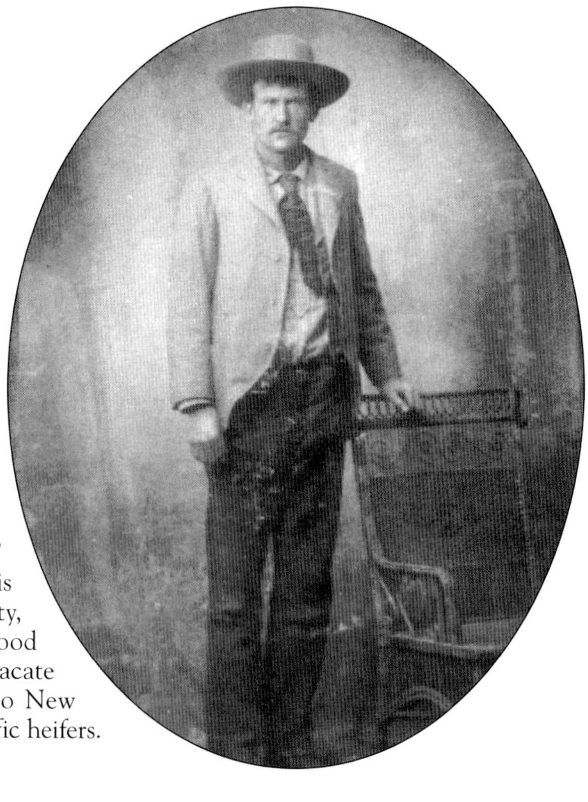

Carl Washburn, shown in this 1909 photograph, became a neighbor to the Reeds and Maloneys about 1907 when he started ranching at a former woodcutters' camp in the canyon named for him. His cattle increased with astounding rapidity, and he married Katie Noland, as good at working cattle as he. Ordered to vacate forestland, the Washburns moved to New Mexico and continued to acquire prolific heifers. (Zola Stoltz.)

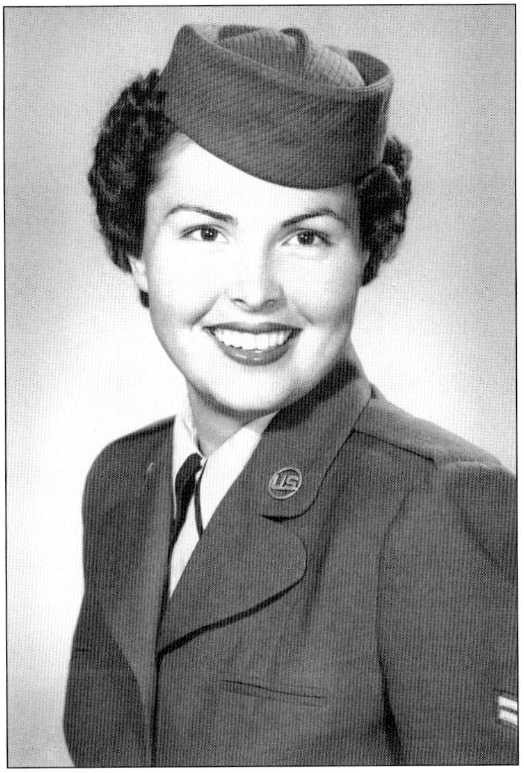

December 7, 1951, ten years after Pearl Harbor, Zola Bellwood (right) met the young man in photograph below, George "Pat" Stolz, at a Los Angeles recruiting center where both enlisted in the United States Air Force. She went to basic training while he attended jet mechanics' school. During a two-and-a-half-year long-distance courtship, there were many letters and phone calls but only 30 dates. They married in Las Vegas on May 9, 1954. (Both, Zola Stoltz.)

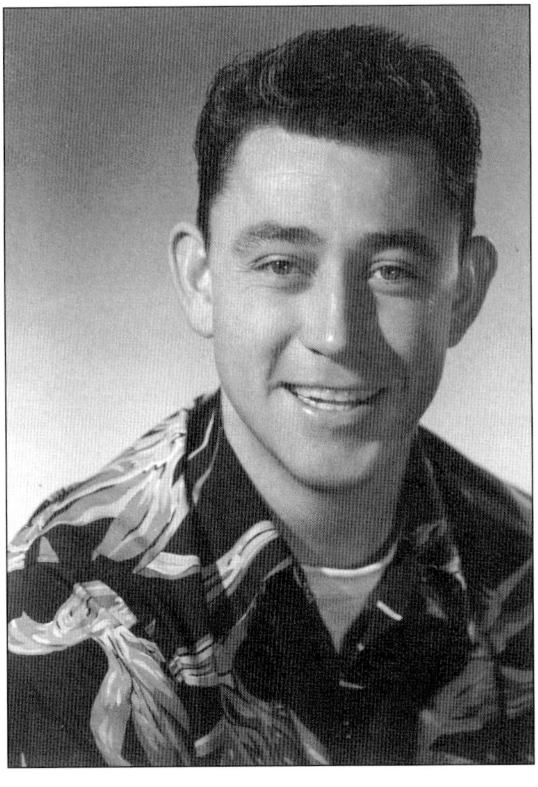

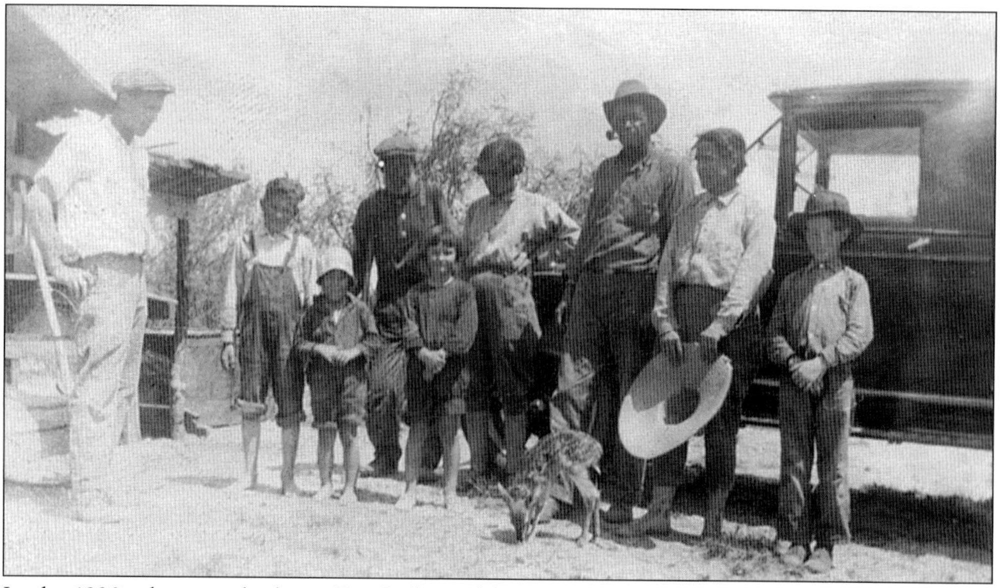

In the 1930s photograph above, Pat Stoltz and friends surround Grandmother Emma's pet deer, Betty. When Stoltz came for summer visits, he would shout Betty's name as they neared the place, and the doe would be waiting for him. Emma found the baby deer in a tree crotch, perhaps dropped by an eagle. Betty followed her around like a dog. Betty went in the woods to have her first fawn but in a few days returned to get Emma to come admire the baby. He, too, was tame, until claimed by the wilds. (Zola Stoltz.)

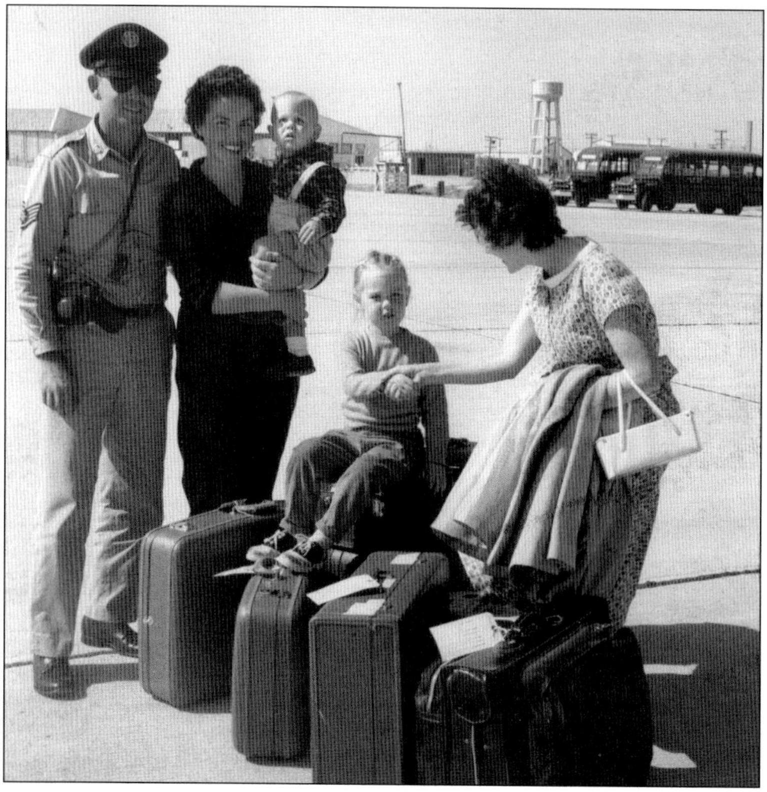

Pat and Zola Stoltz with 18-month-old Kurt and four-year-old Lynette are welcomed to Zaragoza, Spain, in this 1958 photograph. After discharge, Stoltz tired of civilian life and reenlisted. Son Scott was born in Columbus, Ohio. Stoltz's postings included Tucson and Korea. After retirement, the family lived in Denver until his death in 2003. Zola then built a home, still in the family, on the place inherited from the Maloneys. (Zola Stoltz.)

Three

Miners in Paradise

The Mining Law of 1872 made mineral extraction the sovereign use of public lands. The border survey was completed, and townships and section boundaries were defined. A claim could be staked by a pile of rocks holding a can containing location, date, and a signature witnessed by two people. One claimant declared his witnesses were "God and my dog, Mollie." Claims were recorded at the Cochise County seat of Tombstone. By 1900, a scatter of persistent optimists were swinging picks at promising outcrops and glittering ledges in the mountains. Valuable ores, with the coming of electricity, included the copper that drew Phelps Dodge to Bisbee. To attract investors, prospectors along Silver Creek and East Turkey Creek, John Duncan, George Walker, fellow Klondike gold rusher George Myers, and others pooled their claims, creating the California Mining District. Late in 1902, Phelps Dodge's chief competitor, the Calumet and Arizona Company, powered by Michigan investors, put up most of the money for the Chiricahua Development Company.

Machinery shipped to Rodeo was freighted by teams 15 miles across the valley and up the last tortuous climb to the Chiricahua Mine. In 1906, besides saloons, general stores, and "the district," there were two doctors, a lumberyard, several restaurants, a meat market, hotel, newspaper, barbershop with bath facilities, and a blacksmith shop that kept busy, though the mine had its own smiths to keep tools sharp.

With prospects of a railroad spur from Rodeo to Paradise, optimists hoped to rival Tombstone in spite of the territorial legislature's April 1907 ban on public gambling and women working in saloons. The cleanup raised saloon licenses to $300 from the previous $12–$20 that allowed 14 Paradise saloons to prosper at the same time. Only four survived. Then, in faraway New York in October, Westinghouse Electric Company went bankrupt; reckless speculation in mine, banking, and railroads led to bank failures and financial chaos. Copper prices fell until there were no buyers. The Calumet and Arizona Company, chief backer of the Chiricahua Mine, pulled out. In early 1908, the mine closed.

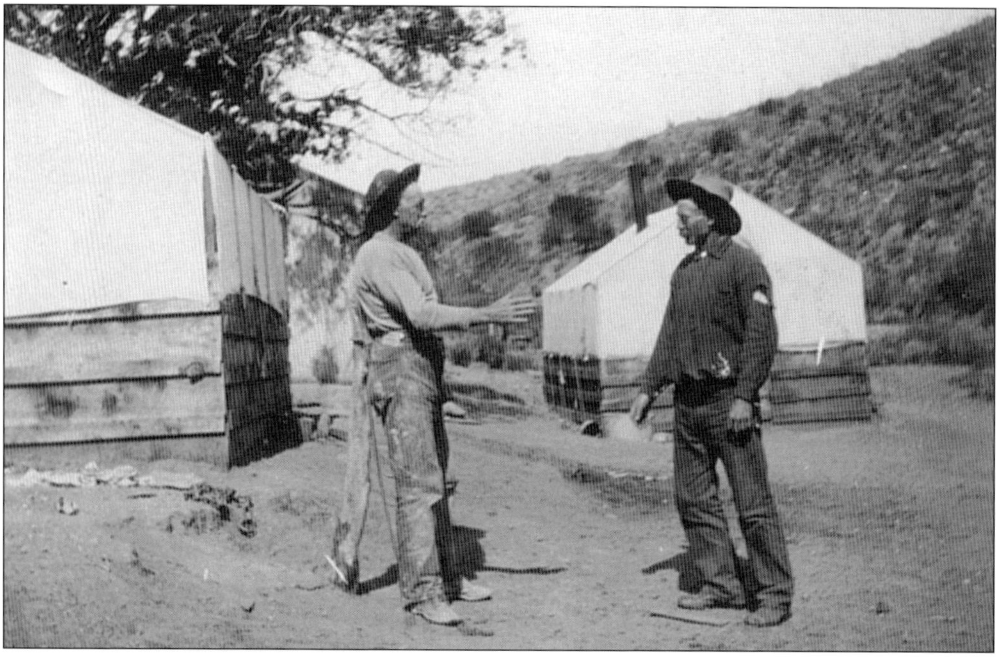

In 1901, George Walker and George Myers laid out a 20-acre townsite along East Turkey Creek with lots on both sides of Market Street, where they opened the first businesses in tents: Myers, a saloon, and Walker, a general store. The store had a cubbyhole for the Paradise Post Office, with Walker as postmaster. The town's name is sometimes attributed to Walker's happiness with Lula, Stephen Reed's eldest daughter, whom he married that summer, but the camp had been called Paradise for a year. Walker's bride was alarmed by drunken revelers galloping past her canvas-topped dwelling, so he built her a frame house well off the road. Edward Sweeney's lumberyard/hardware store sold rough lumber from Pinery sawmills that soaked up paint so fast that many buildings were left plain. Water dipped from the creek became risky to drink as privies increased. Some people dug wells, but hauled water could be bought for 25¢ a barrel. Woodcutters brought in fuel on donkeys fitted with carefully balanced packsaddles. (Both, Duffner Brothers History Project.)

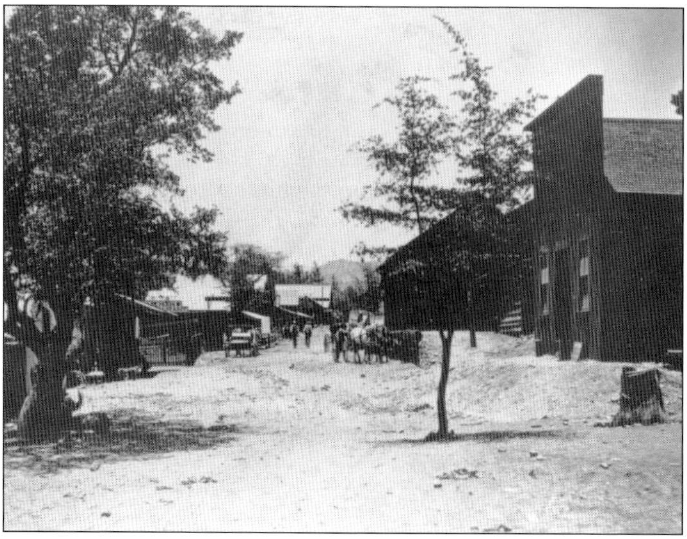

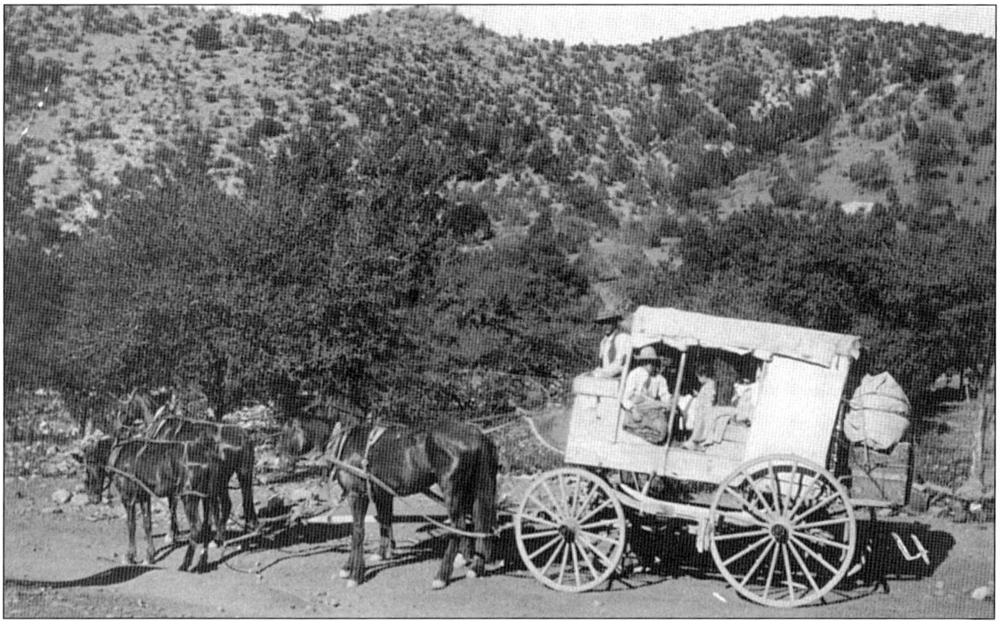

Driven by George Coryell, the Rocking Stage stops in Graveyard Canyon. The stage carried mail and passengers between Paradise and Rodeo. The axle-breaking track was much improved when Coryell's partner, Sheriff Mart Moore, got Judge James Hancock to sentence prisoners to work on it. Mostly arrested as drunk and disorderly, they doubtless preferred labor to being attached to the log chain jail or the sturdy building that succeeded it. (Pamela Hulme.)

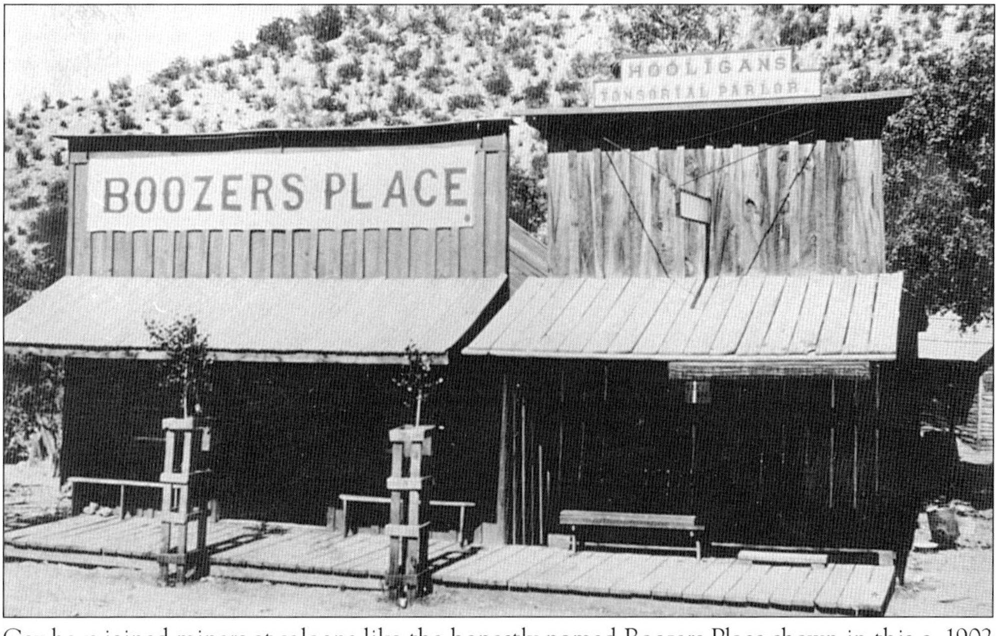

Cowboys joined miners at saloons like the honestly named Boozers Place shown in this c. 1902 photograph. One saloon had a billiard table, but drinking and playing faro, roulette, monte, and rolling dice were the most common pastimes. Madge's Place on the east side of the creek was soon joined by similar establishments to offer feminine companionship to lonely bachelors. (Pamela Hulme.)

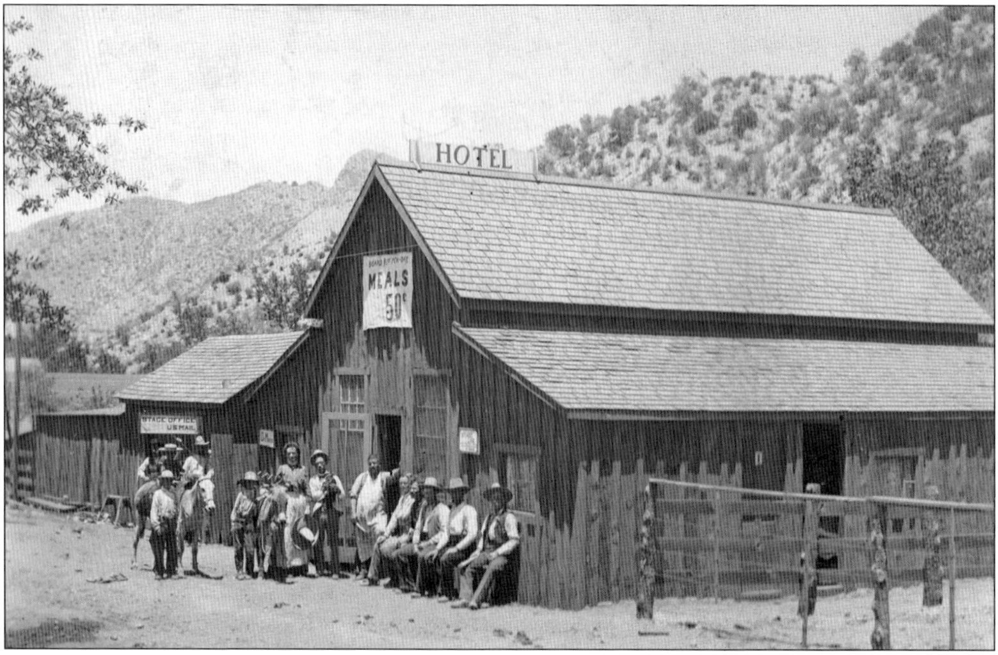

The people in this 1904 photograph await the coming of the stage at the Hayes Hotel, which had a popular restaurant and bakery. The stage office is at left. Travelers were glad to stop in Portal for a jolt of whiskey from Edward Epley's barrel lodged in the hollow of a giant sycamore behind his store/post office, while the teams, just as thankful, drank from the spring. (Alden Hayes.)

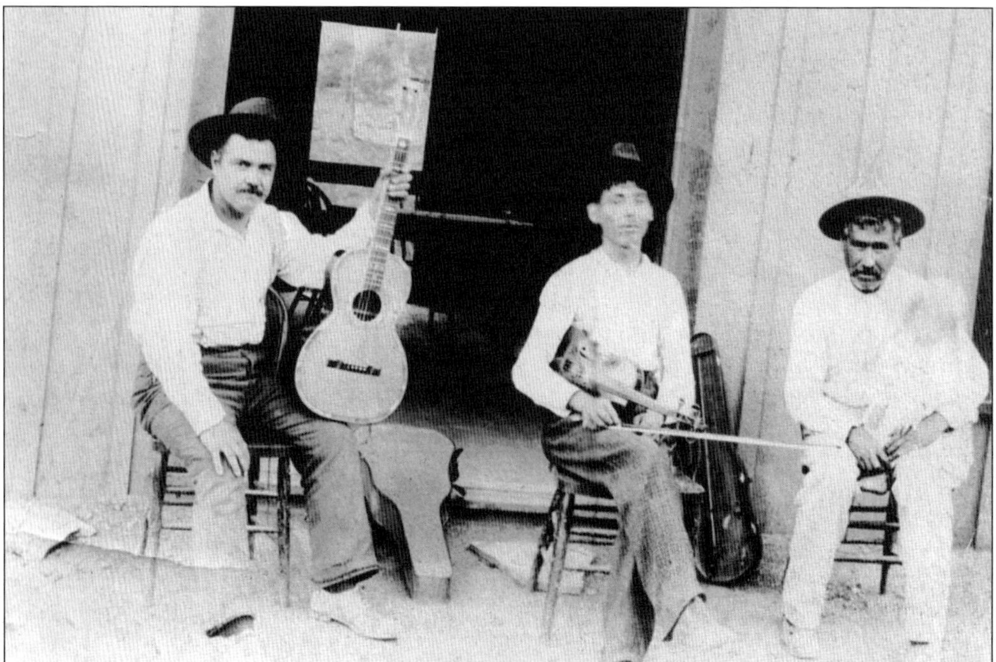

Those who were there praised the musicians and singers of Paradise. In this c. 1904 photograph, Max (right) and Otto Duffner, brothers from Pennsylvania, sit with an unidentified man between them, ready to tune up. (Duffner Brothers History Project.)

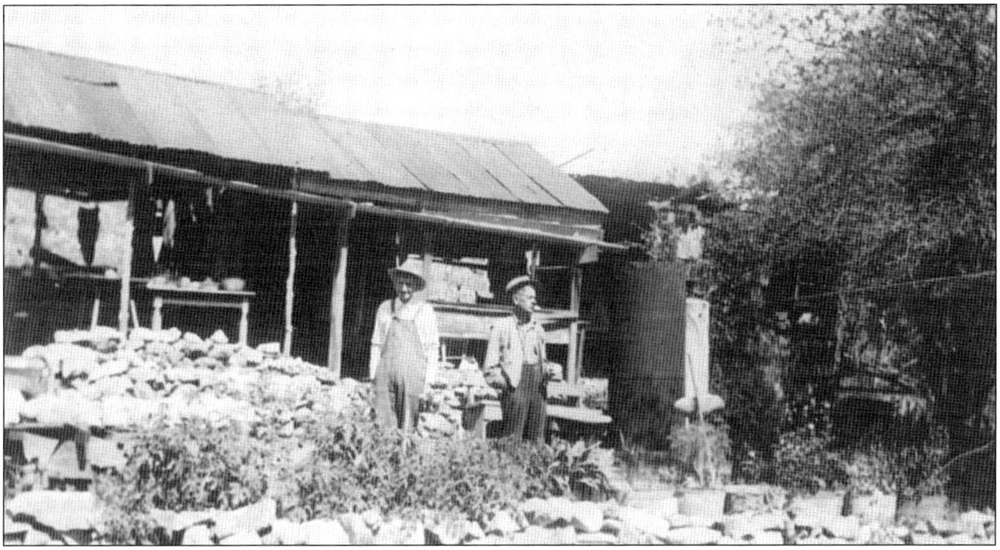

The c. 1906 photograph above shows Max (right) and Otto Duffner beside this comfortable home they built on a slope above Paradise after living for a time in an old adobe on Silver Creek where they had mining claims. They could afford a corrugated iron roof, though tar paper covered many buildings. Always believing Paradise would prosper again, they lived here the rest of their long lives, amassing collections of sun-colored glass, butterflies, mineral specimens, and anything that caught their fancy. Both were expert watch and clock repairmen. Otto, seen in 1904 photograph below, clerked in stores and kept accounts. William Wesley "Bill" Sanders, the only son of old Joe and Susan Sanders, called him "very upright and straightforward in all his dealings." (Both, Duffner Brothers History Project.)

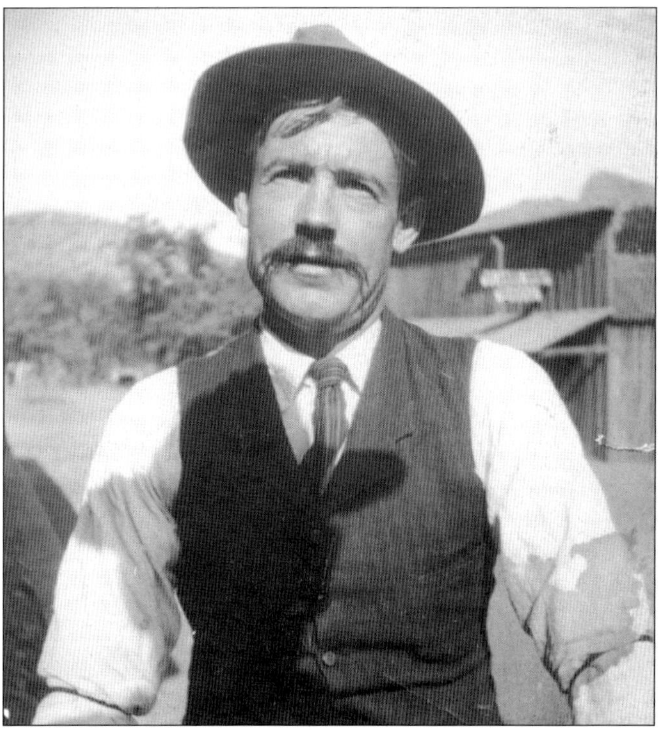

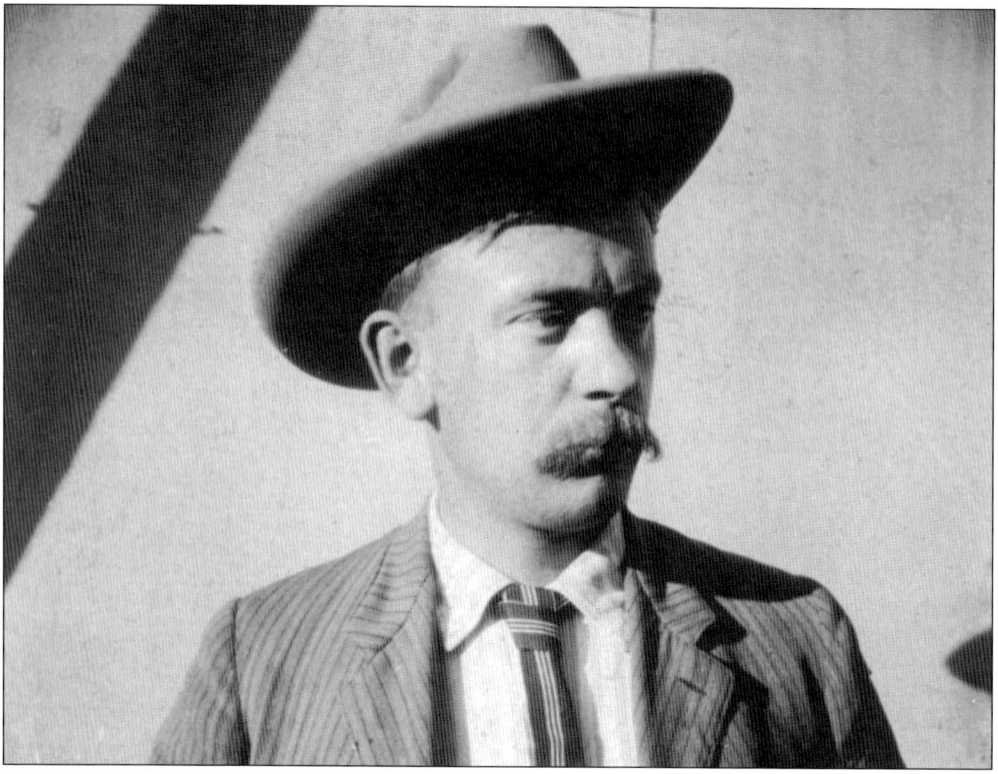

It was commonly alleged that Max Duffner, above in 1904, had become so addicted to narcotics that Otto urged him to come west, hoping new surroundings and challenges would help his brother overcome the habit. Instead, Max began drinking heavily. Besides working their claims, he was a blacksmith, carpenter, and cabinetmaker. Bill Sanders called him "very accommodating and trustworthy." Max outlived Otto by a few years. Their remains were shipped back to Pennsylvania for burial. In the c. 1906 photograph below, Otto kneels by a windlass at their Silver Creek claim. (Both, Duffner Brothers History Project.)

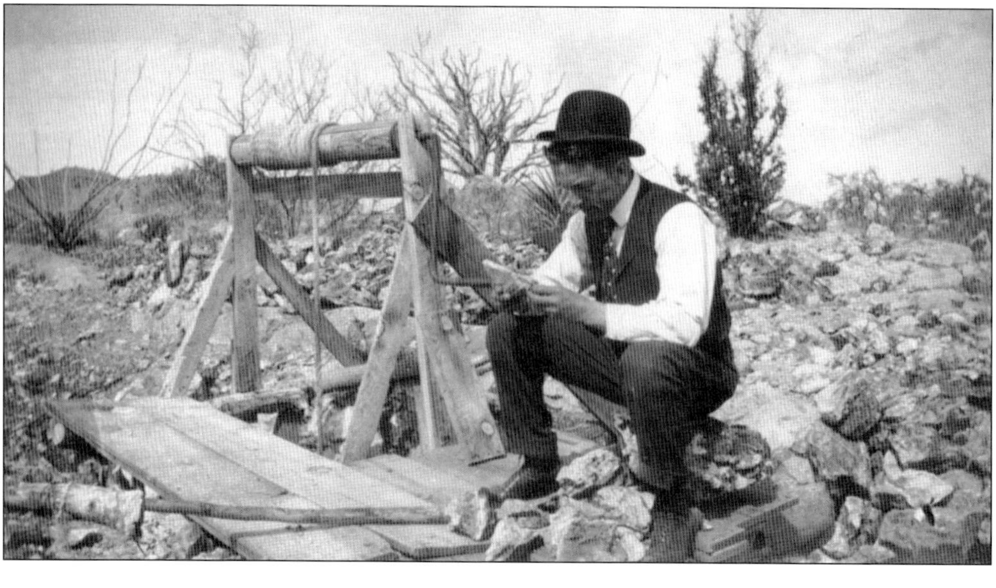

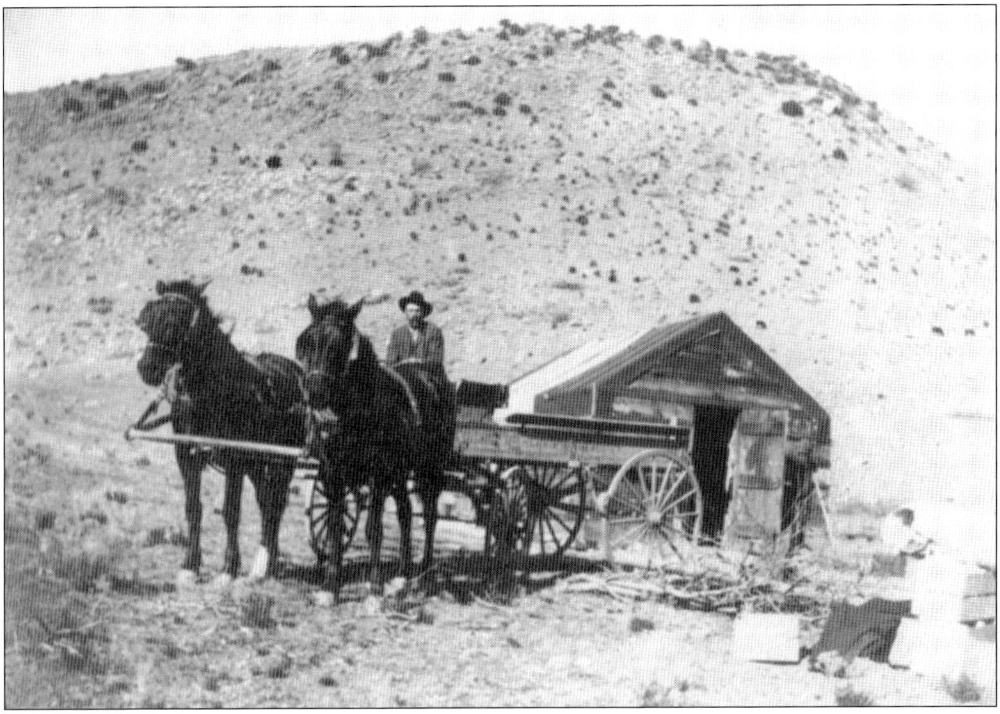

In this c. 1904 photograph, Otto Duffner drives a team hauling ore. The brothers also sold chunks of crystal from Crystal Cave up Cave Creek Canyon until the Chiricahua Forest Reserve's first supervisor, Charles T. McGlone, declared it closed to such ventures. McGlone himself planned to exploit it. It is now barred to casual visitation in order to protect bat colonies and sensitive formations. (Duffner Brother History Project.)

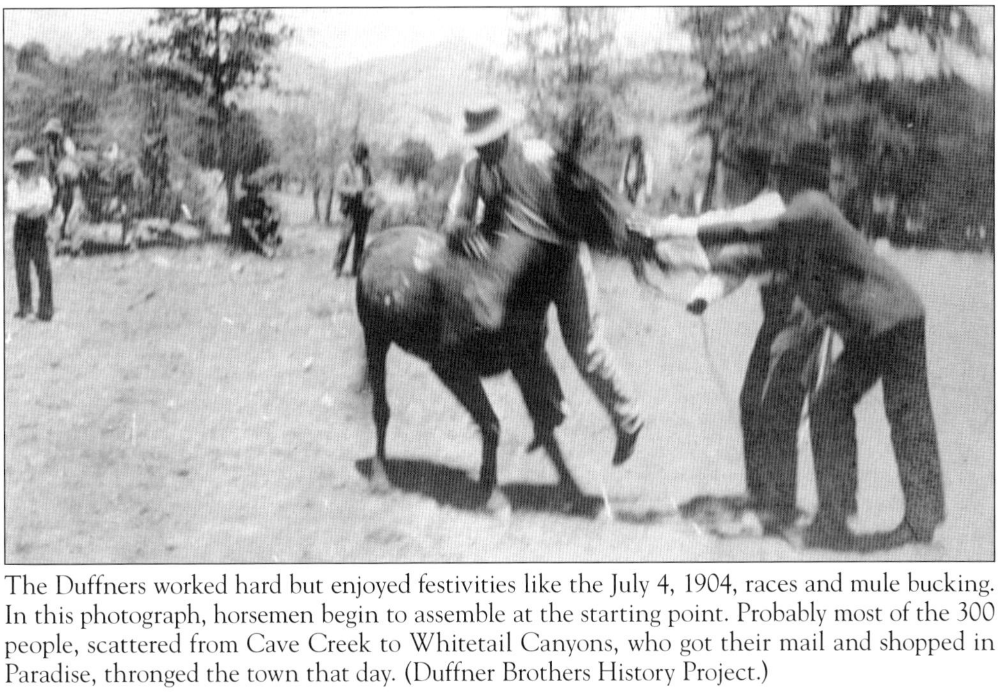

The Duffners worked hard but enjoyed festivities like the July 4, 1904, races and mule bucking. In this photograph, horsemen begin to assemble at the starting point. Probably most of the 300 people, scattered from Cave Creek to Whitetail Canyons, who got their mail and shopped in Paradise, thronged the town that day. (Duffner Brothers History Project.)

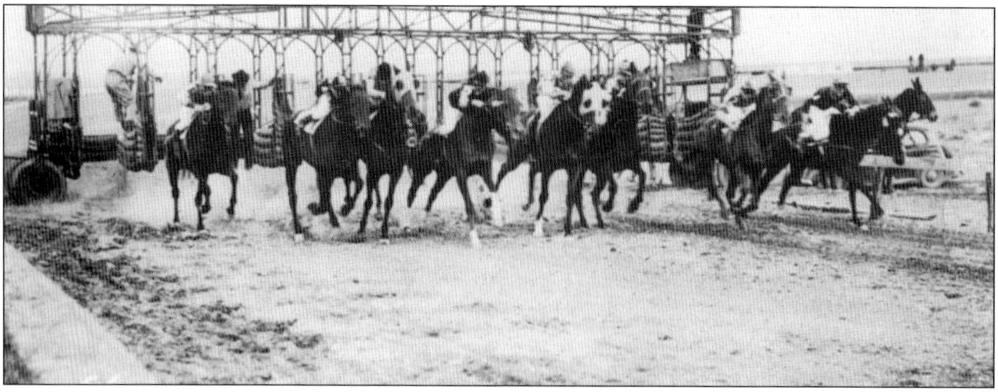

Horses surge from the starting gate in this 1904 photograph. Who could have guessed that a few weeks later, torrential flooding would send the creek roaring high over its banks, sweeping tents, buildings, uprooted trees, and huge logs out to the San Simon Valley? Townsfolk and friends cleared the debris shown in photograph below and usually rebuilt with more-solid structures. (Both, Duffner Brothers History Project.)

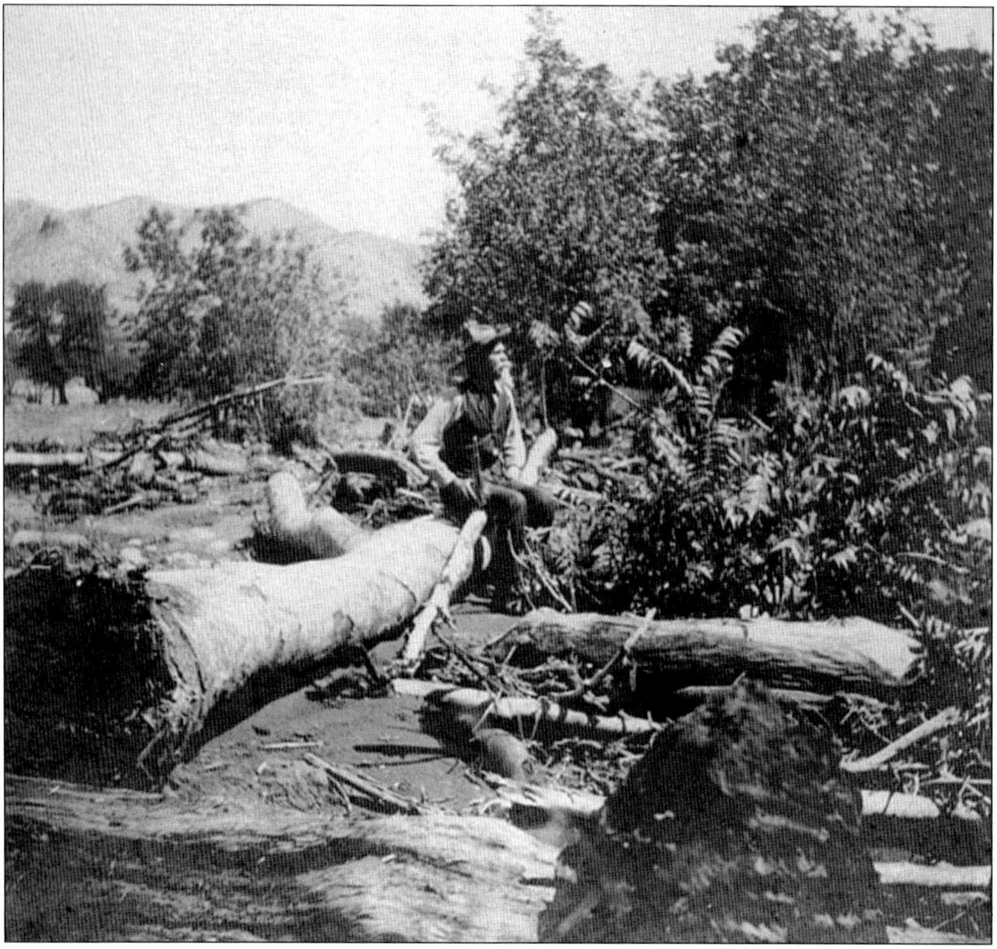

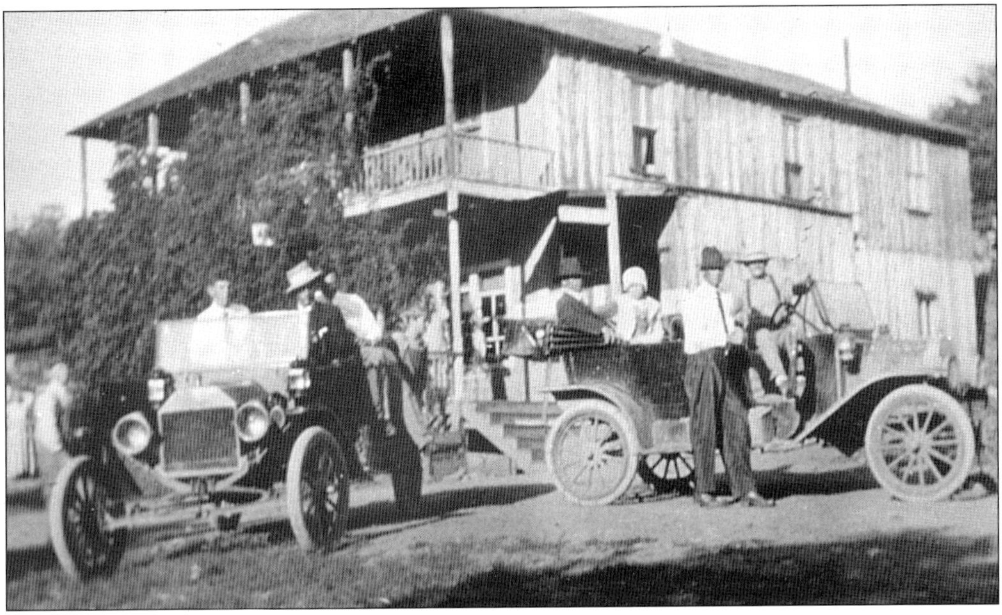

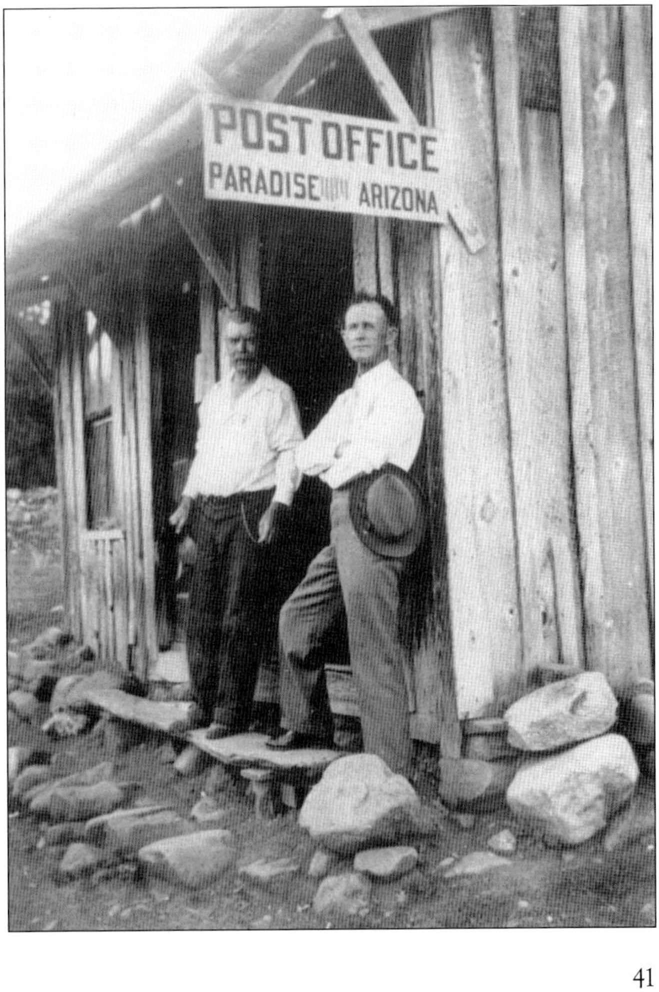

The c. 1915 photograph above shows the Arcadia Hotel with the Autostage, which succeeded the Rocking Stage. The driver, John Lee, was one of the famed mountain lion–hunting brothers. Judge James Hancock, on the left in the photograph at right with son-in-law John Kennedy outside the post office, always believed Paradise had a bright future. (Above, Morrow family collection, © 2015; right, Alden Hayes.)

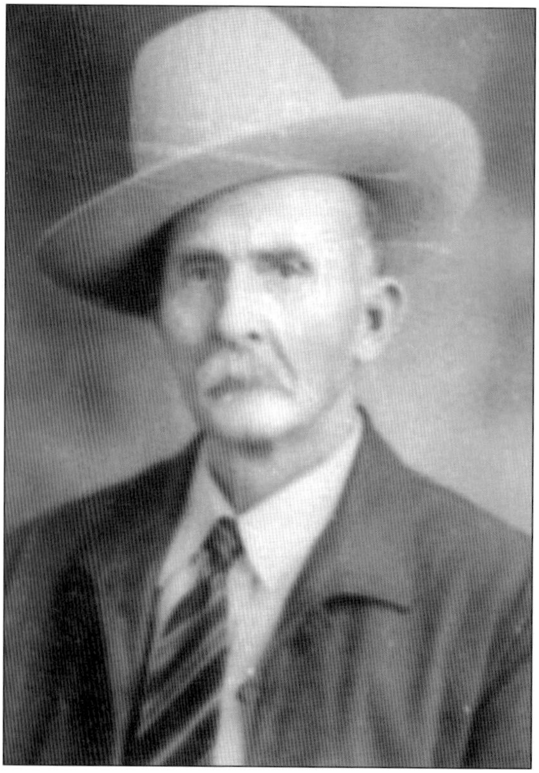

William King "W.K." Morrow, pictured at left around 1910, came from Texas to Roswell with his divorced mother and nine siblings. There, he met and married Eva Corn. When she was eight, her mother had died of measles. Her father, Martin Corn, sold his Texas ranch and moved to Roswell with his eight children. After Eva married Morrow, they homesteaded in Oklahoma until "starved and froze out." She had daughter Rosaline there; Carson, Ralph, and Chester were born near Roswell. The family moved to Douglas, then Paradise. Morrow opened a profitable meat market and invested in mining and ranching. John, Kittie, who died in the flu epidemic, and Dorothy were born before the Morrows moved to Hilltop in 1916. They built a store, but the camp never boomed as expected, so Morrow and the older sons worked at the mine. (Both, Morrow family collection, © 2015.)

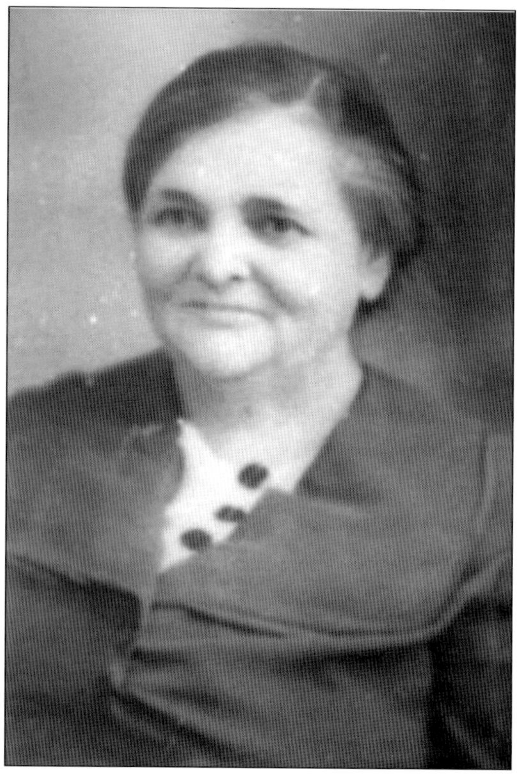

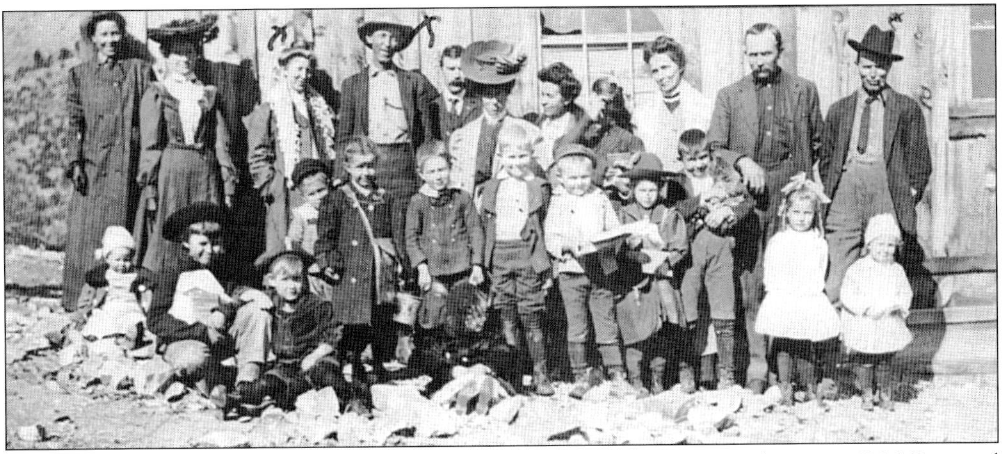

The citizens built a school in 1905. This photograph was taken the second year, in 1906. Pictured are, from left to right, (first row) Bendele baby, Carson Morrow, Erle Hancock, unidentified, Bertha Bendele, Mart Moore, Jerry Chamberlain, Chester Morrow, Irene Hancock, Ralph Morrow, and Dottie and Ted Chamberlain; (second row) Maggie Bendele, teacher Ola Martyr, Gertrude Chamberlain, Tom Hawkins, James Hancock, Laura Hancock, Eva Morrow, Rosaline Morrow, Holly Sweeney, W.K. Morrow, and Harry Chamberlain. (Morrow family collection, © 2015.)

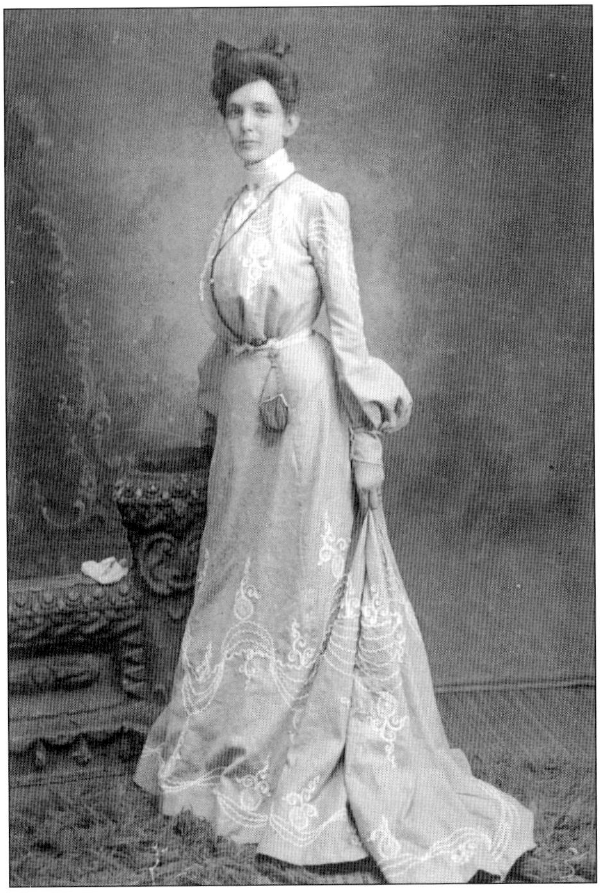

Hollis "Holly" Chamberlain Sweeney is elegant in one of her own creations in this c. 1907 photograph. Briefly returned to San Saba, Texas, her brother Henry Chamberlain invited her to come with him to Paradise where he had opened a general store. She soon married Jack Sweeney, son and partner of Edward Sweeney. Having left a logged-out part of Michigan, the Sweeneys operated a prospering lumberyard. (Pamela Hulme.)

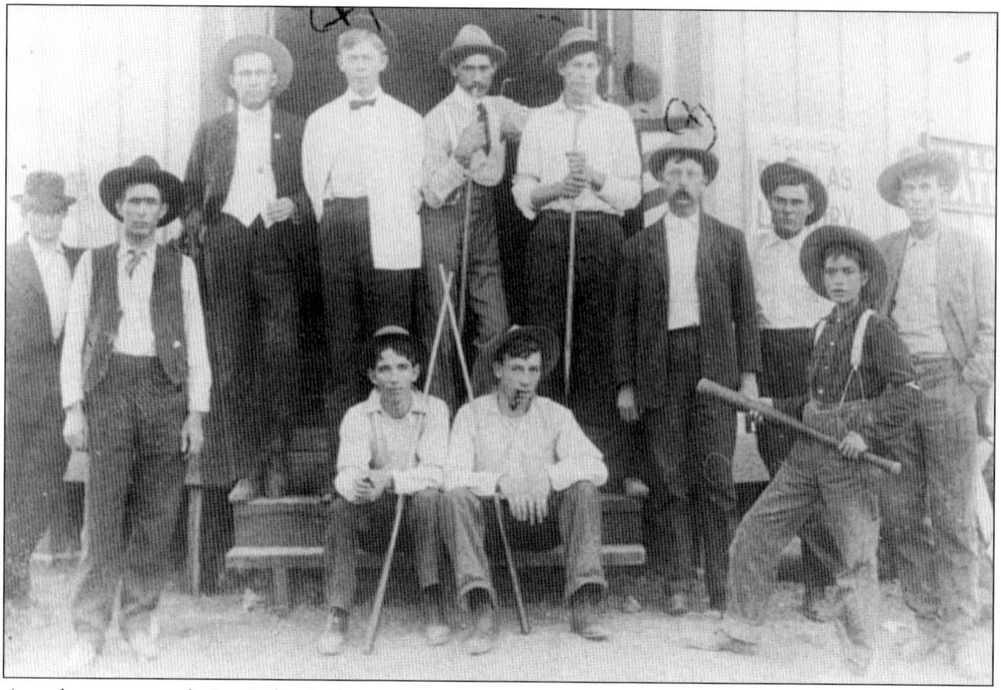

A gathering outside Joe Wheeler's popular saloon in this 1910 photograph shows Carson Morrow (front, right) gripping a bat. When it was clear that the mine would not reopen, businesses closed, including this saloon. Wheeler had been a cowboy in Texas for James Parramore and was welcomed at the 7 Lazy HH, where he became a longtime foreman. (Alden Hayes.)

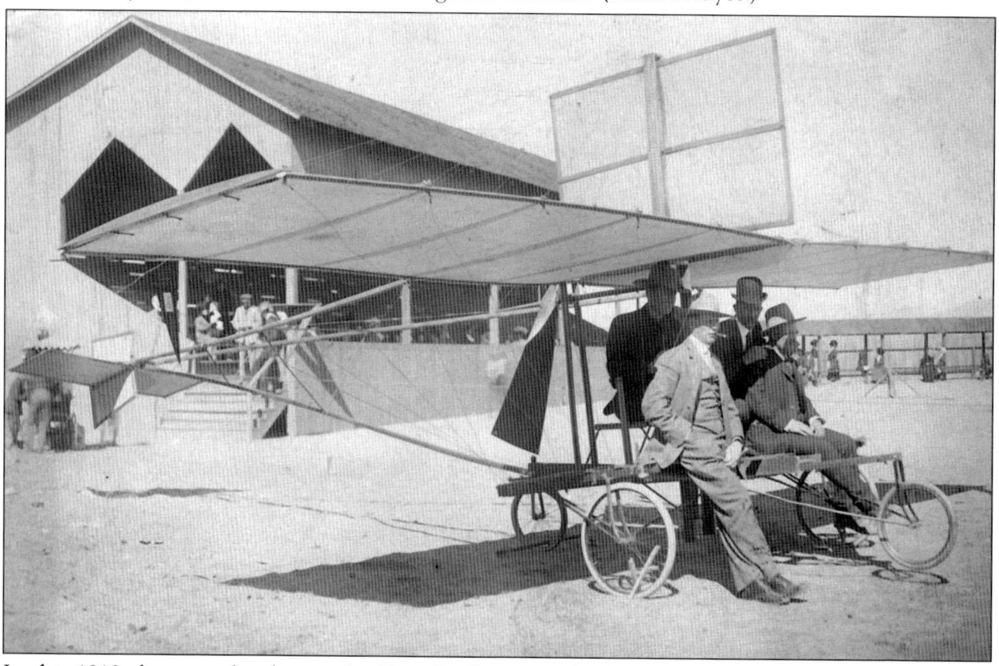

In this 1910 photograph taken at the Douglas fairgrounds, Carson Morrow's father, W.K. Morrow (in a bowler hat), studies an experimental monoplane, possibly designed by Richard Pearse, a New Zealand inventor who pioneered in aviation. (Morrow family collection, © 2015.)

In the 1953 photograph at right, W.K.'s grandson Ralph Wayne "R.W." Morrow climbs into his F-86 Sabrejet at Webb Air Force Base, Big Spring, Texas. During the Korean War, he was one of the youngest flight leaders in the United States Air Force. Cowboy, firefighter, deputy sheriff, and engineer, he designed power lines in California, explored for oil in Texas, and supervised Arizona copper mines. As a real estate broker, respected by buyers and sellers alike, R.W. sold properties for 30 years. His *Chiricahua Journals* proves him a master storyteller with, as his son says, "a playwright's ear for wit and a journalist's eye for detail." Below, in 1934, Deputy Sheriff Ralph Morrow holds a Thompson submachine gun. He was one of the security team when John Dillinger, caught with his gang in Tucson, changed planes in Douglas on his way to Chicago. (Both, Morrow family collection, © 2015.)

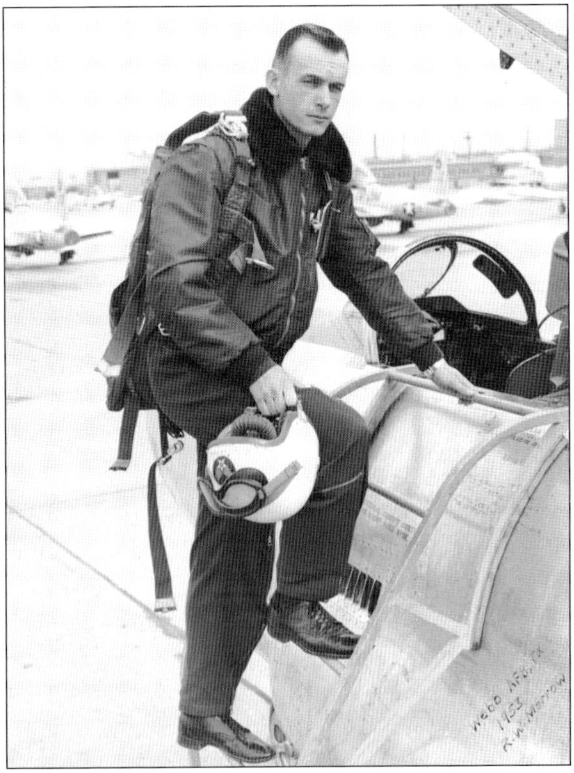

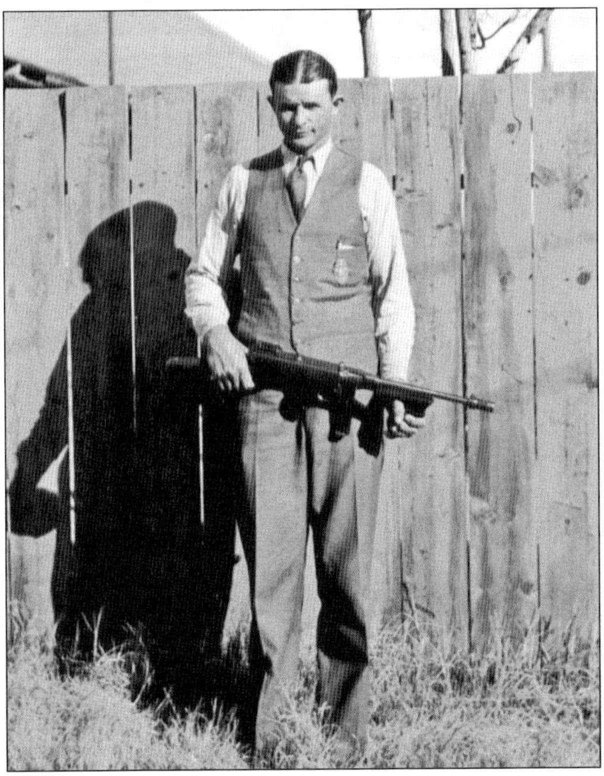

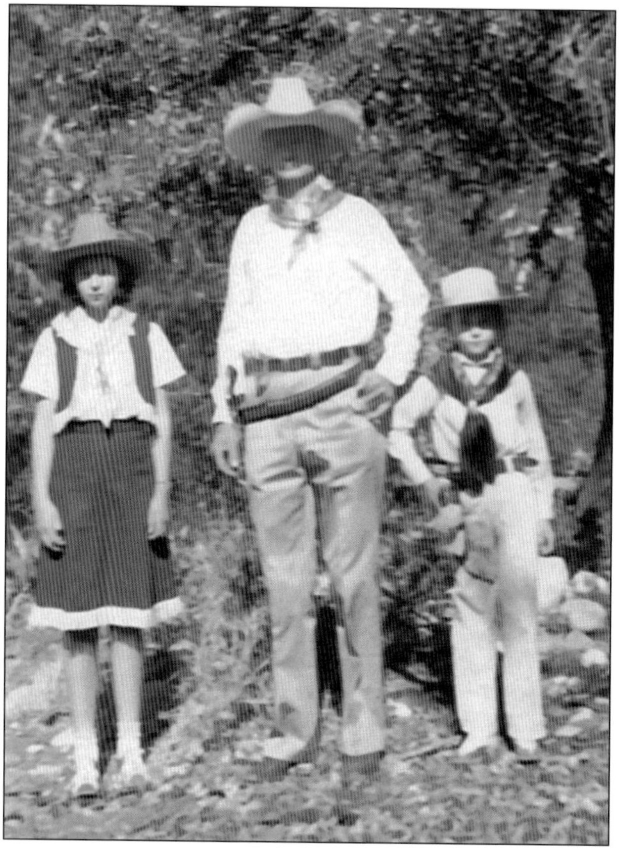

Ralph Morrow grew up in Paradise and Hilltop. As a 12-year-old, he operated the steam hoist that brought buckets of ore to the surface of the Malachite Mine. Working at Hilltop, he fiddled at dances and had an eye on Juanita Kuykendall. They married when she was 15 and he was 27. A Hilltop teacher who knew them the rest of their lives said theirs was the happiest marriage she had ever seen. Left, in 1938, Morrow stands between children Audrey and R.W., who helped rear the orphaned bear Maggie, shown in photograph below. Until Morrow became game warden in addition to deputy sheriff in 1929, Cochise County hunters ignored bag limits and seasons. Morrow changed that, riding horseback where his motorcycle or V-8 Ford could not go. (Both, Morrow family collection, © 2015.)

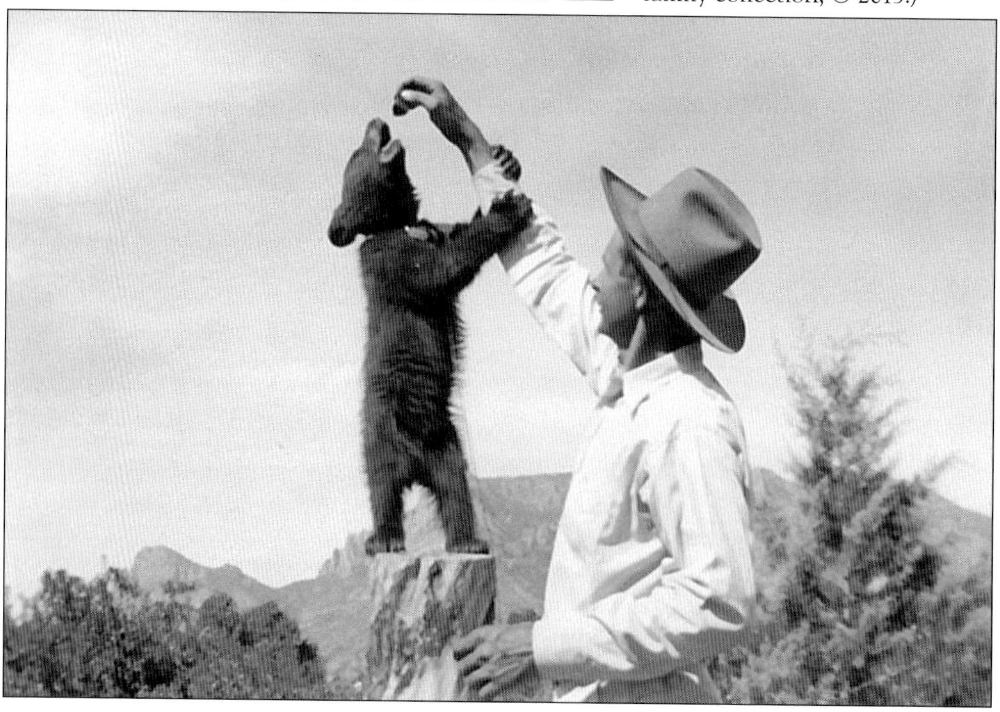

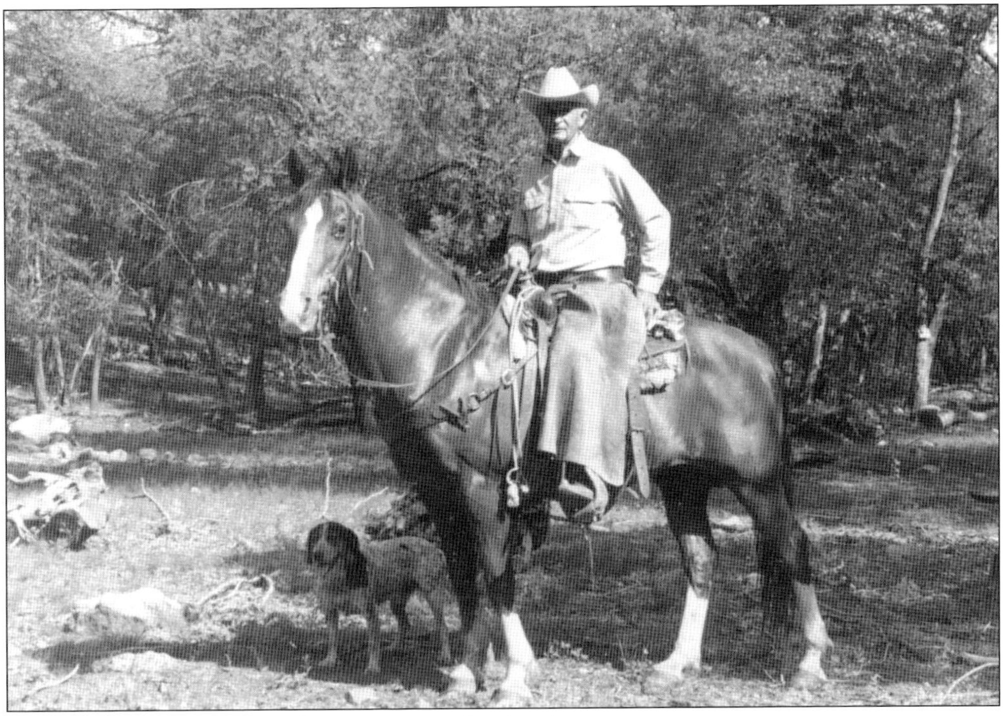

Ralph Morrow, above in 1957, was promoted to head of law enforcement for Arizona Game and Fish. Not a paper pusher, he continued to patrol. Coming upon the governor of Arizona and friends with an illegal elk, he cited them and would not back down. Back in Cochise County, he got no more promotions, retiring in 1963. In 1964, he became the Arizona Game and Fish commissioner. (Alden Hayes.)

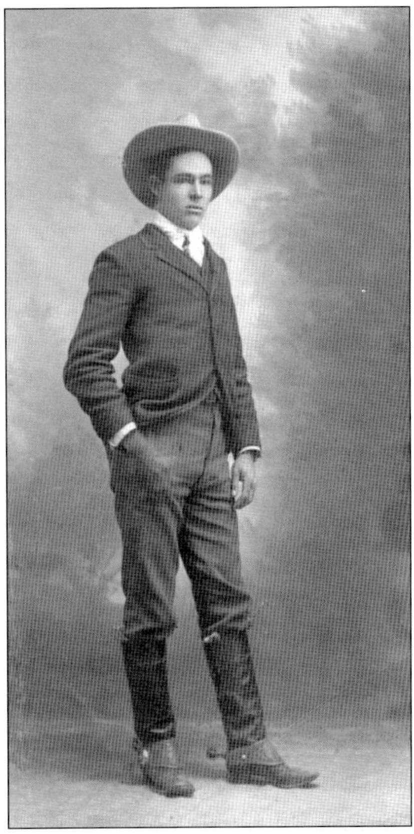

Roland Rodolph Wakefield of El Paso, posing in this c. 1900 photograph, worked on family ranches and had a reputation for taming bucking horses. A thirst for adventure brought him west to Tombstone where he met young Willie Mae Lesuer at a dance. They walked up a hill in the moonlight and fell in love. (Pamela Hulme.)

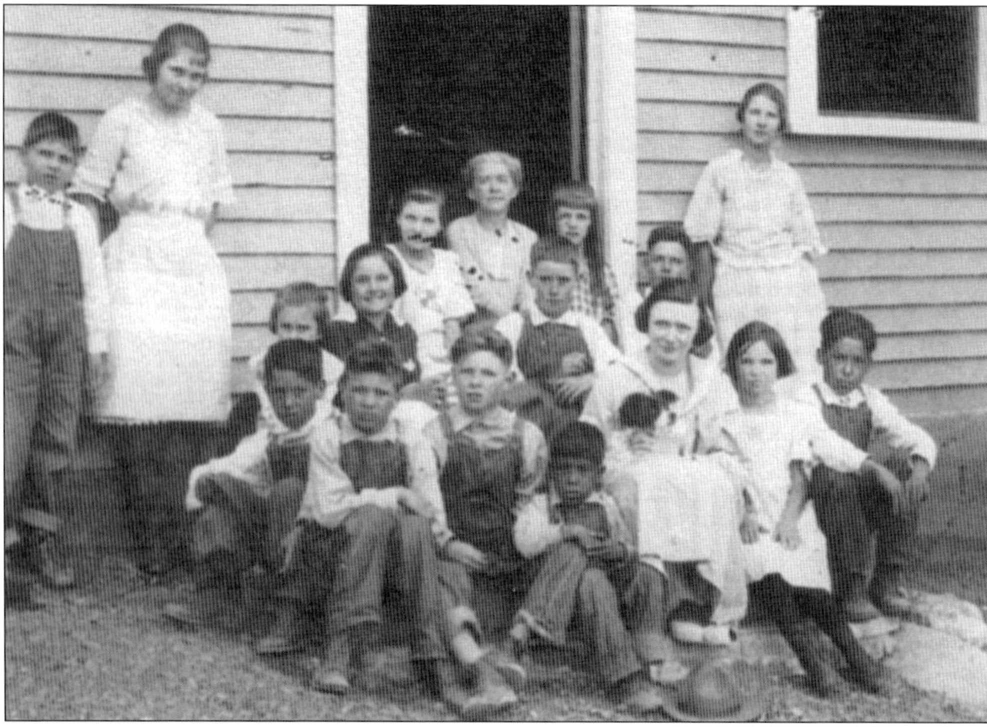

In the 1923 photograph above, Hilltop School students surround teacher Ruth Wynne (second row, second from left). Upper and lower grades had separate entrances to rooms divided by wooden doors that folded back for dances. The dances helped pay for half the cost of a piano; the county school district contributed the rest. People came from miles around, and though these were Prohibition days, bootleg whiskey was often stashed in the bushes outside. The money was collected and the piano enjoyed by students and the community until the struggling mine closed permanently in 1937. Seen below in 1923, Wynne walked through Casper Tunnel, hollowed through the mountaintop, to visit her pupils who lived on the Paradise side and made that journey, using a headlight, twice daily. She wears a popular cloche and practical high boots. (Both, Barbara Miller.)

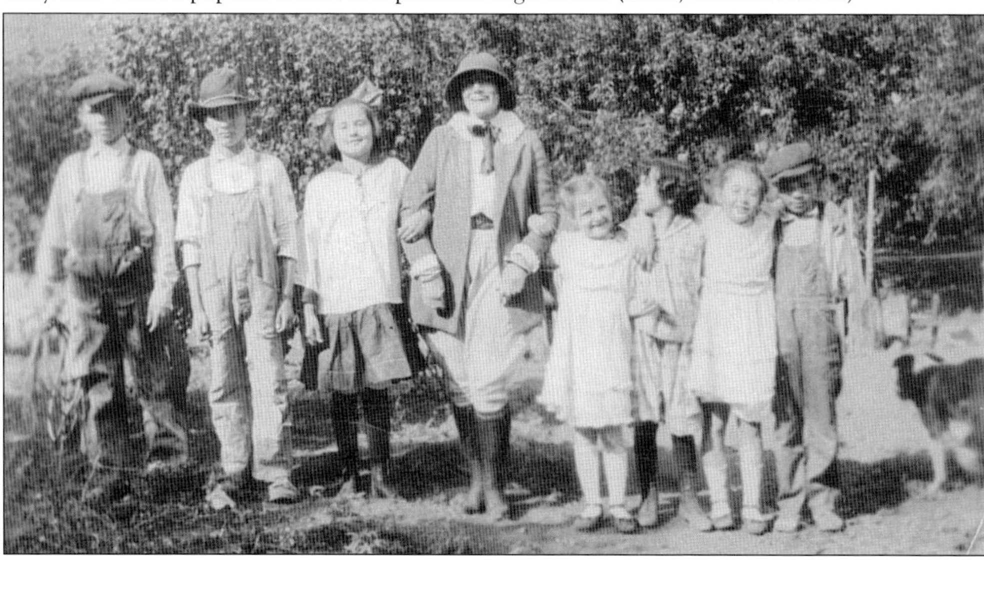

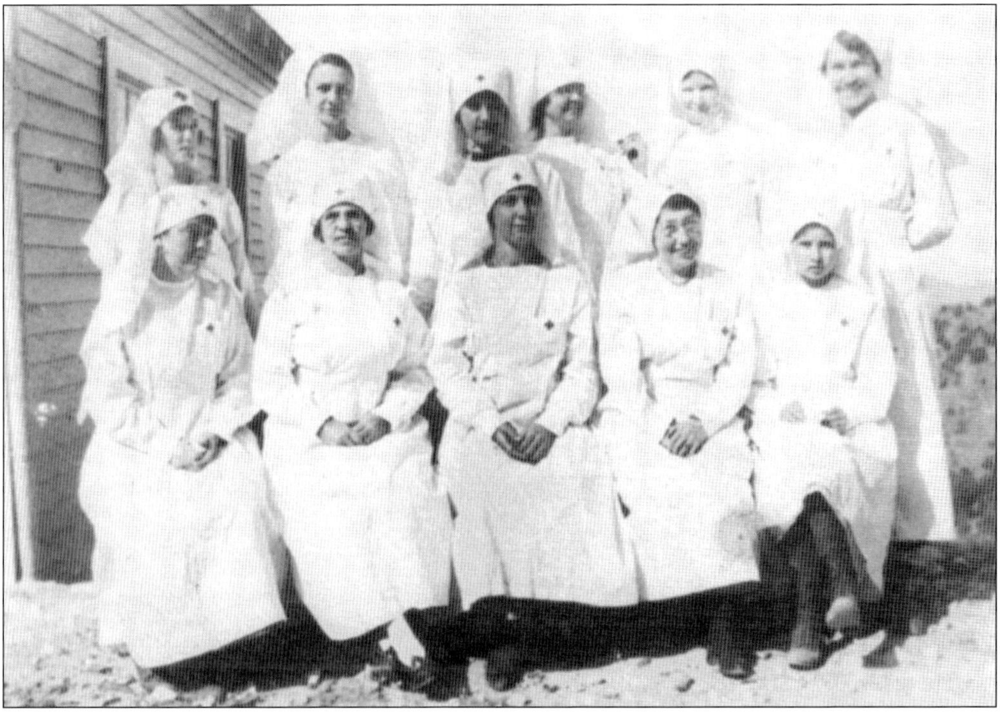

Towards the end of World War I in 1918, influenza broke out among soldiers on the front and spread swiftly through many countries, killing more than 500,000 in the United States. Hospitals and medical professionals were overwhelmed. Thousands of women, like these at Hilltop in a 1919 photograph, volunteered to nurse the sick. Willie Mae Wakefield's mother, "Mudge" Walters, is in the first row, second from left. (Pamela Hulme.)

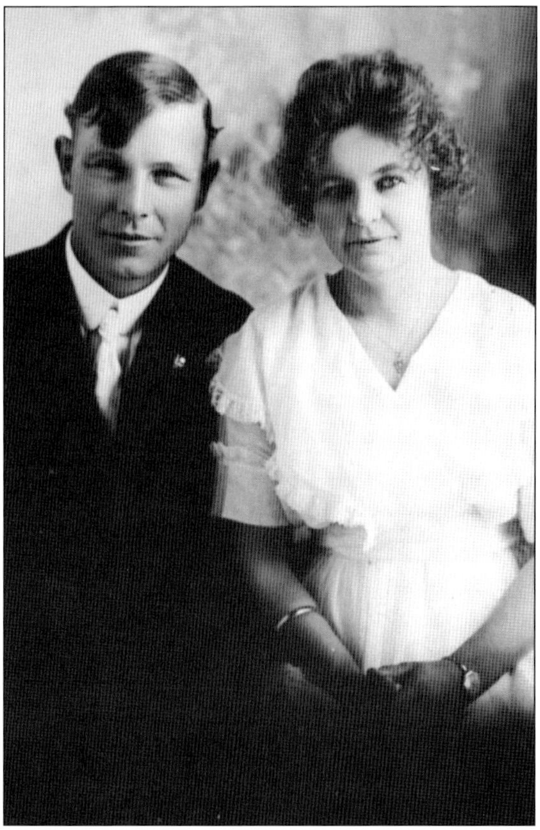

Women were scarce at mining camps, especially the kind to marry. When Willie Mae Wakefield drove into Hilltop, two young miners, Bill Sanders and Mark Chapman, were determined to win her. Chapman courted her successfully, and they were married, as seen in this c. 1920 photograph. Chapman died young, though, possibly from lung disease, which afflicted miners who worked long shifts underground. (Pamela Hulme.)

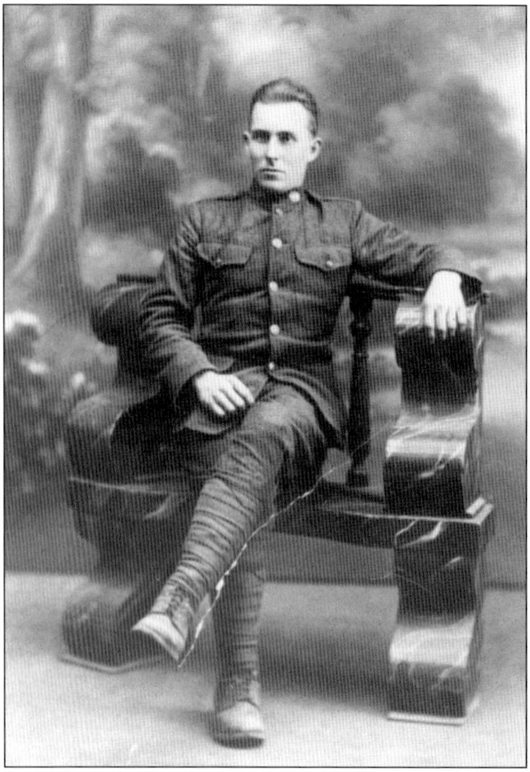

Pictured at left in 1919 is Bill Sanders, back from World War I, where he served in Siberia. He would never talk about it. Sanders worked at the Hilltop Mine when it opened in 1915 and again after the war. He had longed for Willie Mae ever since she drove up with her fatherless boys. After Mark Chapman died, Sanders moved fast. Standing by their Paradise home in this undated photograph, he and his wife had a long and happy marriage. His Leadville Mine above town produced several tons of lead ore before it played out. (Both, Pamela Hulme.)

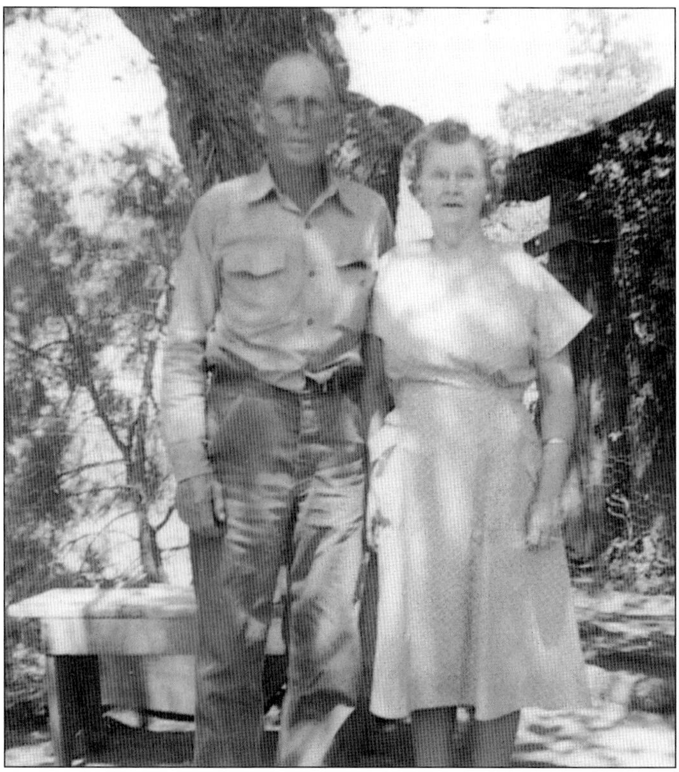

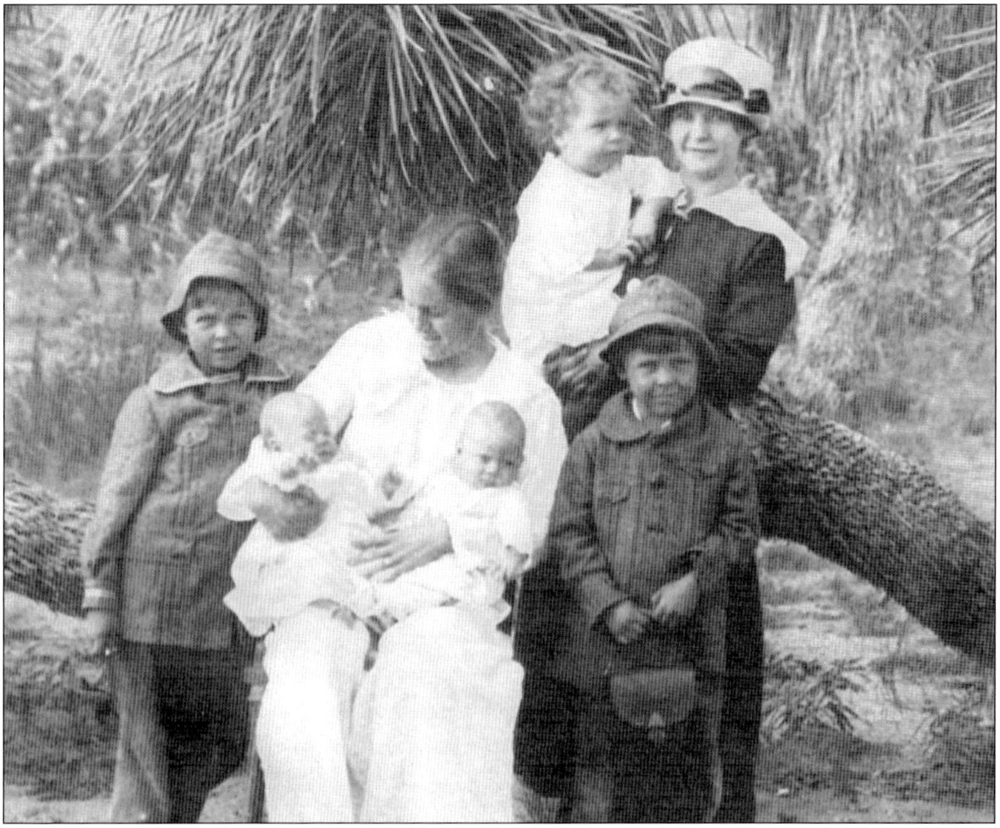

In the 1920s photograph above, Willie Mae, standing behind her two elder sons with baby Eugene, wears a stylish hat. From left to right in front are Albert, the Jones twins with their mother, and Dana. Eugene Wakefield grew up loving the wild country, but rather than be a cowboy or miner, he got a teacher's degree. He returned to his mountains when Pinetop School, seen below in the 1940s, was established for children of loggers and sawmill workers. (Both, Pamela Hulme.)

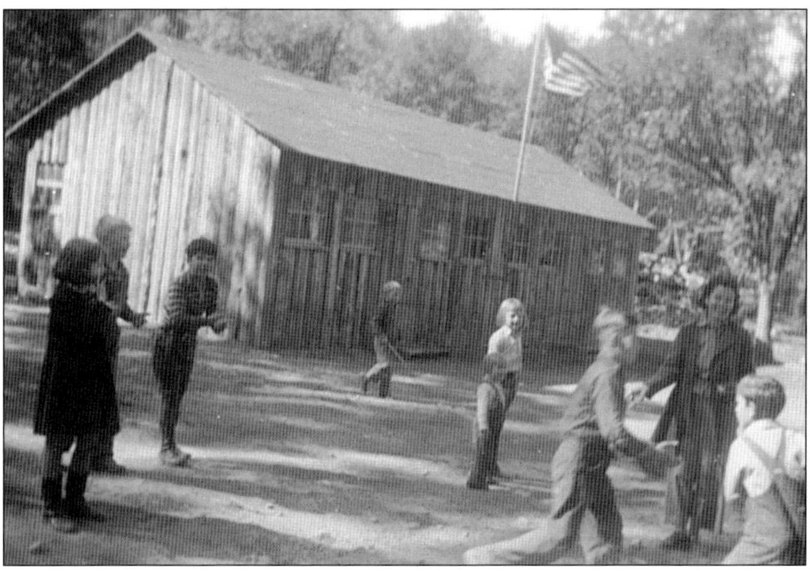

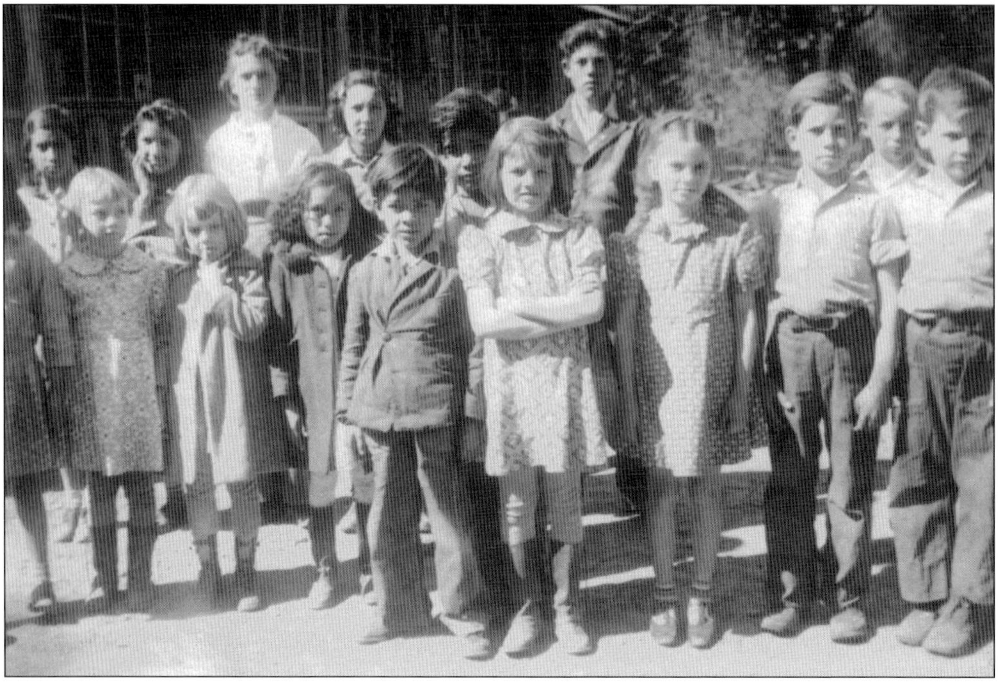

This 1940 photograph of Pinetop School students shows how they dressed a year before the start of World War II. Girls wore skirts. Those made to wear long wool or cotton stockings often rolled them down below their knees until they neared home after school. Bib overalls were usual for boys. (Pamela Hulme.)

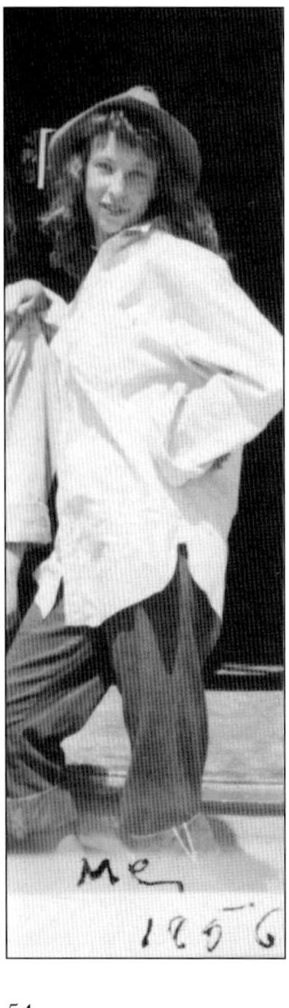

Sadie Hawkins Day, an enduring folk event, originated in Al Capp's *Li'l Abner* comic strip that ran from 1934 to 1978. Girls could pursue boys, and there were often dances where girls invited their partners. A big part of the fun was dressing sloppily, in men's garb. In this 1965 photograph, Pamela Wakefield, granddaughter of Willie Mae and daughter of Eugene Wakefield and his wife, Bella Lou, models her father's shirt at Miami High School. (Pamela Hulme.)

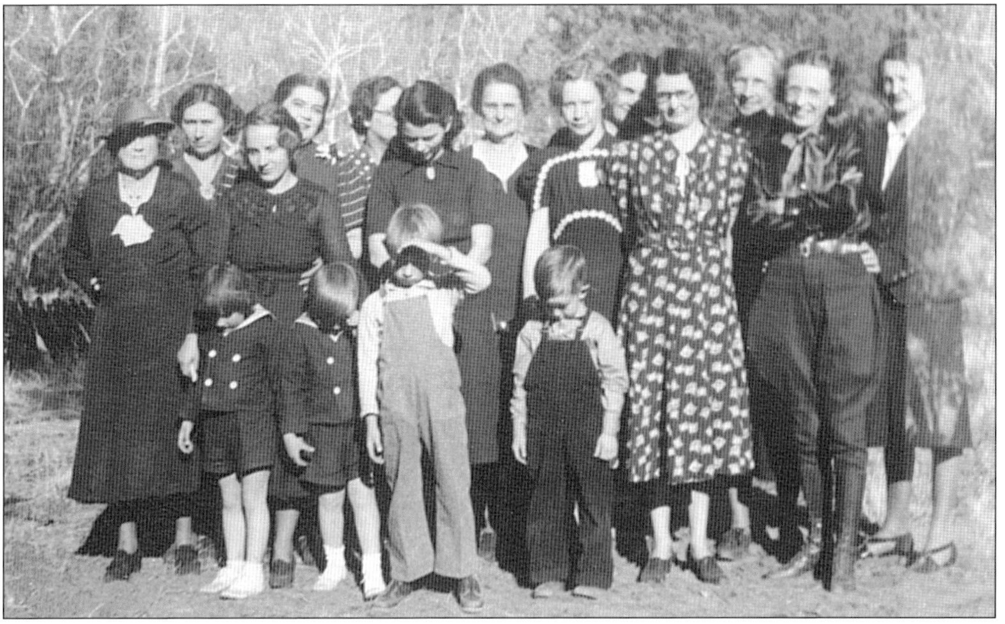

This 1938 photograph is labeled Women's Club of Paradise. Children are unidentified but presumably stand in front of mothers. From left to right are Bellah ?, ? Wheeler, unidentified, Ruth ?, wife of a Civilian Conservation Corps (CCC) man, wife of CCC man, Elizabeth "Bea" Epley, two unidentified women, wife of CCC man, ? Virmond, Ruth's helper, and Belle Erickson. Paradise School closed in 1930 so these children rode the bus to Portal. (Sew What Archive.)

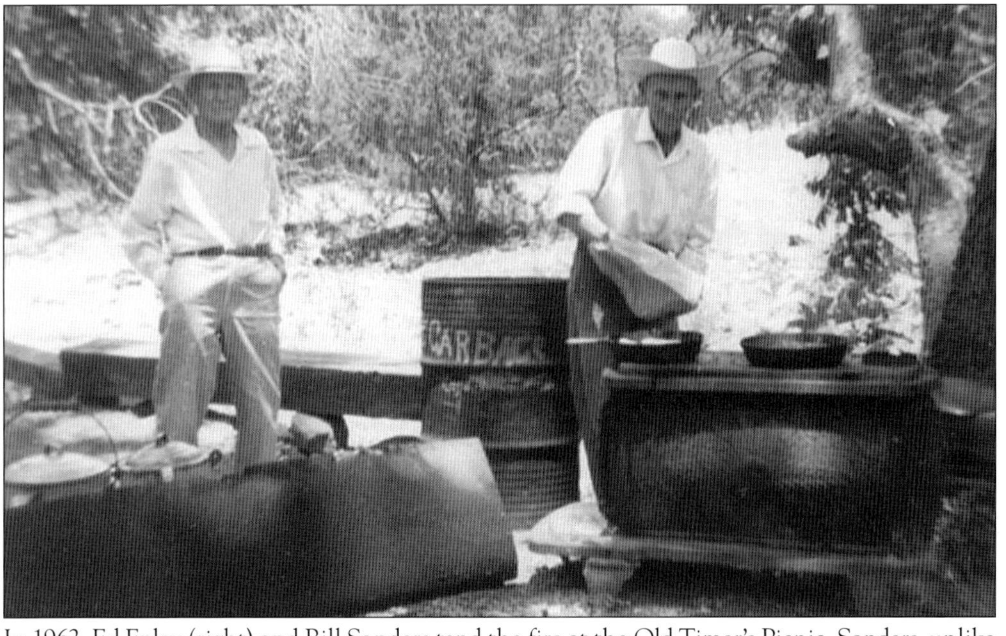

In 1962, Ed Epley (right) and Bill Sanders tend the fire at the Old Timer's Picnic. Sanders, unlike his roving father, spent most of his life around Paradise. As a boy, he helped his stepfather, George Coryell, herd goats in the foothills. Before backhoes existed, he blasted out bedrock at the Paradise Cemetery and was the last local person licensed to use dynamite. Epley bootlegged to pay for his first car. (Pamela Hulme.)

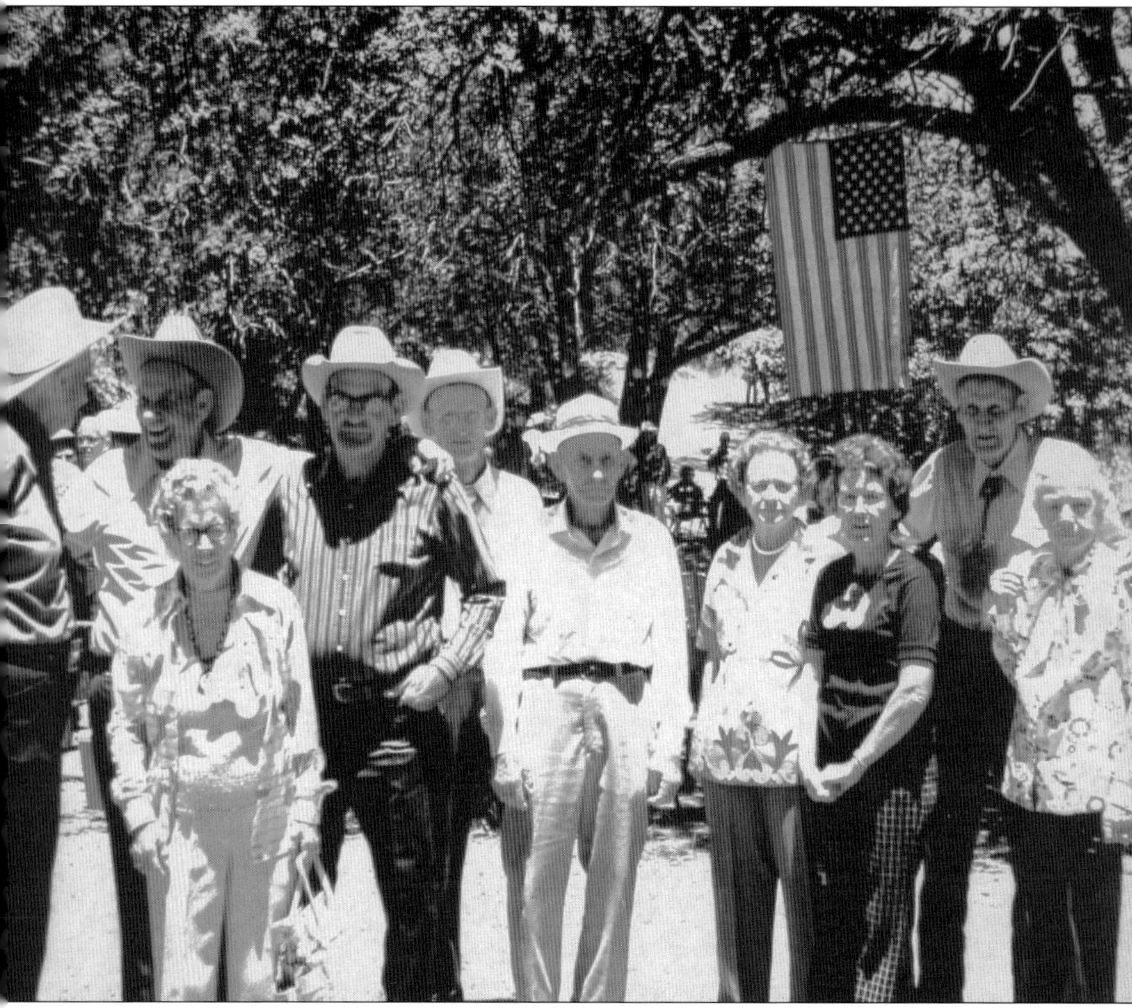

In this Old Timer's Picnic photograph, taken around 1962, are, from left to right, Ralph Morrow, former Hilltop school bus driver Alma Pague, Jimmy Coryell, a Lee brother, Bill Sanders, Laverne Olney, former Portal postmistress, Maurine Reed Walker Hicks, another Lee brother, and Mary Church Reay, a teacher at Portal and other local schools. (Pamela Hulme.)

Four

PORTAL

Portal existed because shade and water in the broad mouth of Cave Creek Canyon made a welcome resting place between Rodeo and booming Paradise, especially for weary travelers on the Rocking Stage. Ed Epley sold whiskey from a barrel to the men and let teams water free at the spring. He ran a little store from a tent and applied for a post office, which opened in 1905 with him as postmaster. Surely the railroad would run a spur line to pick up Paradise's ore. The camp was crowded into a narrow canyon so dwellings and businesses could be built in Portal. Besides, the Ajax Mine near Whitetail Canyon was hiring miners, as was the Savage Mine just over Limestone Ridge.

A townsite laid out by Emmett Powers and son-in-law Fitch McCord was dedicated in 1906. They themselves bought eight lots where they built a general store and hotel. Epley took seven lots, and A.C. Boswell bought five. He opened a saloon but sold out and moved to Rodeo after he was forced within nine months to kill the second drunk customer who threatened him. By 1908, only 46 of the 1,186 lots platted had sold. Why pay for a town lot when a person could settle on any unclaimed land and homestead, as both McCord and Powers did?

While Paradise was a mining camp with scenery but scant arable land, Portal's agricultural potential was proved by Stephen Reed's and Jack and Emma Maloneys' orchards and gardens. Most settlers planted fruit trees and grew vegetables, while some also kept chickens, turkeys, goats, and hogs. Woodcutters' camps hauled logs to sawmills and sold fuel for households and powering engines. Thousands of fence posts and innumerable cords of wood were sent by rail to Douglas.

The eagerly awaited railroad was never built. No bonanza was found. After Paradise's brief glory days, it dwindled, while Portal slowly grew. Abandoned mine shafts, inhabited only by barn owls and bats, scar the mountains, but the true treasure is Cave Creek Canyon itself, which draws nature lovers from around the world.

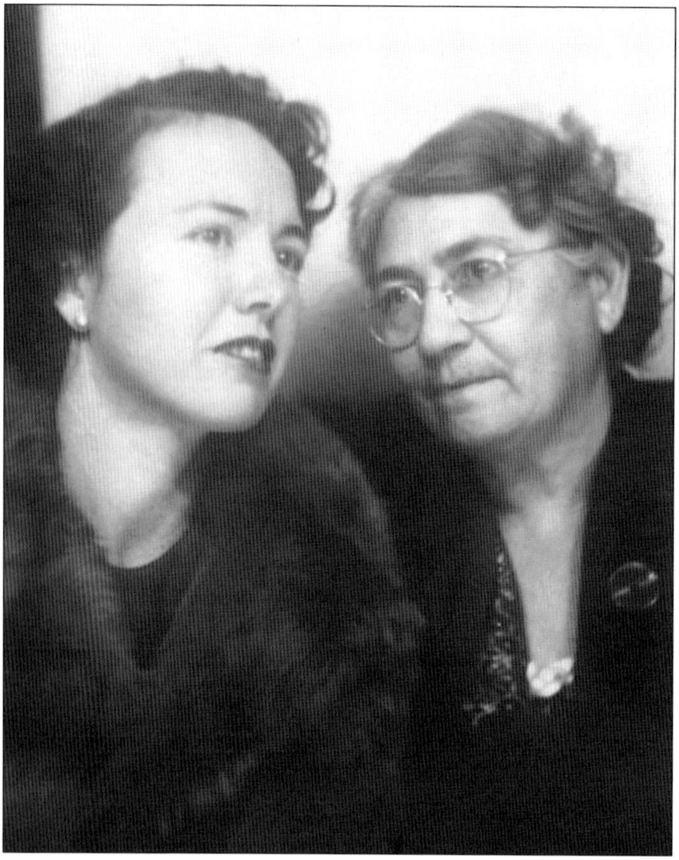

The mid-1930s photograph at left shows teacher Elsie Munda with her close friend Nancy English Sanford. The children of Civilian Conservation Corps and National Forest Service families added to those from Paradise, necessitating the construction of a larger adobe building, known as the "Big Room," next to the small existing Portal School, called the "Little Room," which was attended by the younger students in the 1938 photograph below. From left to right are (first row) Melvina Salon, Geneva Hughes, Mary Dominguez, Audrey Morrow, and Gene Lynch; (second row) Virginia Alvardo, Nancy Cox, Barbara Pague, Elsie Munda (teacher), Betty Jo Walker, and Pete Dominguez. (Both, Jim Frank Cox.)

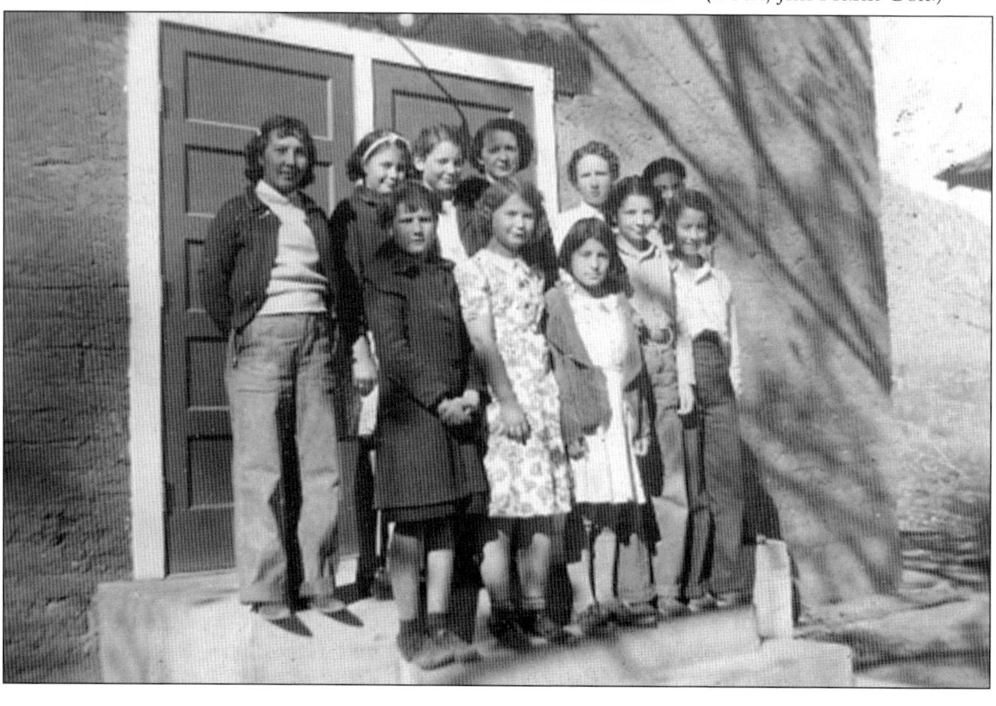

In front of the Portal School in this 1970 photograph are, from left to right, (first row) Clarissa Somoza behind flagpole, Chistine Somoza, and Jimmy Hicks; (second row) Rachel Terrazas, Patsy Somoza, Lucia Dominguez, Dolores Terrazas, Lupe Dominguez, Michael Richards, Eddie Rivers, Steven Dominguez, Cruzie Lopez, Judy Richards, Max Rothpletz, Mary Somoza, and Frankie Terrazas; (third row) Sally Rivers, Rosie Terrazas, Sheila Rivers, Virginia Cutler (substitute teacher), and Lillian Marshall (teacher). (Virginia Cutler.)

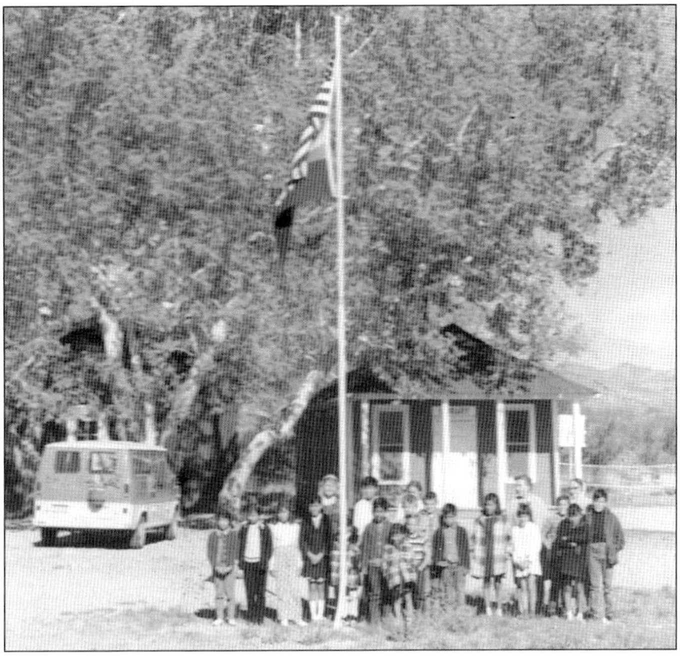

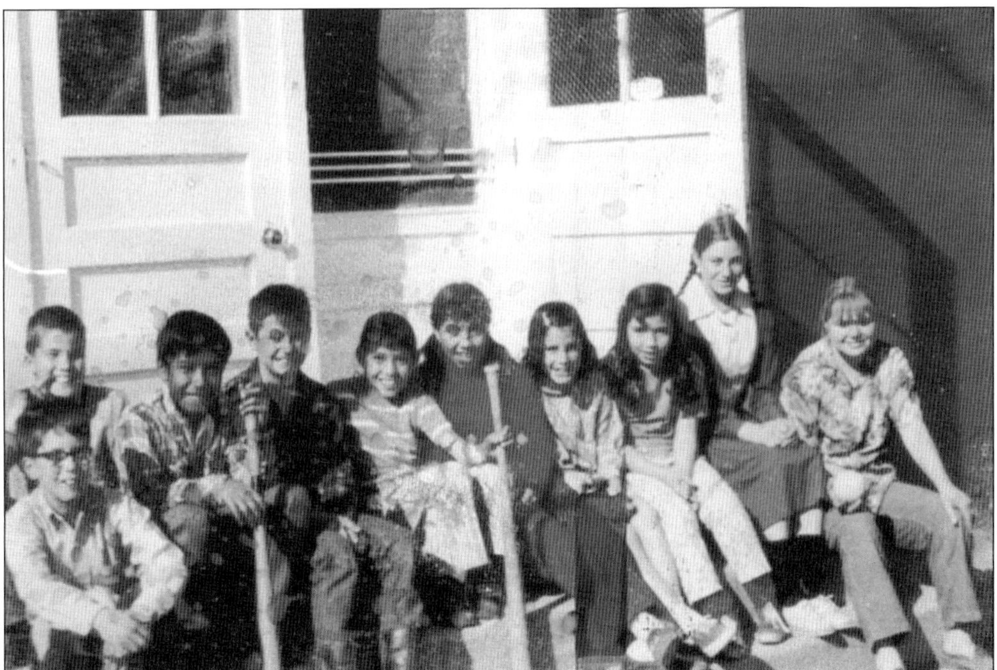

Seated on the steps of the Big Room in this c. 1968 photograph are, from left to right, Michael Richards, Max Rothpletz, Lupe Dominguez, Eddie Rivers, Mary Somoza, Lucia Dominguez, Judy Richards, Patsy Somoza, Sheila Rivers, and Sally Rivers. Sheila Clark was in the last eighth-grade graduation in 1971. The school merged with San Simon in 1973. (Sheila Clark.)

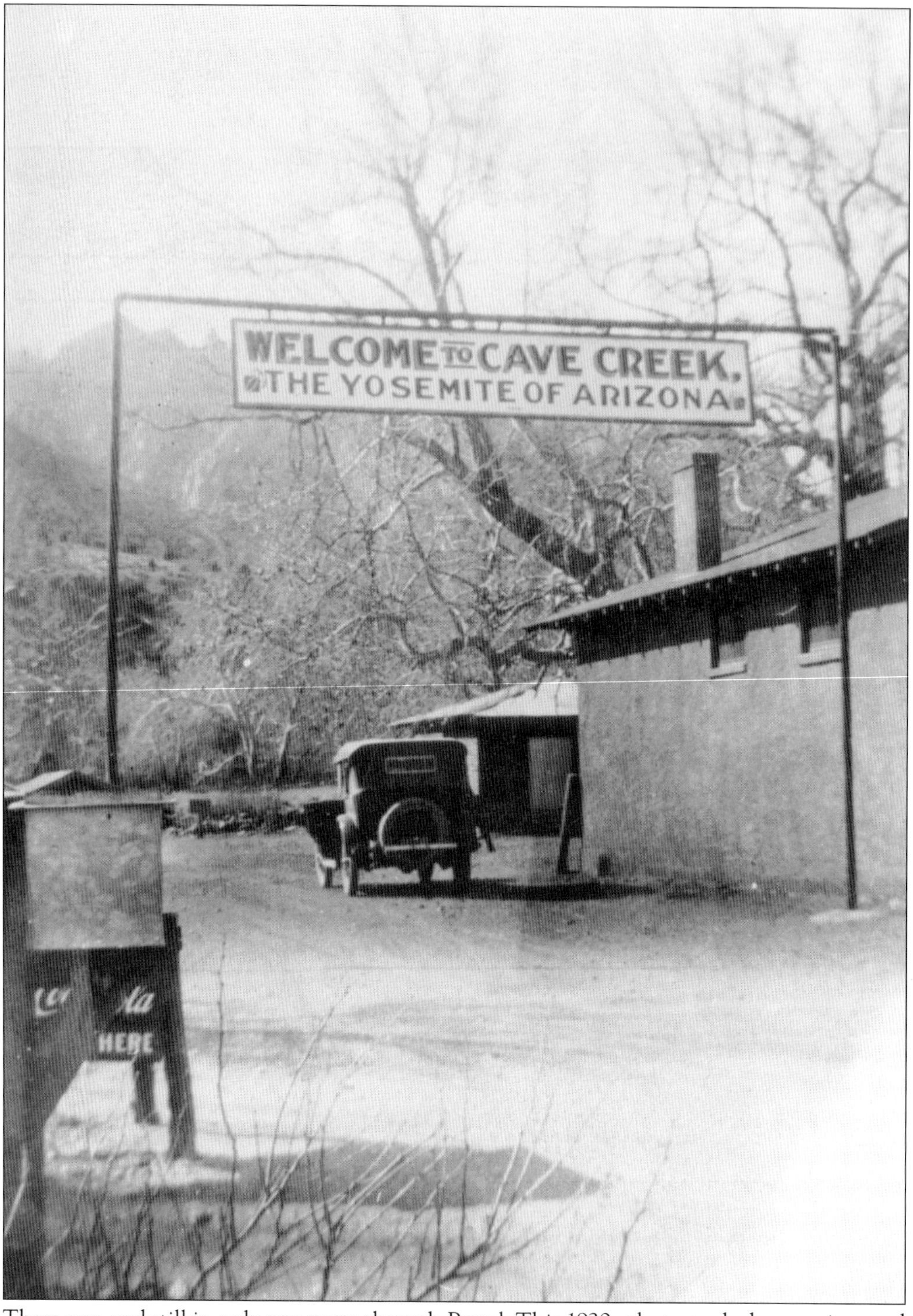

There was, and still is, only one street through Portal. This 1920s photograph shows a sign used to lure tourists in as the road narrows close to Anna Roush's store/post office. The sign vanished long ago, but the building has been a law office and a lodging, and is now a business office. (Barbara Miller.)

Anna Roush Pugsley, pictured at right in the 1970s, separated from her first husband in 1921 shortly after they sold their isolated home in Horseshoe Canyon and moved to Portal. Her brother John Pence built her store/post office and her house on the bank above them in 1921. Dr. W.C. Pugsley, assigned to give medical care to Civilian Conservation Corpsmen near Portal, married Anna in the early 1930s. Below, in this 1970s photograph, Dr. Pugsley sits in his 1930 Ford Model A coupe beside the house he built up canyon after he retired from delivering fresh meat to customers. He still gave free doctoring. Years later, his wife said when she married the 15-years-younger doctor, she thought he could take care of her "but he went and got old on me!" (Both, Myrtle Young.)

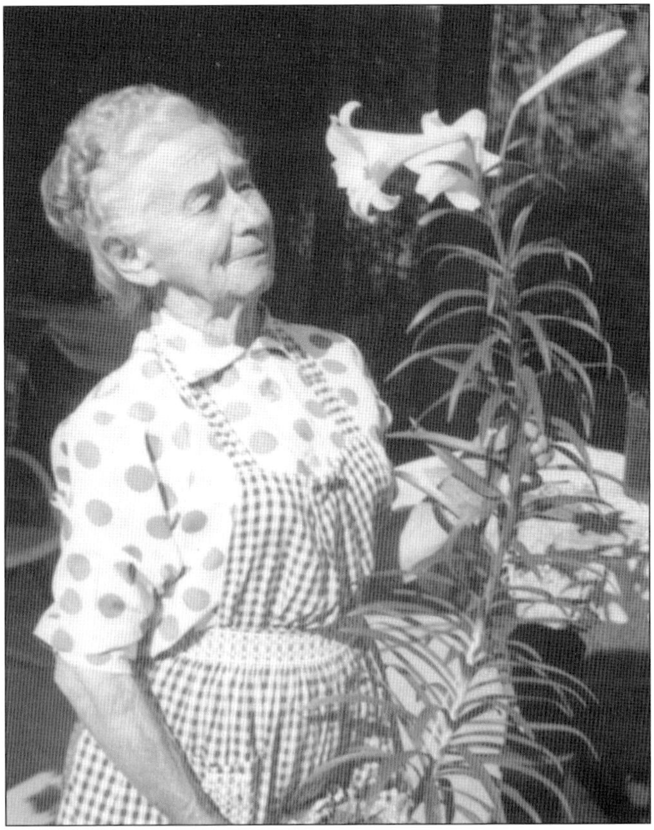

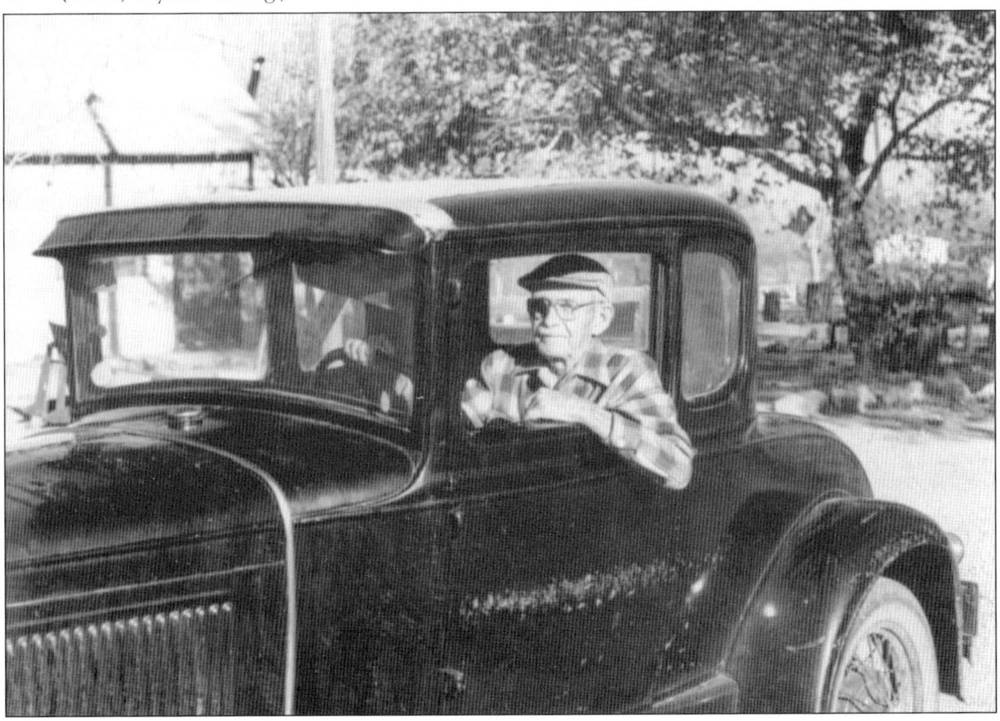

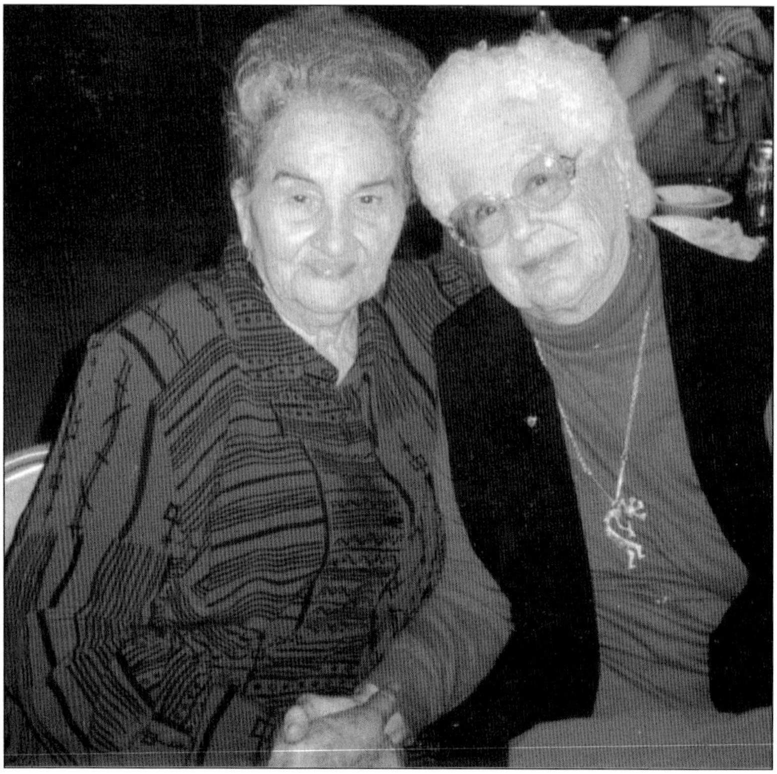

Sisters-in-law Charlotte and Frances Bagwell, shown in 1970s photograph above, remained close after Frances and Philip Bagwell divorced. Frances kept the Valley View Ranch acquired in 1957 but taught school to support her four children. A gifted artist, photographer, musician, and poet, she wrote several copyrighted religious songs, directed the Rodeo Portal Youth Choir, and was pianist at the Rodeo Baptist Church where Dr. Pugsley loved to sing. Charlotte and Ed Bagwell moved near the aging Pugsleys to help them, and Frances often visited with her children who loved "Lady Ann" and "Pug." On February 14, 1975, at right, at the ranch, one daughter, Myrtle, who would have a distinguished career in juvenile justice, helps her husband Charles "Red" Young cut their wedding cake. She is radiant in grandmother Myrtle Belle Ferguson's 1910 gown. (Both, Myrtle Young.)

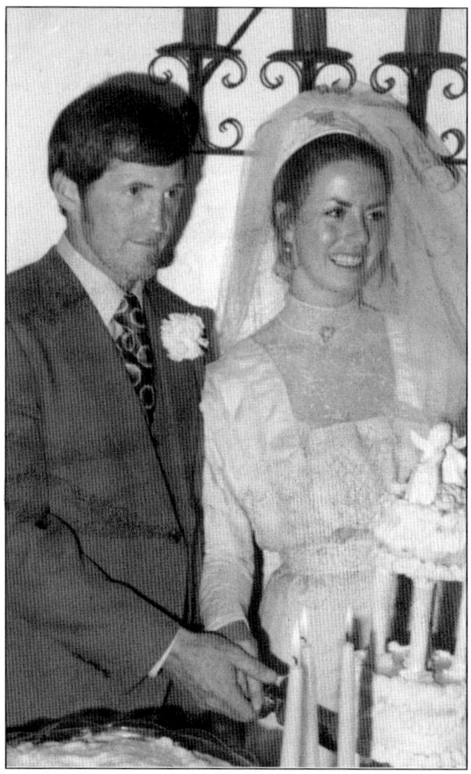

John Hands used some of his money from the sale of Hilltop to acquire ranches and homesteads whose owners were forced to sell in the hard times following World War I. He took over James Reay's Oasis Orchard in 1927, moved there, and renamed it Desperation Ranch. He always kept a kettle of beans cooking in this kitchen, where University of Arizona archaeological students are shown gathering in this 1930s photograph. (Alden Hayes.)

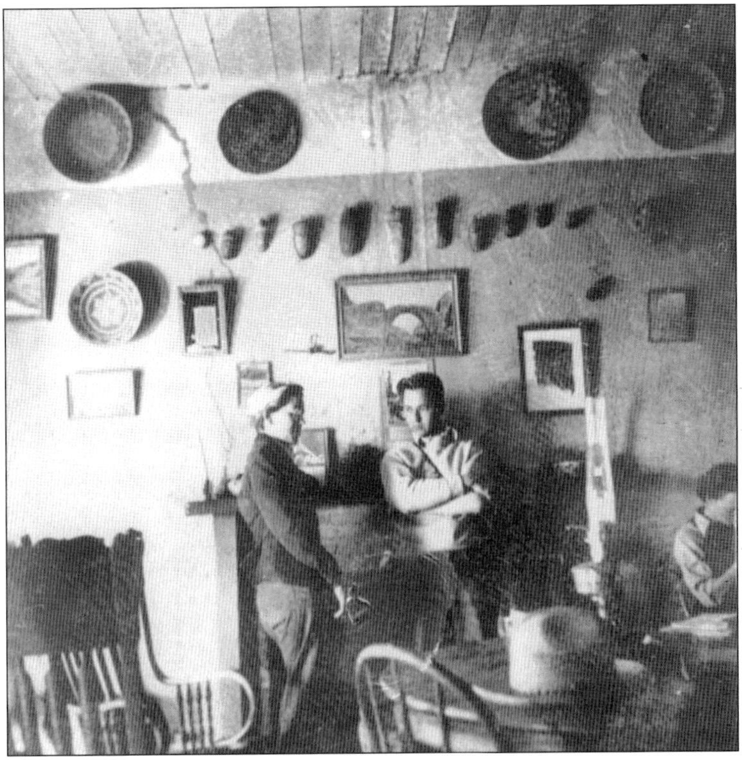

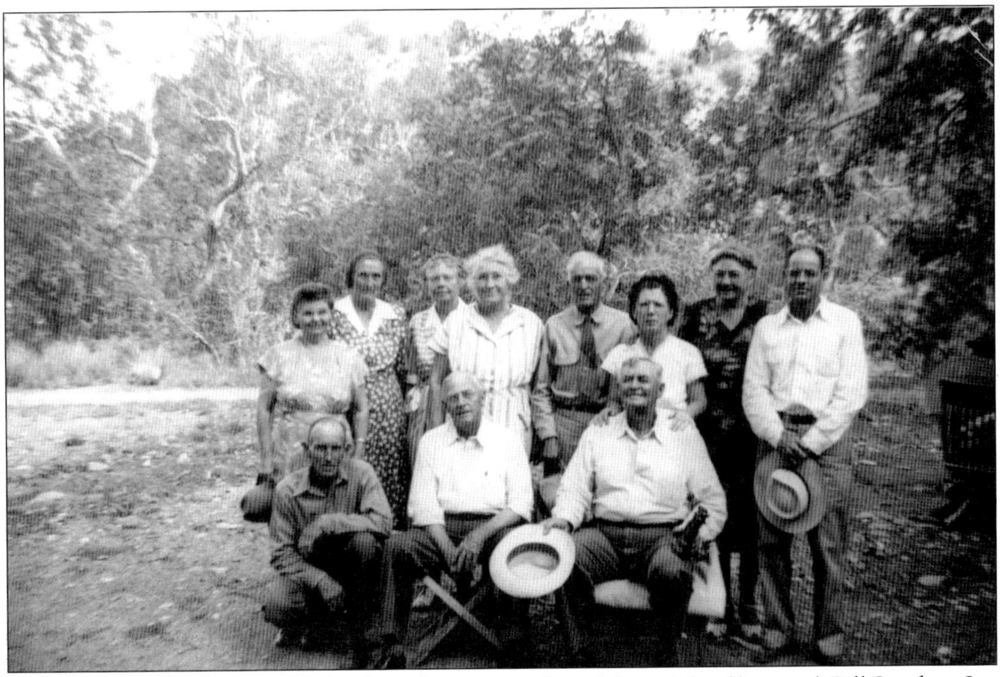

Gathered outside the Portal School teacherage are, from left to right, (first row) Bill Sanders, Joe Jones, and Ben Sanders; (second row) Willie Mae Sanders, Lula Walker, Agnes Andress, Mabel Jones, Andrew Andress, Carmen Walters, Nancy English Sanford, and Roland Walters. (Jim Frank Cox.)

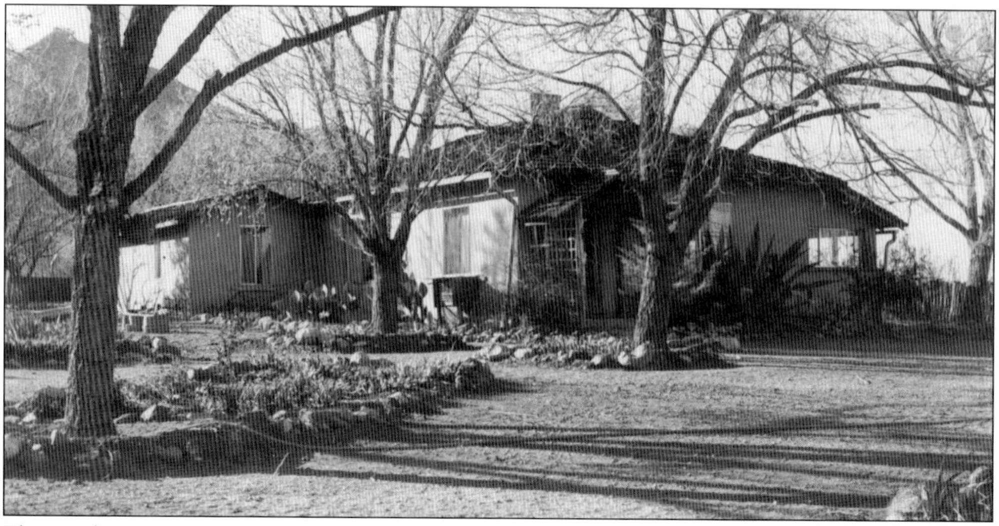

Elsie and Myriam Toles, daughters of a Bisbee mining executive, bought Frederick Finnicum's homestead above Portal where they taught school and wrote several children's books. Elsie became Arizona's first woman superintendent of education. They built and lived in the large house at right in the 1990s photograph above; in addition, they operated a girls' boarding school in the cottage at left, which also served as a guest house. Vladimir and Vera Nabokov stayed here in 1953 while he pursued butterflies and worked on *Lolita*. Neighbor Ted Troller recalls hearing Vera play the piano. Legend says they left after finding a giant rattlesnake on their doorstep. Dr. Ralph Willy looks suitably western in the 1961 photograph below, a year after he and his wife bought the place. He brought fresh ideas and new energy to the Douglas hospital. (Both, Mary Willy.)

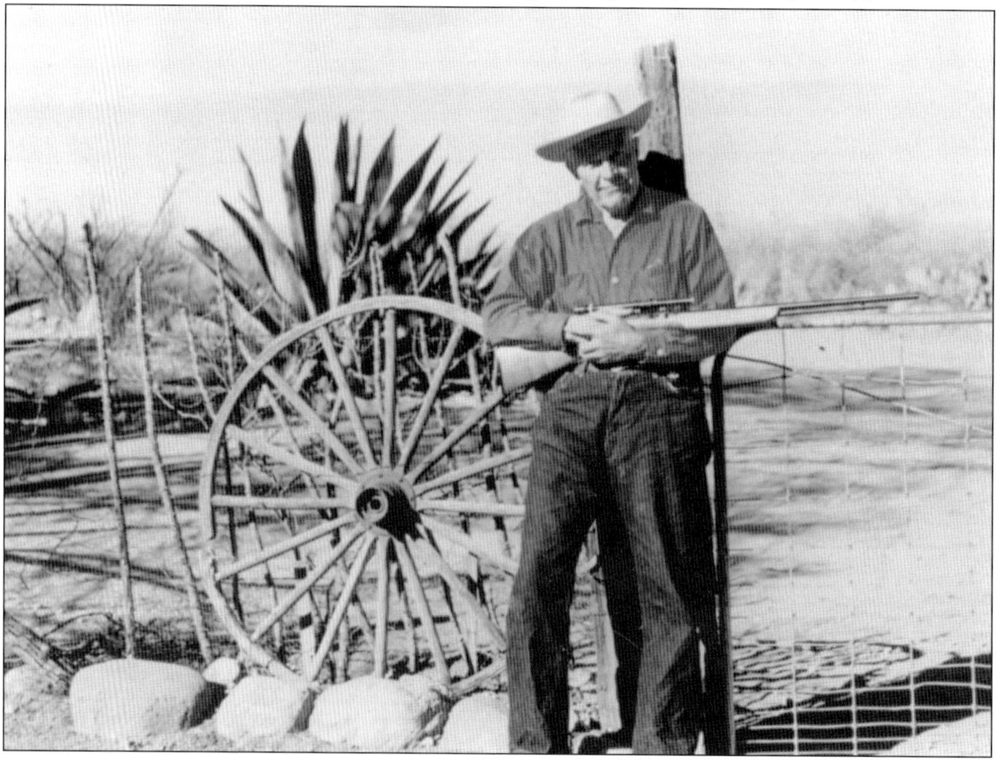

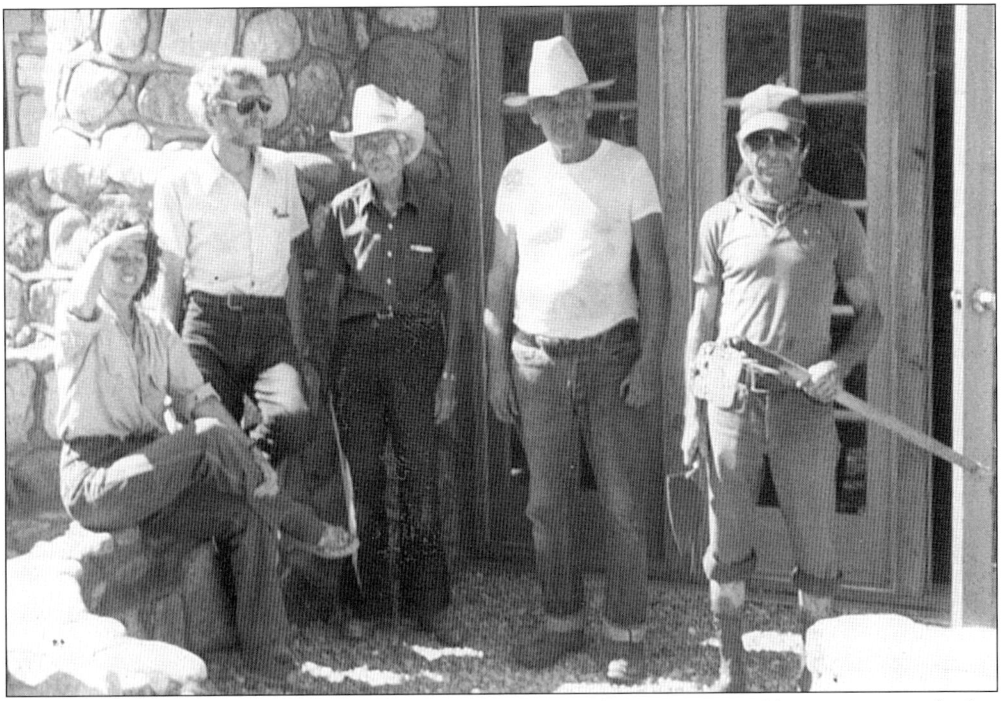

Patrick "Pat" Willy, son of Dr. Ralph Willy, left his teaching career in Chicago to care for his widowed mother. After her death, he planned this unusual house of creek stone built into a slope. From left to right in this 1984 photograph are architect builders Susan and David Nelson, Russ Crutcher, Willy, and Lupe ? The clay floor, sealed with three coats of oil, took a month to dry. (Mary Willy.)

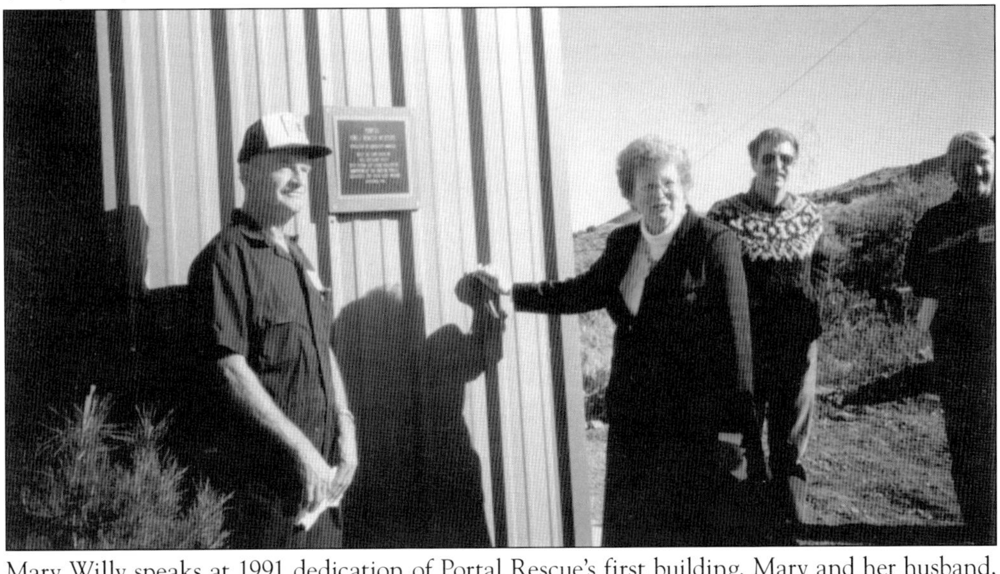

Mary Willy speaks at 1991 dedication of Portal Rescue's first building. Mary and her husband, Ralph "Bill" Willy, a volunteer emergency medical technician, donated the site. Later, she gave more land for a helispot; patients could be transferred from Portal's well-equipped rescue van into a helicopter where a nurse and paramedic could administer medications and treatment during the 40-minute flight to a Tucson trauma center, a lifesaving advance. (Portal Rescue.)

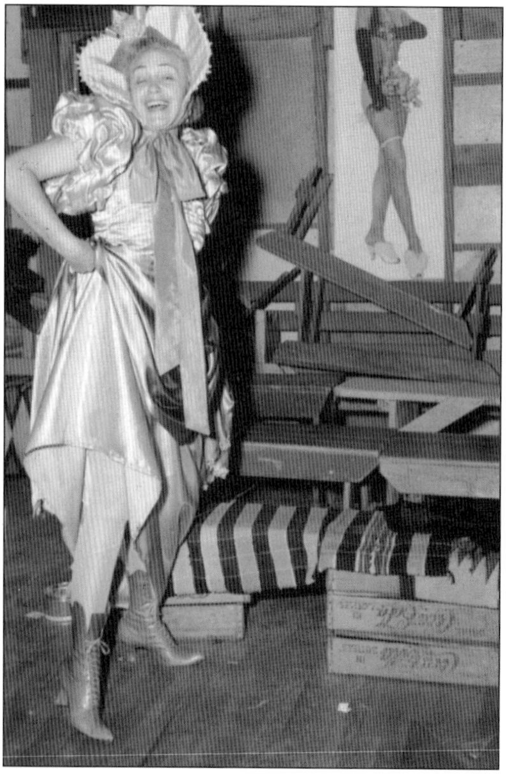

Ruth Swinford, master of ceremonies, gets in the spirit of Sew What's Gay Nineties skit in this 1957 photograph. She wrote the play and designed costumes for all the performers. Ruth Newman, as an opera singer, strives for a high note in the photograph below. She ran Newman's Store, but as a nurse, she took care of the sick and injured (sometimes schoolchildren) and delivered babies. The store had a beer license, a gas pump, and a bench in front for loungers. The competing Cave Creek Grocery had a bench, gas pump, and post office. Instead of making a long trip to town, even those who had vehicles usually bought supplies and groceries, including meat, from both stores and swapped news and views in the late evening when they picked up their mail. (Both, Sew What Archive.)

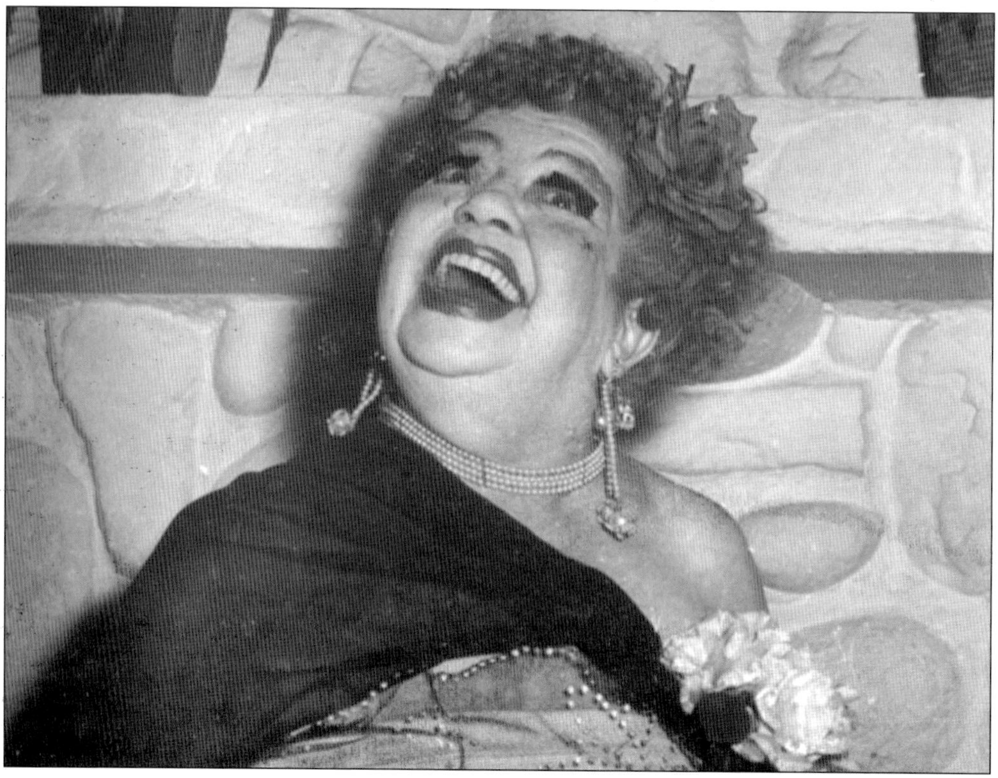

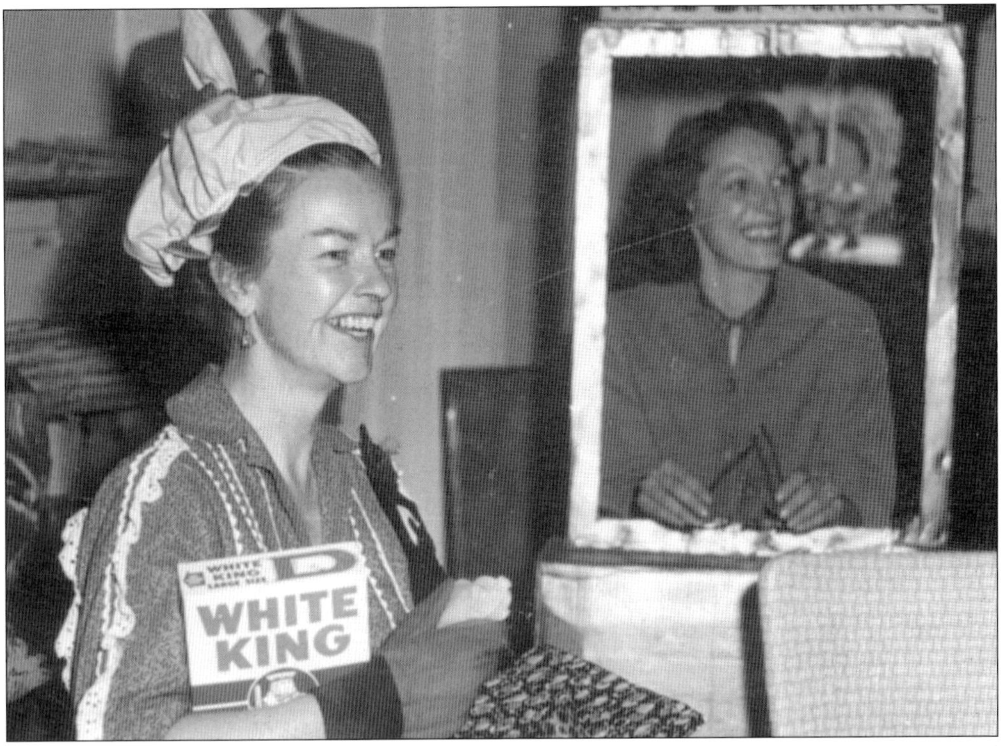

Gretchen Hayes (right) and a Mrs. Fisher enjoy a 1950s Sew What event. Gretchen married archaeologist Alden Hayes in April 1941. With their belongings in two vehicles, they drove through a valley ablaze with poppies to the Sierra Linda Ranch, which her parents, Jane and Arthur Greenamyer, had recently bought. They invited Alden to help with the work, but Pearl Harbor sent him to World War II while Gretchen waited there. (Sew What Archive.)

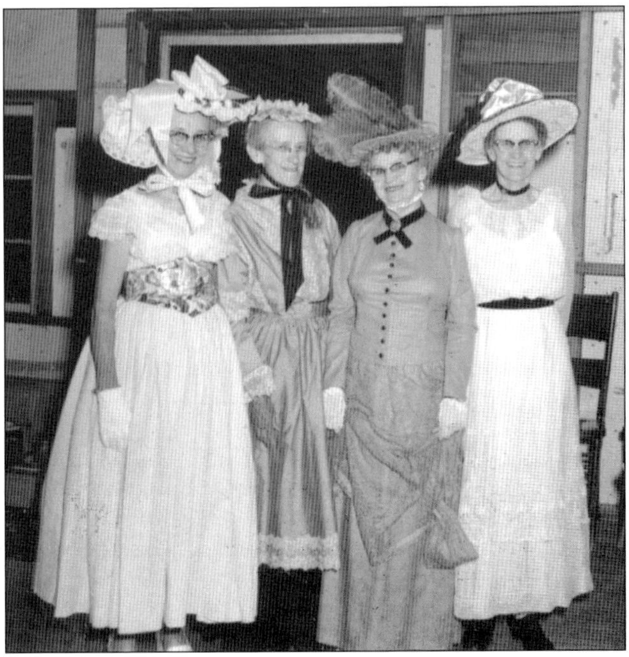

A large room at Newman's Store had a pool table, was often used for dances, and sometimes welcomed members of Sew What. Dressed in 1890s clothing, the club members in this 1958 photograph are, from left to right, Florence Koehler, Jane Greenamyer, Willie Mae Sanders, and Bea Epley. A 1919 visitor describes meeting such local women at a home canning demonstration she attended with the housekeeper of John Hands's Bide-a-Wee guest ranch. (Sew What Archive.)

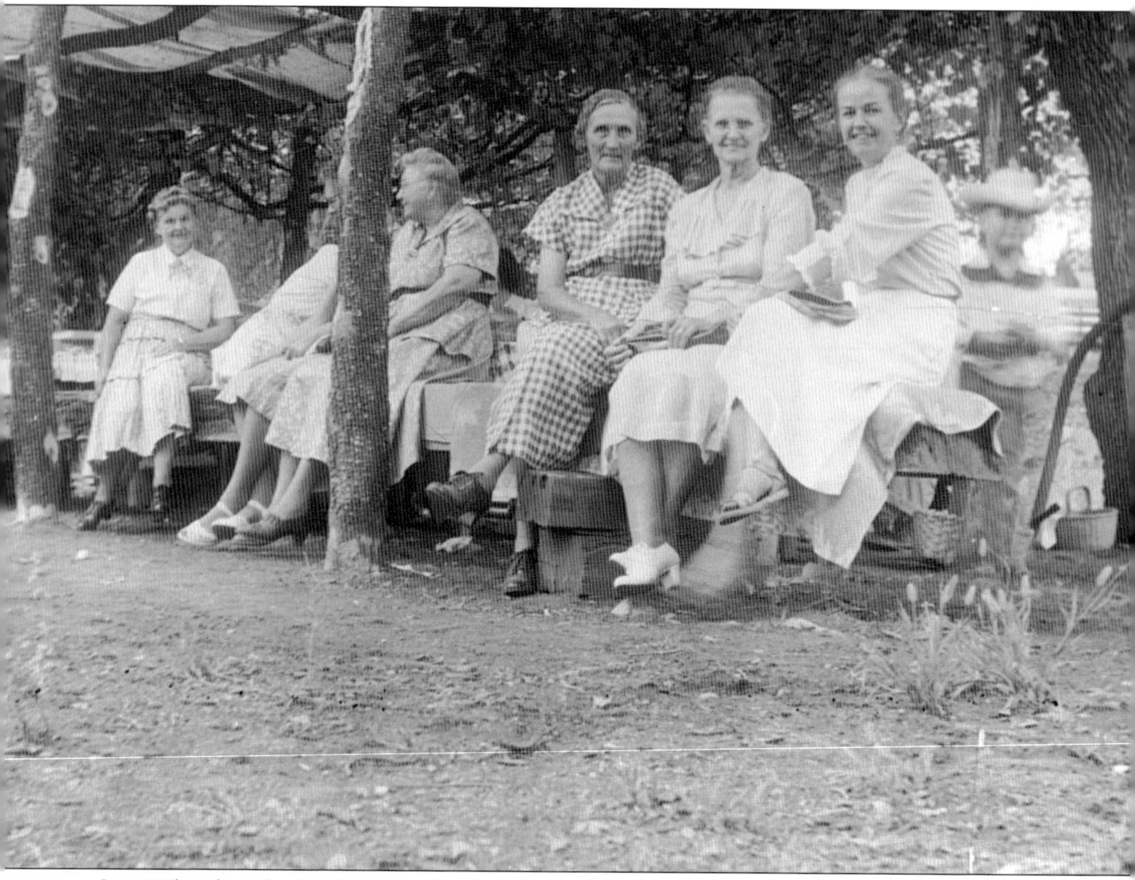

Sew What has doubled its membership in the last few decades, bringing fresh energy for club projects, scholarships, holiday gifts to a nursing home, and community forums, which in election years include a Candidates Night and pros and cons of ballot propositions. Some of the ladies in this 1950 photograph grew up before women got the right to vote. Seated in front of the old Paradise dance hall are, from left to right, Willie Mae Sanders, who worked at her mother's Hilltop boardinghouse and buried two husbands before Bill Sanders won her at last; Jane Greenamyer, who left Buffalo for the Sierra Linda Ranch; Nancy English Sanford, who nursed a young cowboy back to health and married him; Lula Reed Walker, Stephen Reed's eldest daughter; Elizabeth "Bea" Epley, who loved Paradise on first sight; and Gretchen Hayes, whose husband's career took them away for 19 years but who returned to end her days at the Sierra Linda, and her son Marc Hayes. (Pamela Hulme.)

Five

The Rescued Forest and Its Creatures

Millions of board feet had been logged from the Chiricahuas, much of it from the west side. Bisbee's Copper Queen Mine Company was the worst offender, contracting with a sawmill to supply its needs. The US government waged a 12-year court battle, demanding payment for taking trees from public lands. The Supreme Court ruled against the government shortly before Pres. Theodore Roosevelt's July 1902 proclamation of the Chiricahua Forest Reserve. Bureau of Forestry inspectors had reported that remaining trees were valuable enough for protection. This came in time to save much old-growth forest; though along the creeks and springs, livestock seeking shade, grass, and water had trampled bare the surroundings.

Forestry was a new profession. From the 1890s for over a century, policy was to extinguish flames as quickly as possible. Suppression clogged forests with debris so that catastrophic fires bake the soil into sterilized moonscapes. Now, natural fires a safe distance from dwellings are allowed to burn themselves out, and prescribed burns clean away brush to limit a fire when it starts, but increasing drought creates a forest tinderbox.

Down in the valleys, open-range grazing led cattlemen, especially corporations, to overstock. The range never recovered from the drought of 1901–1903, when 75 percent of Cochise County's herds died of thirst and starvation. Dr. Robert Forbes, of the University of Arizona's agricultural department, called the San Simon Valley one of the most devastated grasslands in the whole country. During a 1903 roundup, the creek was bogged with rotting cattle. James Hancock found the cook making coffee from water he reckoned he had strained maggot-free. That summer, a person could walk from one end of Skull Canyon to the other on decaying carcasses.

The Arizona Game and Fish Commission regulated deer and turkey hunting until 1918 when the Arizona Game and Fish Department was organized but had no money. Sheriff's deputies and cattle inspectors were given extra duties as deputy game wardens until 1929 when Ralph Morrow became warden for the southeast corner of the state and trained Kimrod "Kim" Murphy.

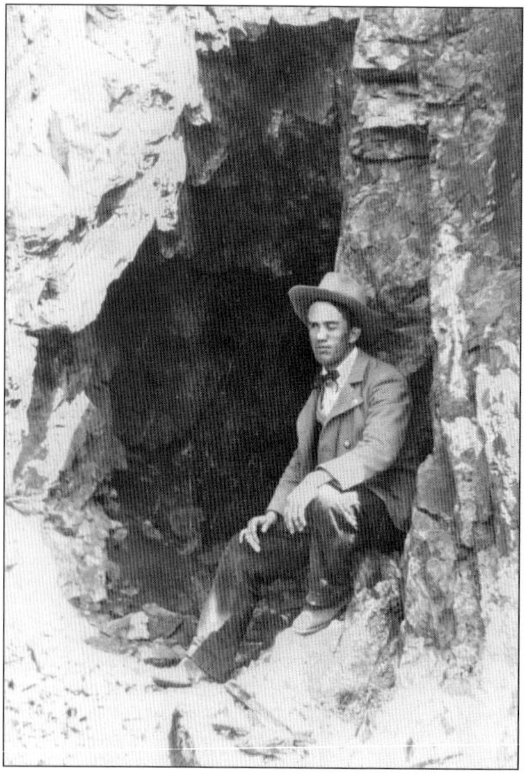

The first supervisor of the Chiricahua Forest Reserve, Charles McGlone, had the formidable task of convincing residents that they must pay for permits to cut firewood and fence posts or graze livestock. McGlone's new bride was unhappy in Paradise, so he moved his office to Douglas, far from the forest. Promoting Cave Creek's Crystal Cave as a tourist destination, he poses at its mouth in this 1907 photograph. (Coronado National Forest.)

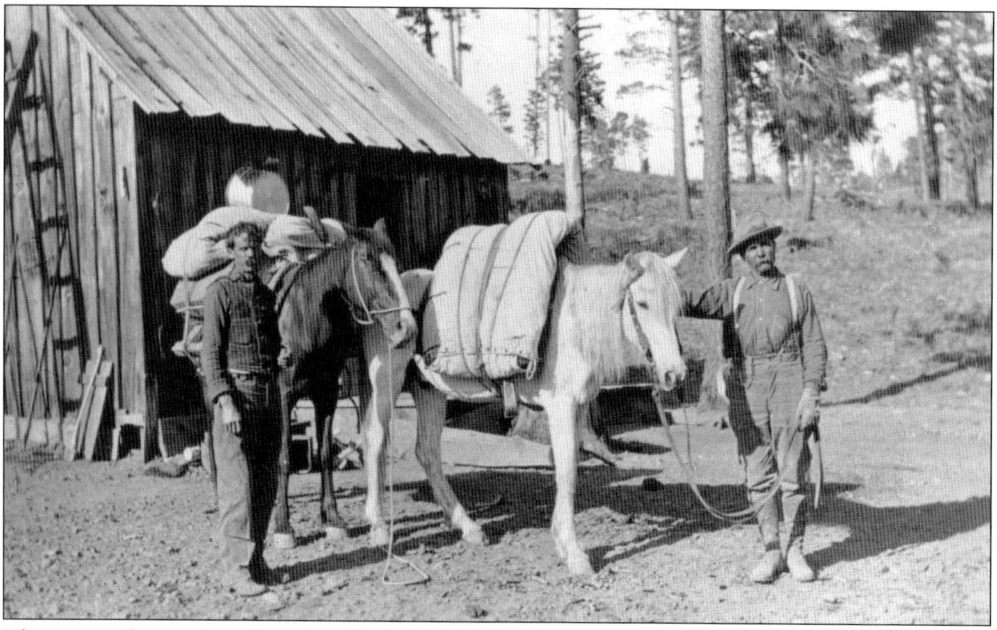

The wisest thing Charles McGlone did was hire Neil Erickson, the retired cavalry sergeant who ranched in Bonito Canyon. Erickson checked mining claims and grazing permits, surveyed and mapped forest boundaries, organized crews to fight fires, and grew saplings that he planted among stumps of trees felled by loggers. Pictured in 1910 at Barfoot Park with ranger John Wethered (left), Erickson (right) prepares to pack supplies to higher outposts. (Coronado National Forest.)

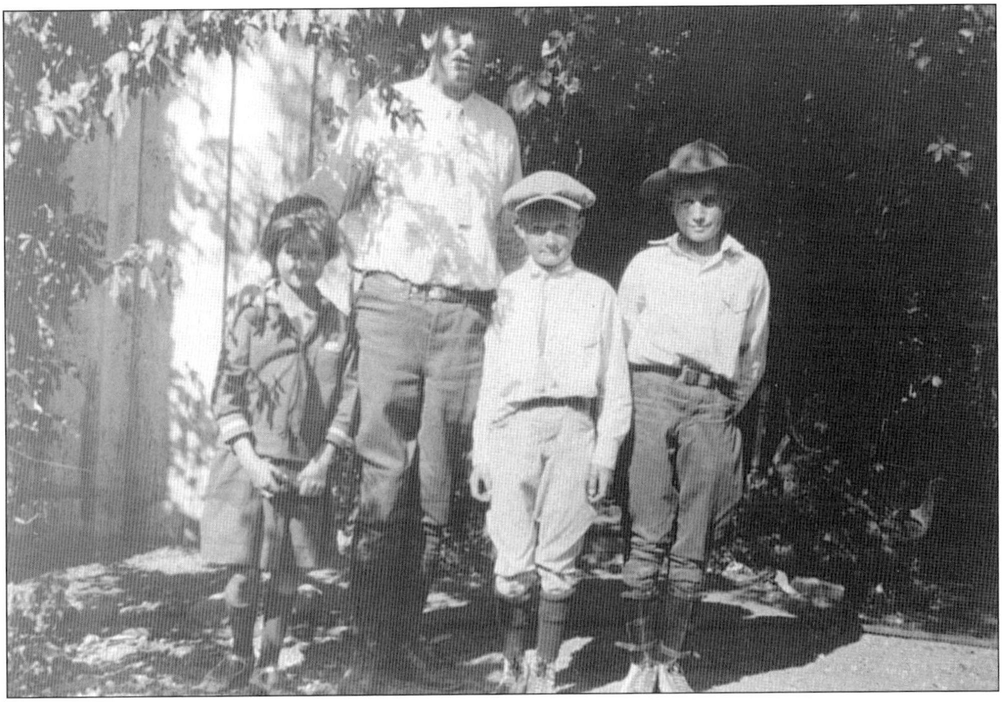

Charles McGlone got Neil Erickson suspended shortly before his own removal in early 1908. Chief forester Gifford Pinchot sent inspectors to every reserve so that incompetent political appointees could be dismissed. Prussian-born Arthur Zachau replaced McGlone in April 1908. Above, in the early 1920s, Zachau stands with his children, from left to right, Elsie Sophia, Walter, and Arthur Jr. By April 15, 1908, Zachau had reinstated Erickson and rode all over the mountains with him. Zachau set up headquarters, a tent built on a platform in the mouth of Cave Creek Canyon, which in 1909 was connected by telephone to ranger outposts. The photograph below shows where John Hands used dynamite to help Erickson string wire around denuded Ida Peak to Erickson's headquarters. Zachau let local folk buy their own telephones and use the forest line. (Above, Alden Hayes; below, Coronado National Forest.)

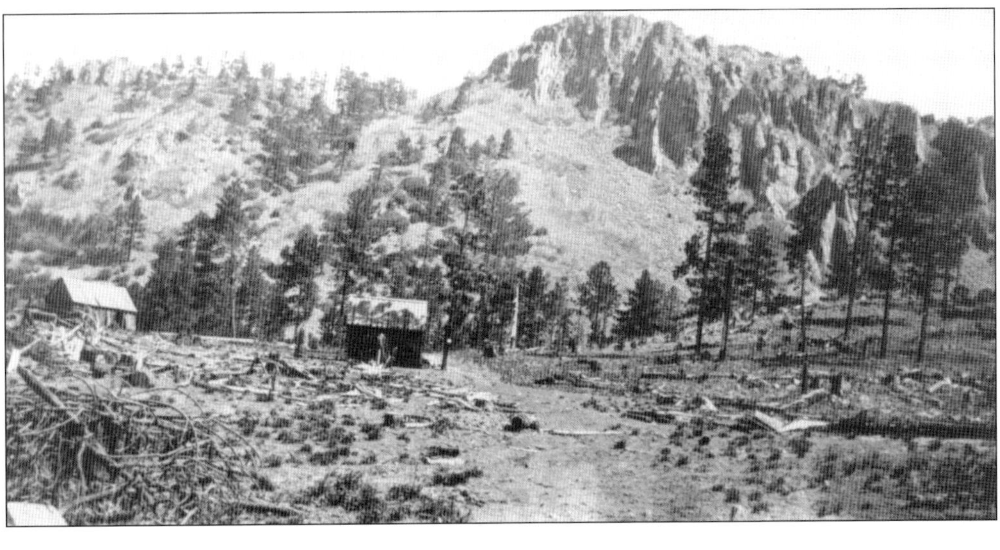

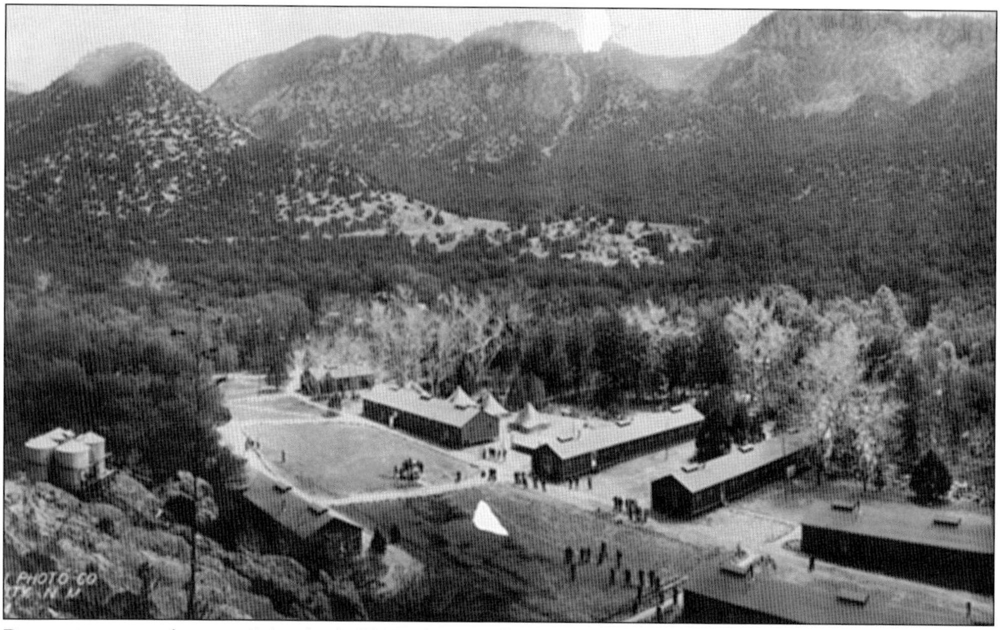

Becoming president on March 4, 1933, during the Great Depression, Franklin D. Roosevelt at once launched his New Deal programs. Perhaps the most successful was the Civilian Conservation Corps. The Cave Creek camp, pictured above in the 1930s, opened June 1, 1933, and did not close until 1942. Young men like those pictured below took basic training at an Army post before their assignments to projects. Of their $30 monthly wage, $25 was sent to their families. Married World War I veterans, placed in separate companies, were added to the program. The Portal Company vastly improved the mountainous roads, put in culverts, and built bridges and the Cave Creek Canyon campgrounds, as well as log and rock check dams to stop erosion. (Both, Coronado National Forest.)

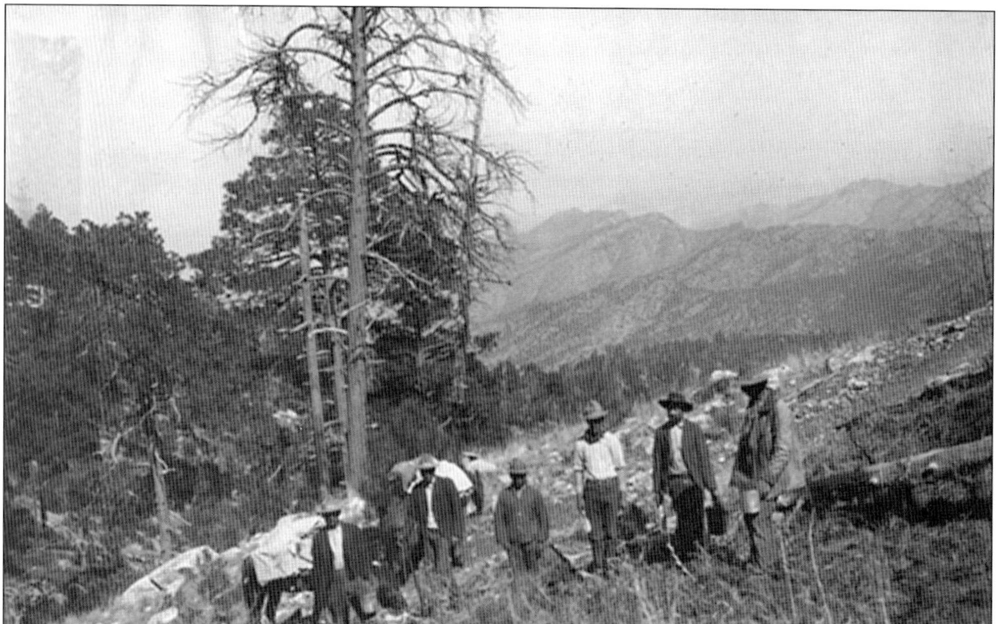

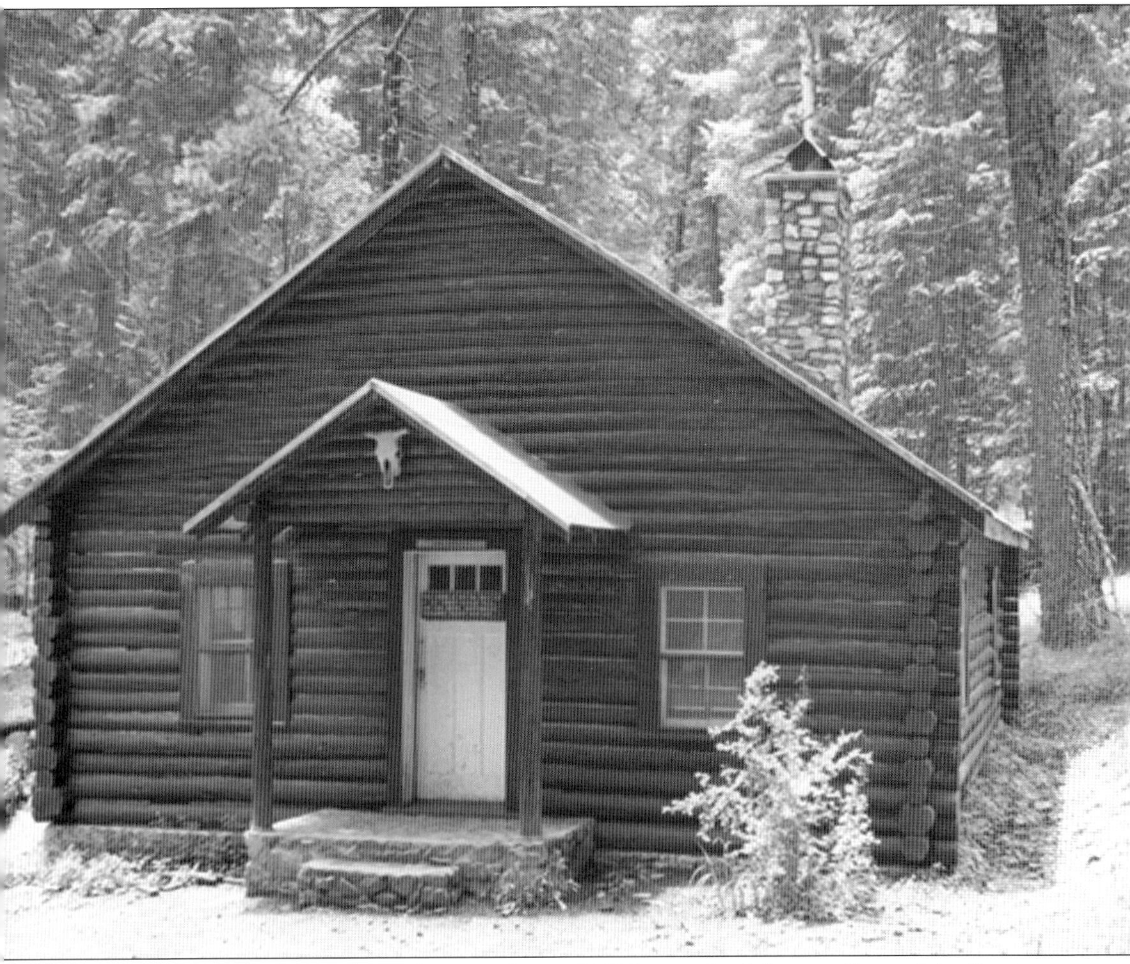

The Cima Ranger Station, shown here in the mid-1930s, was built by enrollees of the Bonito Canyon Camp. It had two bedrooms and a large kitchen warmed by a wood-burning range, which supplied the luxury of water heated in its reservoir by circulating coils. Water was piped into the cabin from a spring above. (Coronado National Forest.)

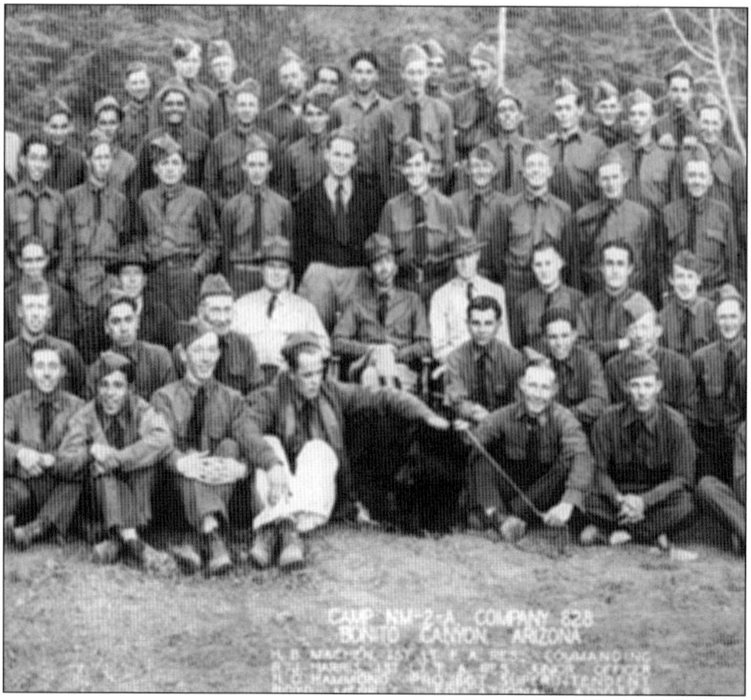

After around 1935, the Bonito Camp men, shown here with their mascot bear, worked on building the campground and headquarters complex of the nearby Chiricahua National Monument. These, with roads and trails they made, enhance visits to the weirdly beautiful Wonderland of Rocks. (Coronado National Forest.)

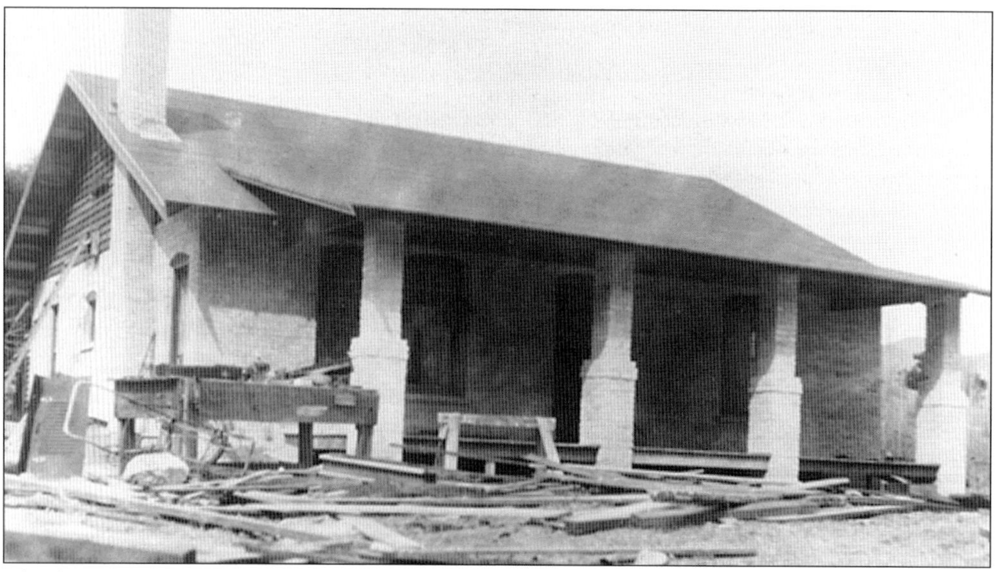

The first Portal Ranger Station was a small brick building on a rise above the one in this 1930s photograph. When Ranger Carl Scholefield was allotted $1,000 to build a home for his family, the bricks of the 1910 station were used in it. One of the oldest Coronado National Forest structures, it is now the Cave Creek Visitor Center, with informative displays and videos. (Coronado National Forest.)

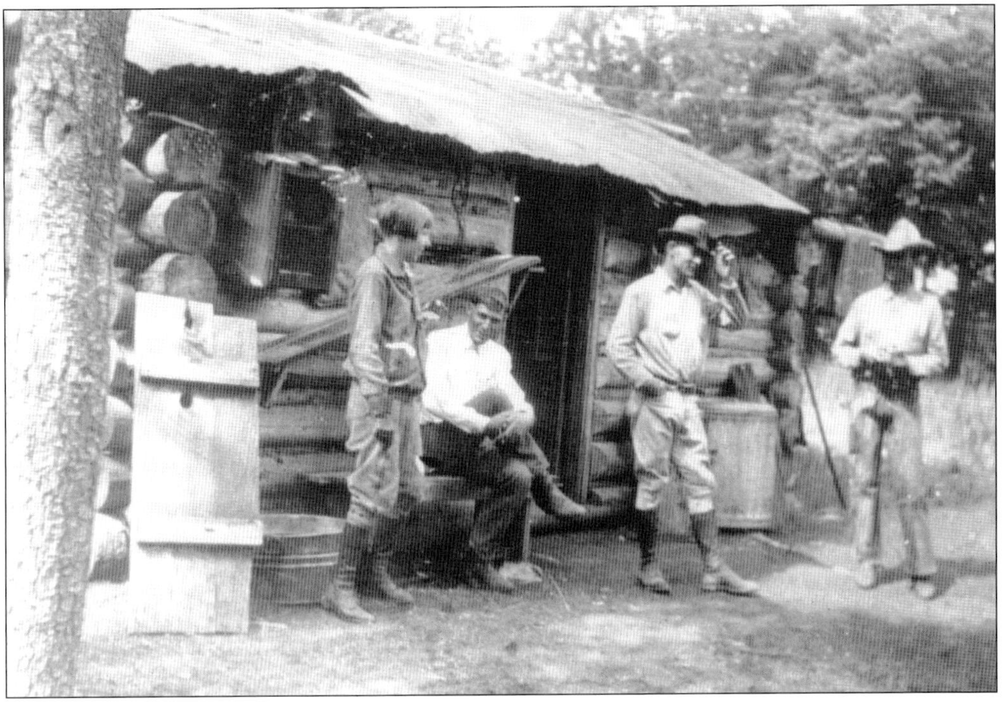

Blackie Stidham, third from left in this 1930s photograph, lounges with friends outside the Fly Peak ranger's cabin. Stidham built roads, houses, and did rock work throughout the region. Near the cabin is the wooden lookout tower built by Cave Creek corpsmen. The peak is named for C.S. Fly, renowned for his photographs of the surrender of Geronimo, who once homesteaded there. (Barbara Miller.)

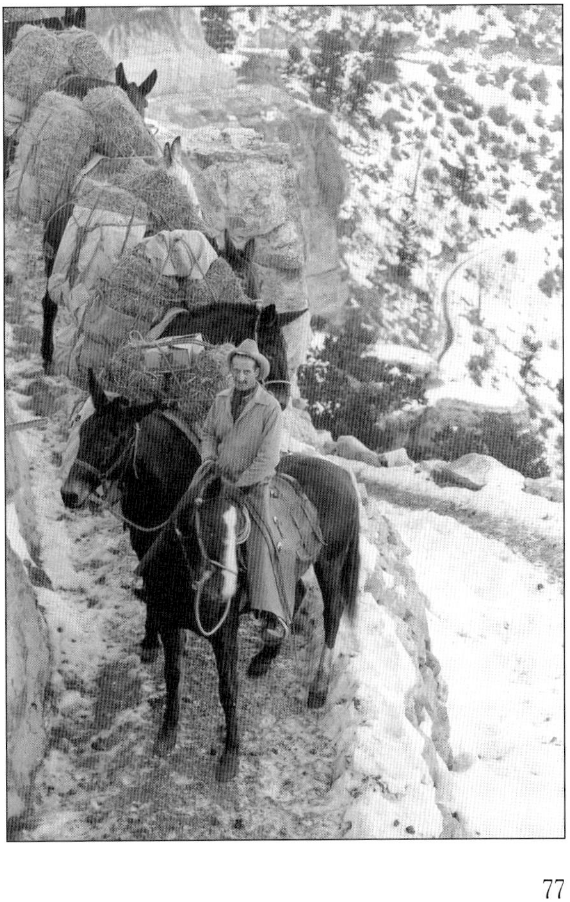

Packers like this corpsman in the 1930s carried supplies on steep, hairpin trails no vehicle could manage. They delivered necessities to work crews, ranger outposts, and lookout towers. These tall structures usually had an enclosed space where the lookout and smoke chaser slept. (Coronado National Forest.)

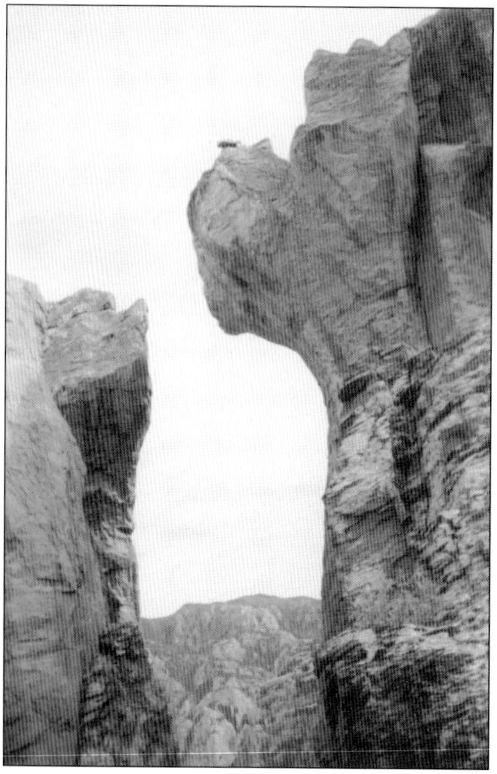

An often hazardous duty of rangers is rescuing people from places they should never have gone, such as this overhang on Silver Peak. The sheriff's trained search and rescue team operate from Bisbee, a two-hour drive, though a helicopter is called in case of serious injury or someone stranded in a spot inaccessible by ground. Area emergency medical and fire departments are often first on scene. (Kim Murphy.)

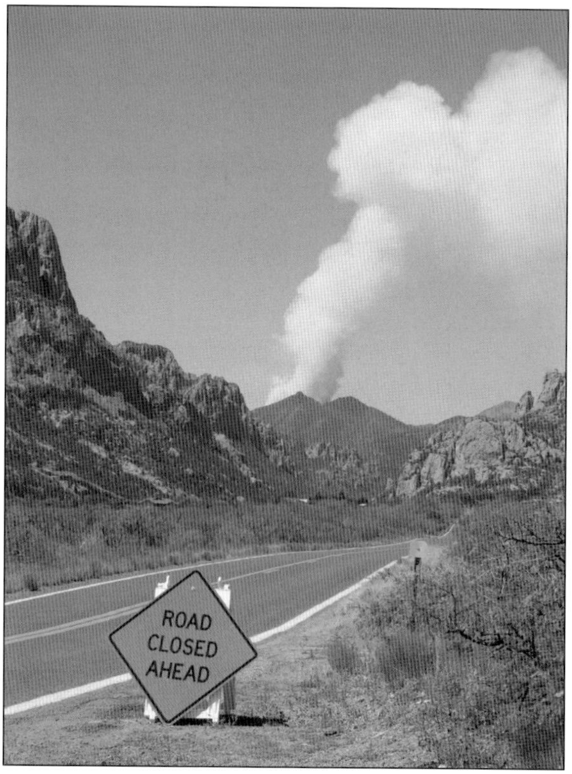

This May 2011 photograph of the Horseshoe II fire shows smoke from the ridges behind the high peaks and the road closure at the forest boundary. Horseshoe I, a few years earlier, smoldered for weeks among rocky crags until quenched by summer rains. Horseshoe II erupted from a campfire, hurtling against the eastern palisades, reaching the summit, and devouring huge trees as it spread in both directions along Cave Creek. (Barbara Miller.)

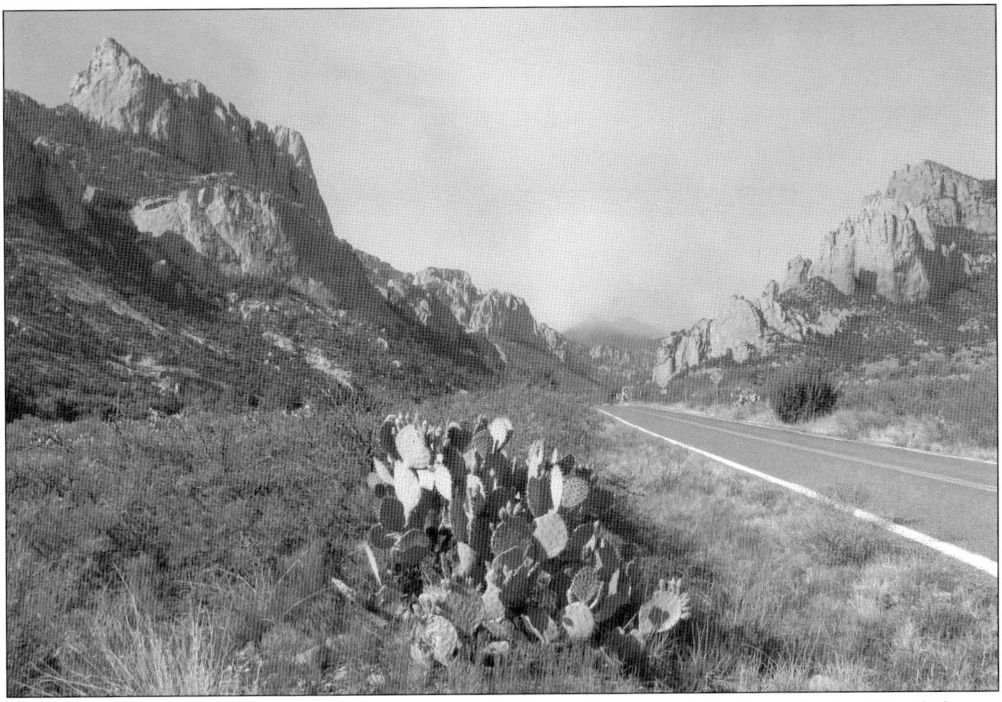

As the fire grew, a command post was setup at Rodeo to house and feed hundreds of firefighters, including elite hotshot crews. Aircraft dropped fire retardants, and backfires were set to burn into the approaching inferno. Above, smoke shrouds the higher mountains. Portal and Paradise were evacuated. The megafire charred 222,000 acres before it ran out of fuel and the rains came. The photograph below shows how flames stoked by accumulated debris, stunted trees, and brush shot into the canopy and destroyed giants that had survived natural fires for up to 500 years. (Above, Barbara Miller; below, Kim Murphy.)

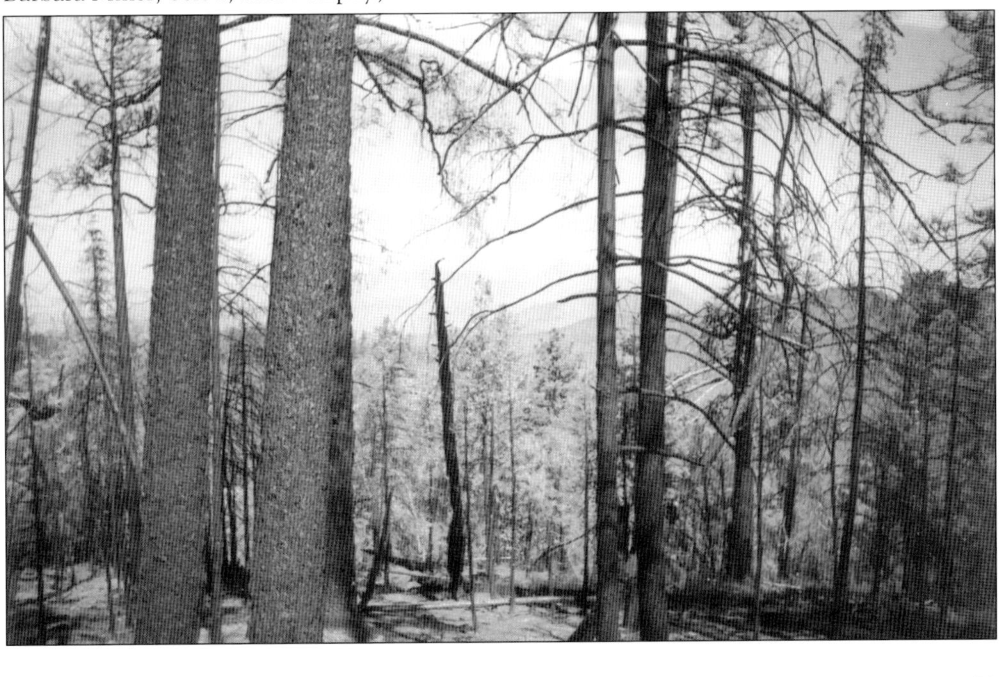

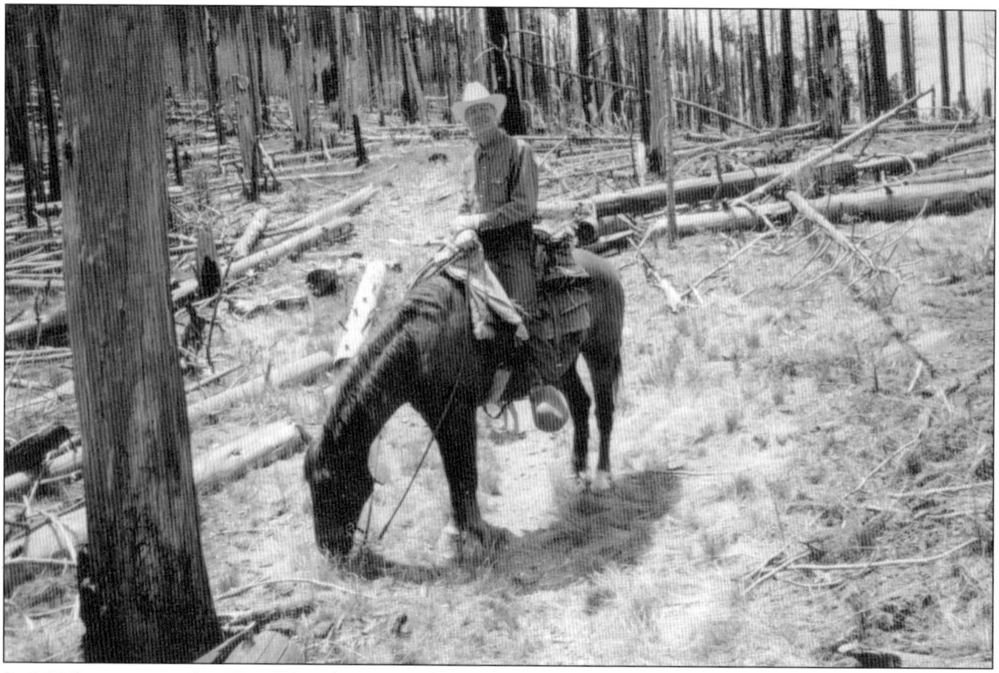

In 2005, game warden Kim Murphy views damage at Long Park 11 years after the 1994 Rattlesnake fire. Caused by a lightning strike, as many fires are, it burned fiercely for three weeks, ravaging 24,000 acres. The intensity resulted from a century of National Forest Service fire suppression policy, which ended the natural cycle of surface fires every decade or so that cleared out combustibles. (Kim Murphy.)

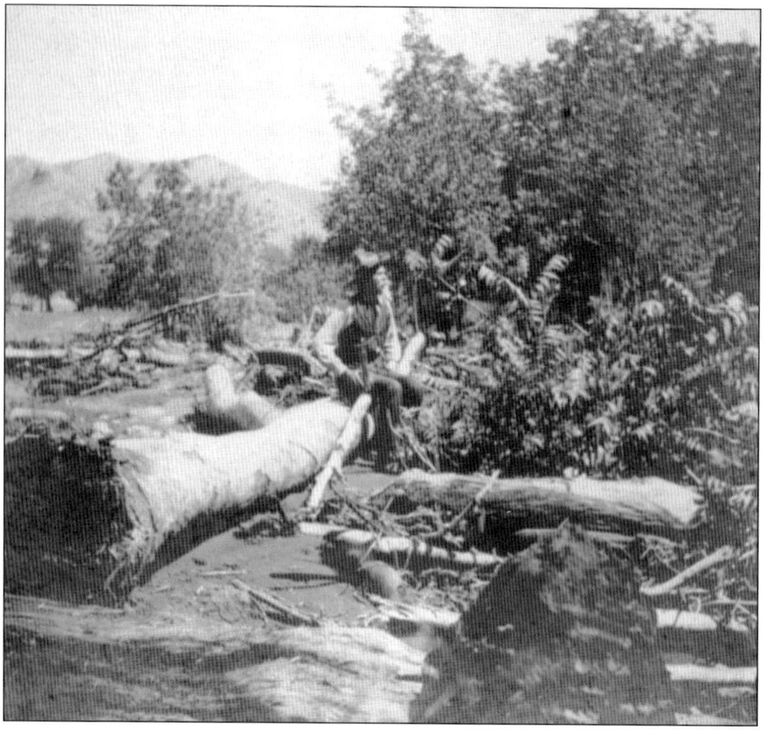

The rain so longed for during a fire can bring disaster. The 1912 flood that almost claimed Stephen Reed did sweep telephone poles and uproot trees down the canyon but did little damage to man-made property, unlike the December 1978 deluge. Warm rain melted a huge snowpack and sent the creek raging over its banks. (Sally Spofford.)

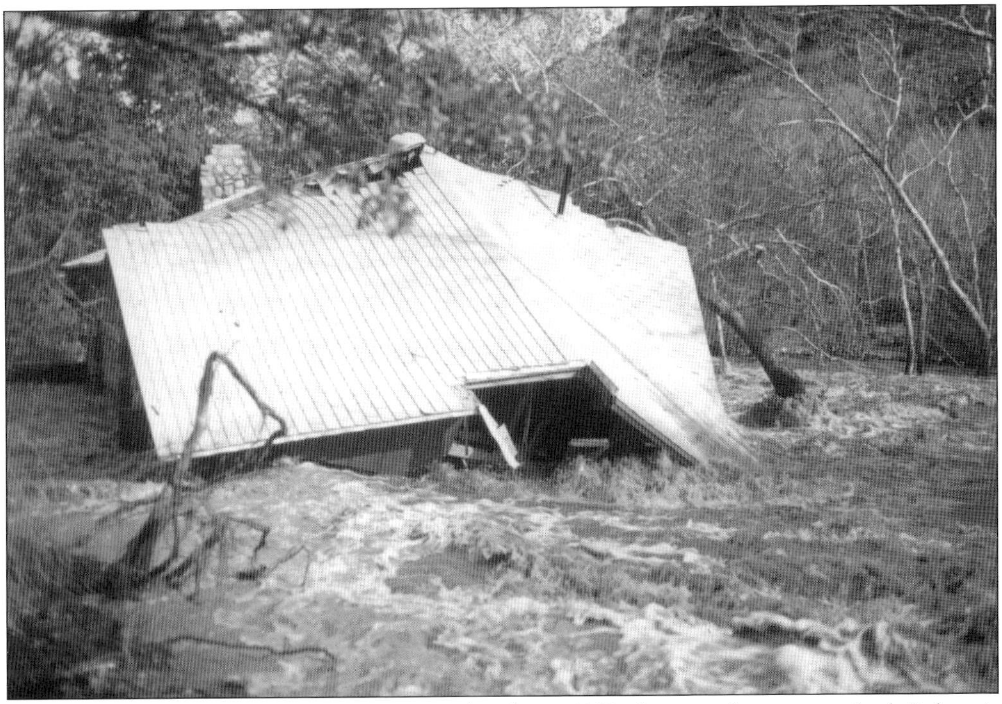

This cabin at Cave Creek Ranch, seen in the above 1978 photograph, was smashed. Below, it is seen in the devastating September 2014 flood. Deeply eroded by sluicing rains, slopes burned naked by the Horseshoe II fire could not soak up and hold torrents caused by Hurricane Odile. Creek-side homeowners heaped up countless sandbags, which did help, but a number of cabins needed extensive repairs. (Above, Sally Spofford; below, Reed Peters.)

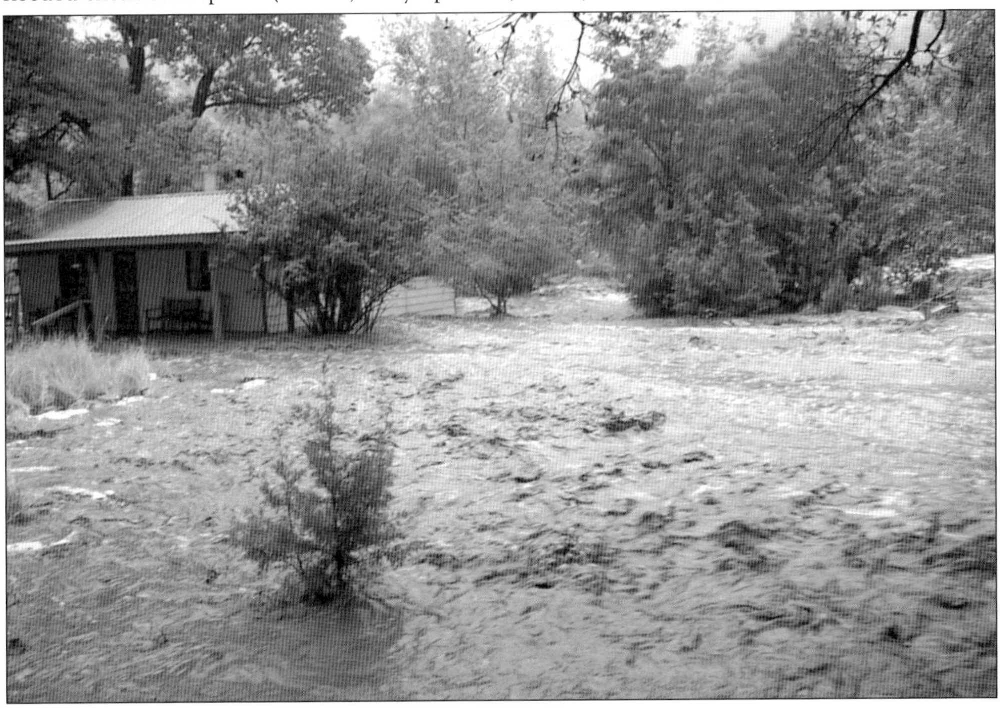

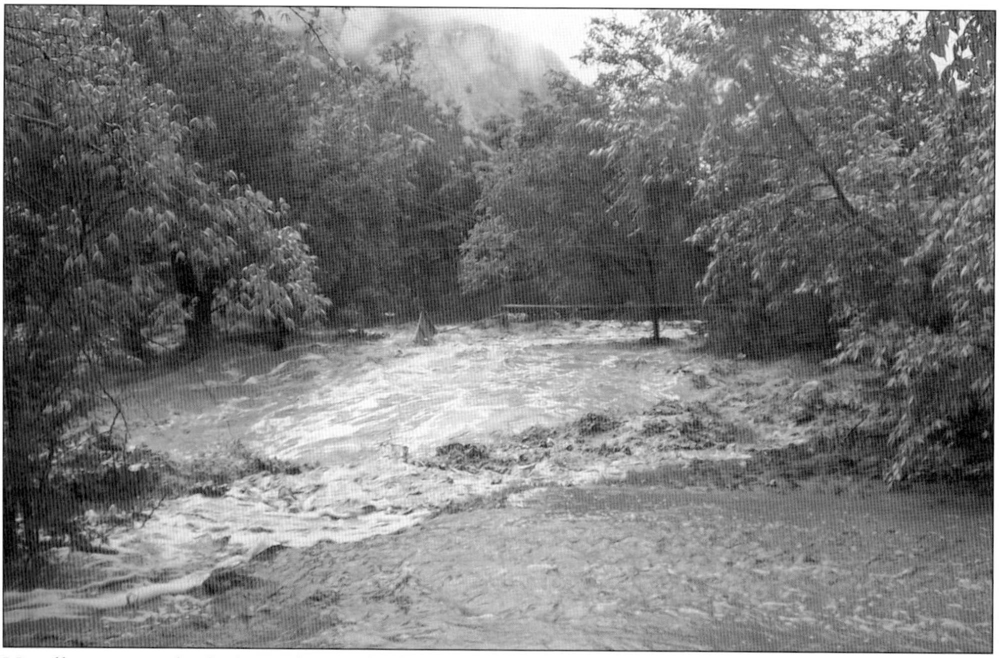

Usually swinging high above the creek, the bridge, shown here in 2014, lost planks while downstream concrete crossing was wrecked. Over a year later, the principal forest road to the Southwestern Research Station and higher mountains is under construction. The dirt road up South Fork was demolished, though, heaped with boulders and downed trees. (Reed Peters.)

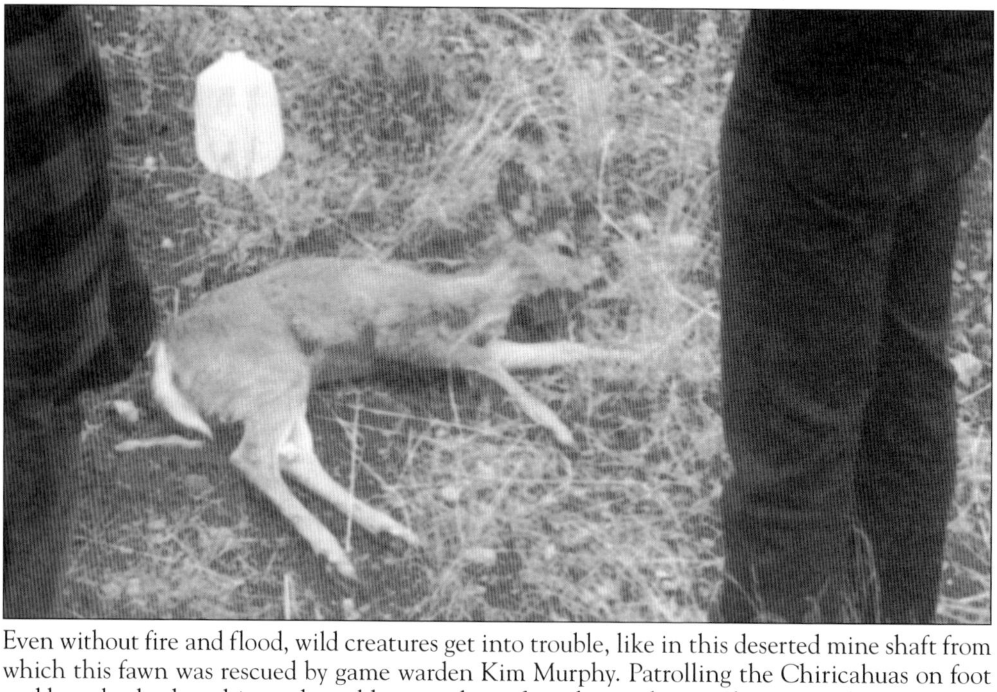

Even without fire and flood, wild creatures get into trouble, like in this deserted mine shaft from which this fawn was rescued by game warden Kim Murphy. Patrolling the Chiricahuas on foot and horseback where his truck could not go, he enforced game laws and monitored wildlife from 1965 until he retired in 1998. Almost to his death in 2014, Murphy voluntarily cleaned out springs and seeps so vital to animals. (Kim Murphy.)

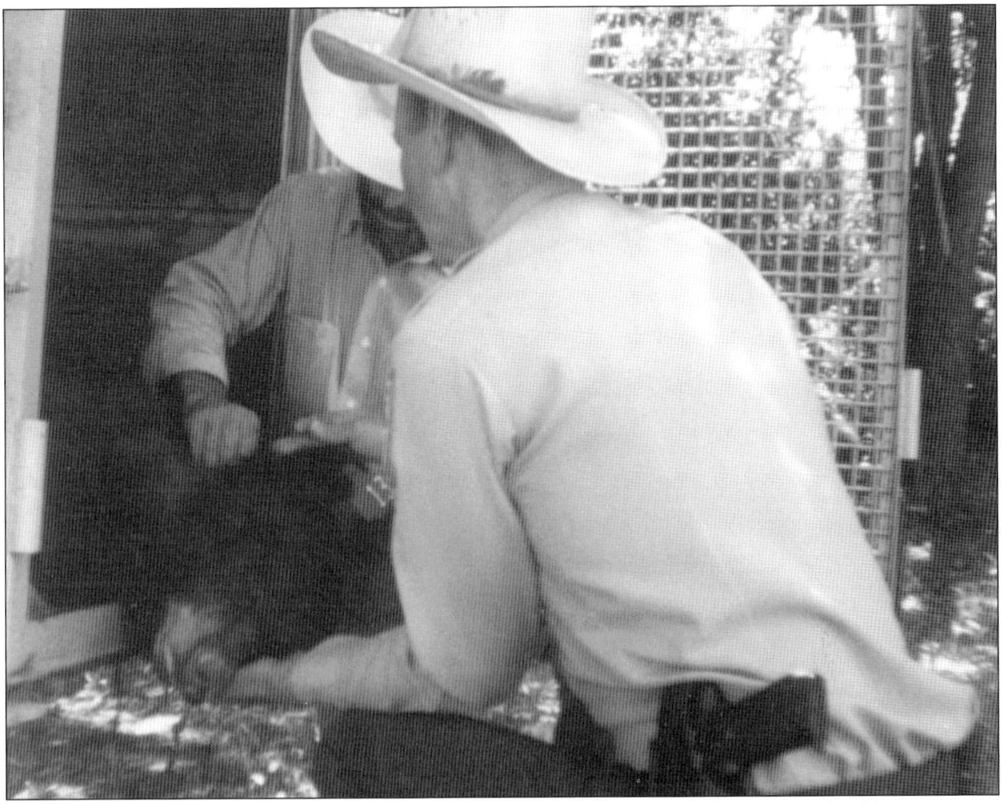

In the 1980s, Kim Murphy and a biologist have trapped a female bear that had become too habituated to people. The photograph below shows her still sedated when taken out of the cage in the wilderness near Fort Bowie. Transporting bears to a safer area does not always work. They may travel 80 miles or more to their former haunts. (Both, Kim Murphy.)

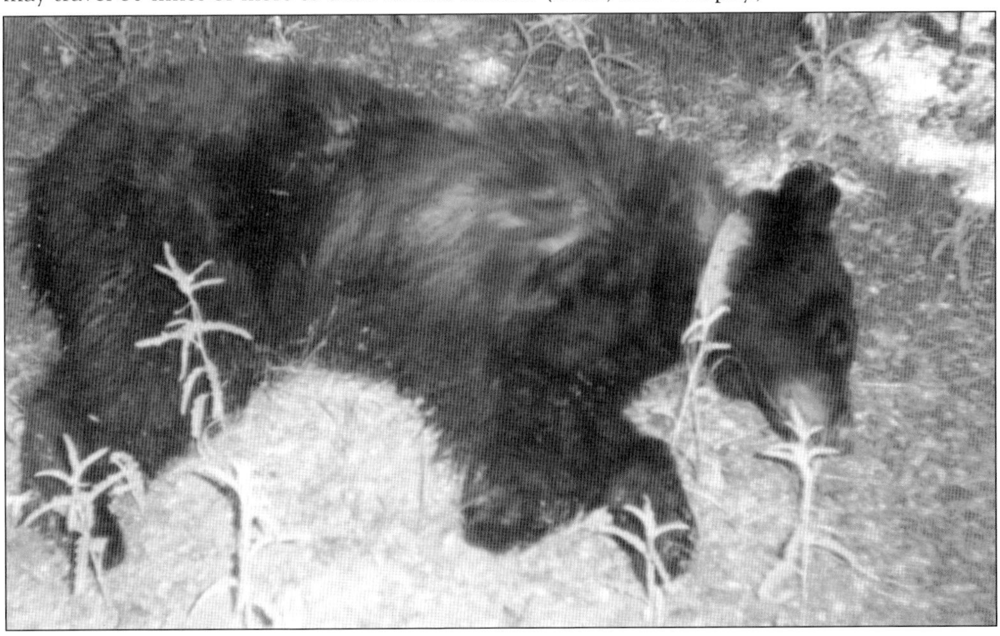

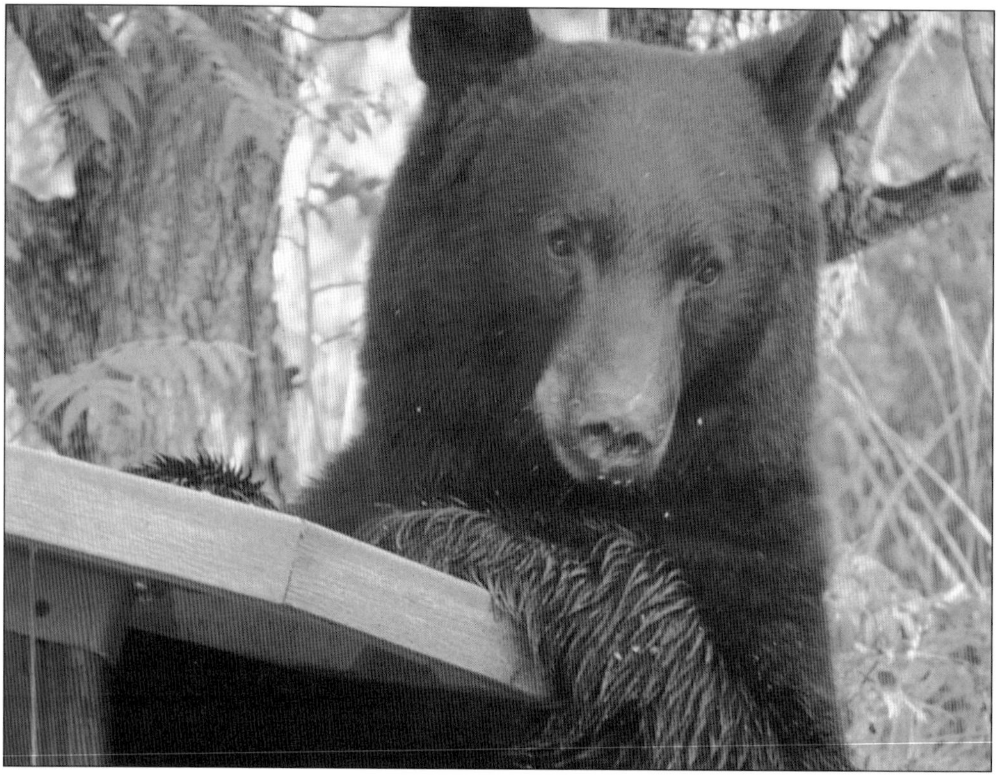

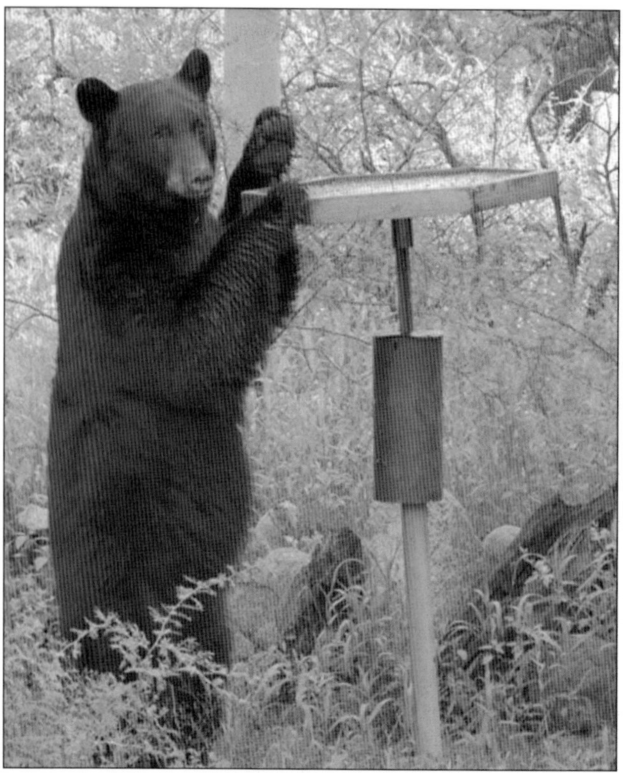

Black bears like the one tilting a feeder above are often brown or cinnamon and are the largest animal in the Chiricahuas. An adult male can stand seven feet tall and weigh about 350 pounds, with females 100 pounds smaller. Juniper berries, raspberries, acorns, cactus fruit, and manzanita are staples, but these omnivores can feast on carrion, grubs, and insects. Usually solitary except when mothering cubs, bears are shy unless they discover that campgrounds and homes offer tasty fare, as proved by the bear in photograph at left. Humans need to bring in feeders by twilight and securely store edibles and garbage lest the prophecy, "a fed bear is a dead bear," be fulfilled. A mother will defend cubs, but most maulings result from human error, like keeping food in tents. (Both, Deborah Galloway.)

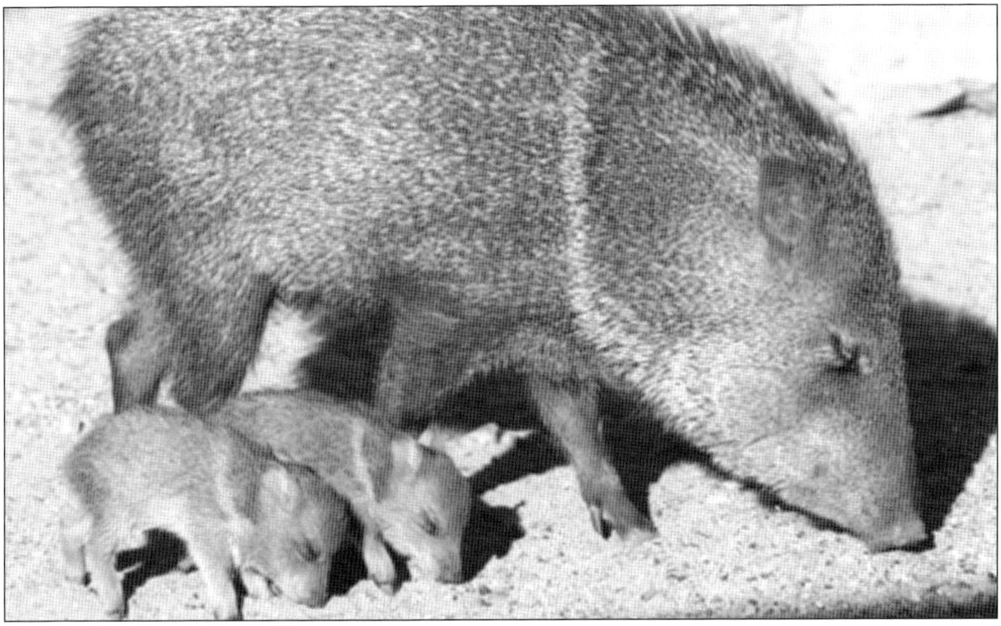

Baby javelinas, like those seen here, are born at any time of year and will not grow coarse dark hair until three months old. Adults weigh anywhere from 35 to 60 pounds. They forage for prickly pear and other plant foods in herds of up to 20 for protection from mountain lions, bobcats, and coyotes. If pressed, they may defend themselves with their sharp tusks, which have been known to eviscerate dogs. (Deborah Galloway.)

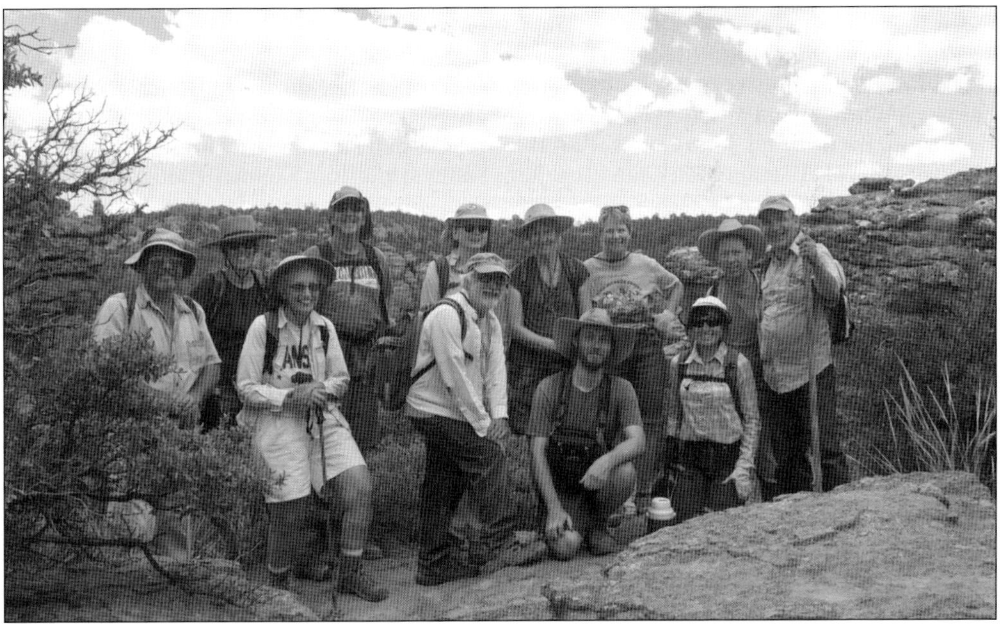

The Portal/Rodeo Hiking Group meets Thursday mornings to explore one of the myriad trails in the mountains or canyons of the Chiricahuas and Peloncillos. This 2014 photograph shows members on the Chiricahua National Monument, Heart of Rocks Loop. From left to right are Jack Hartley, Susan Mittelstadt, Pat Owens, Burt Mittelstadt, Carol Simon, Al Bammann, Elaine Moisan, Jonathan Patt, Linda Pretty, Sheila Clark, Craig McEwan, and Bill Cavaliere. (Jonathan Patt.)

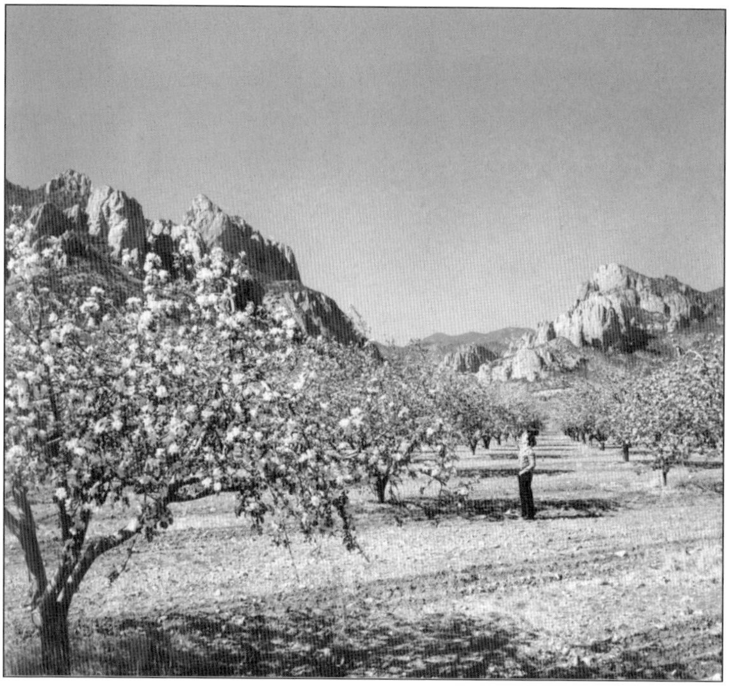

Gretchen Hayes breathes in the fragrance of blossoming apple trees at her parents' Sierra Linda Ranch in this early-1940s photograph. After World War II, her husband, though an archaeologist, ranched for 16 years. A five-year drought compelled him to join the National Park Service in 1954. He worked at Pecos, Chaco Canyon, and Mesa Verde before buying back the Sierra Linda, retiring there 19 years later. (Alden Hayes.)

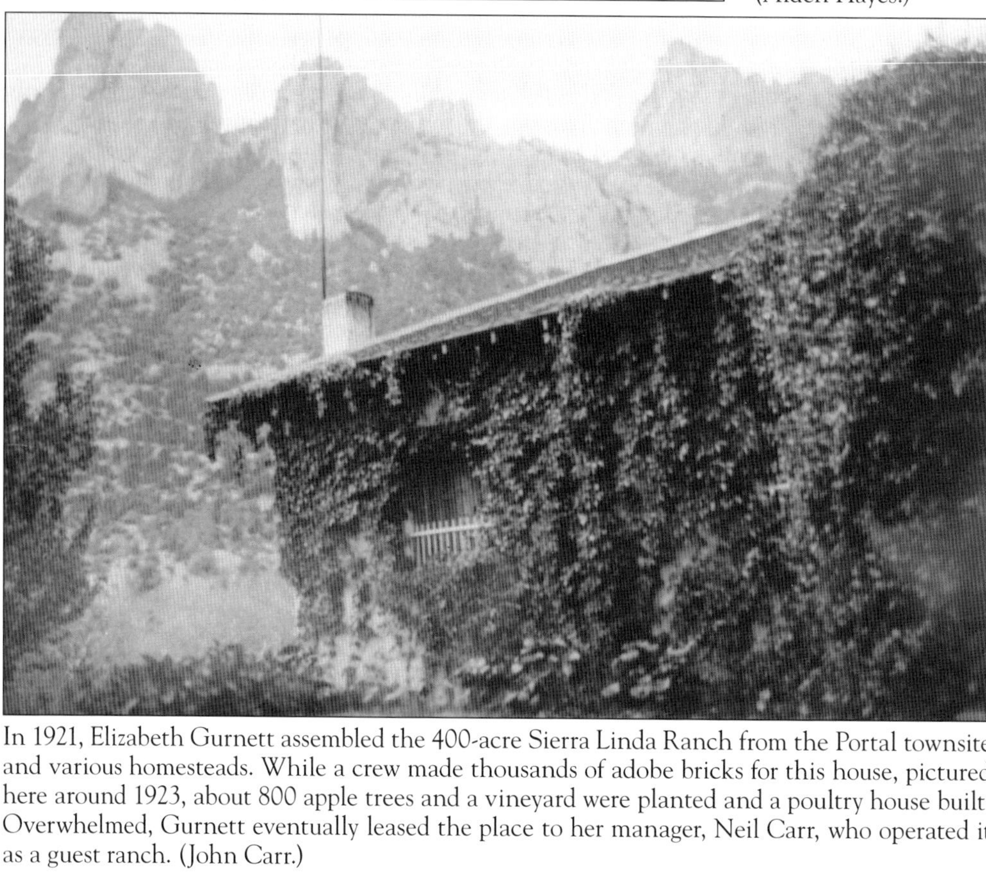

In 1921, Elizabeth Gurnett assembled the 400-acre Sierra Linda Ranch from the Portal townsite and various homesteads. While a crew made thousands of adobe bricks for this house, pictured here around 1923, about 800 apple trees and a vineyard were planted and a poultry house built. Overwhelmed, Gurnett eventually leased the place to her manager, Neil Carr, who operated it as a guest ranch. (John Carr.)

Arthur Greenamyer, a Buffalo, New York, steel executive, had longed to be a farmer since he was a country boy in Ohio. Upon retiring, he fulfilled his dream when he and his wife, Jane, bought the Sierra Linda Ranch in 1941. They invited daughter Gretchen and her new husband, Alden Hayes, to come and help. (Jim Frank Cox.)

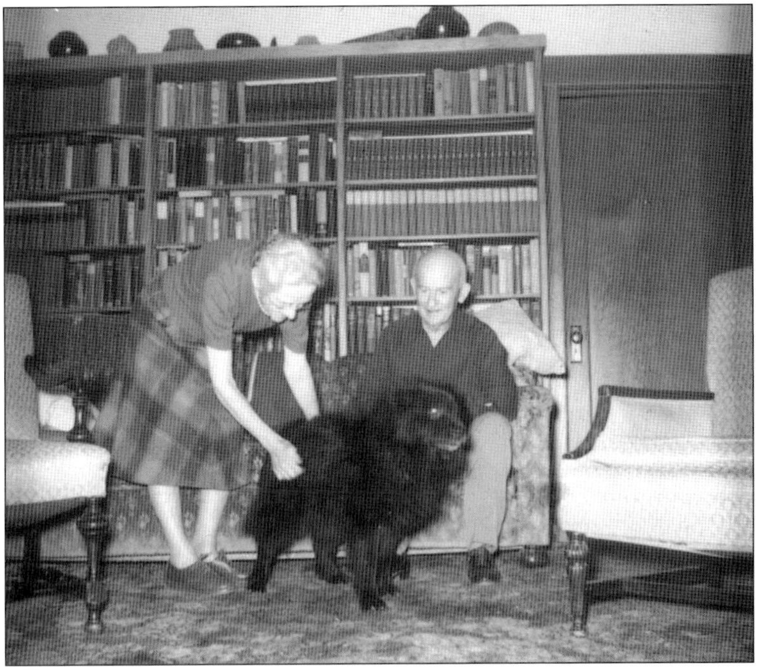

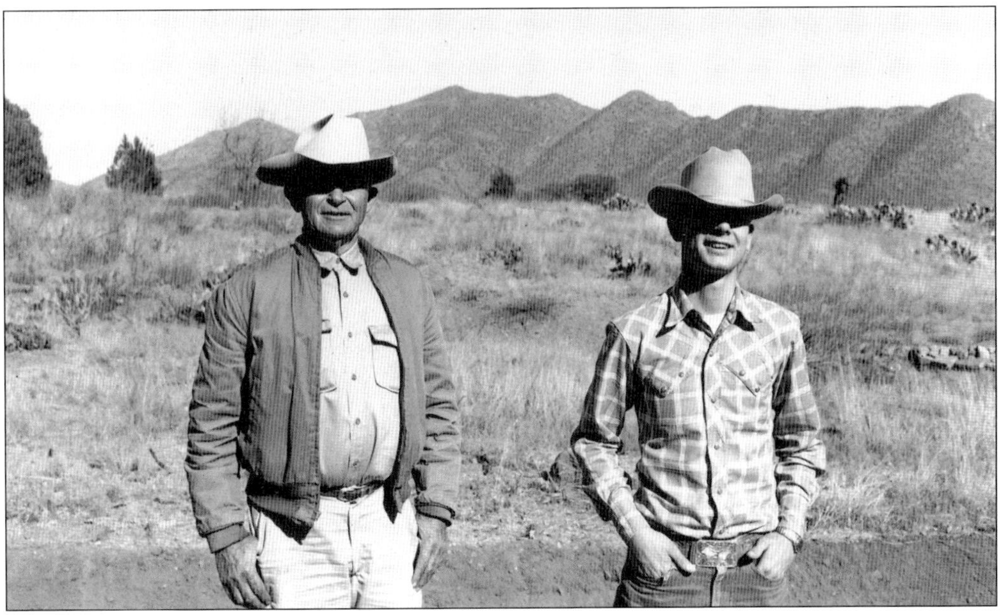

Carson Morrow (left), known as "Chief" from his turbulent years in the Border Patrol, left a humorous but fact-filled record of this region in the mid-1950s. Carol Cazier mimeographed the four-page *Chiricahua Bull Sheet* at the research station—free except for mailed subscriptions. Eric Hayes, still in high school, did the covers and artwork. (Barbara Miller.)

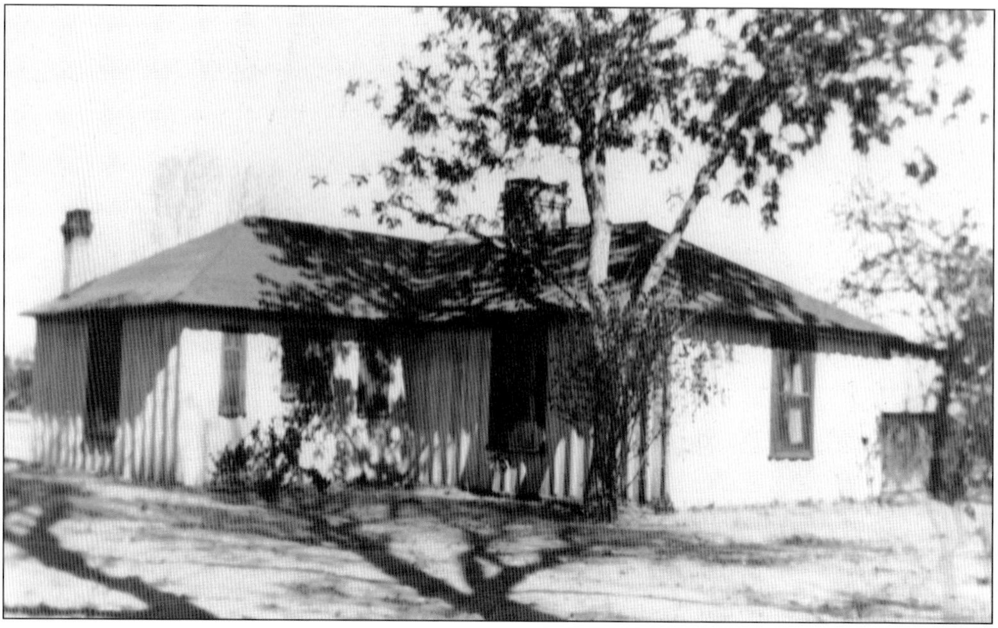

The house in the 1952 photograph above was built around 1914 by forester William "Bill" Stuart and his wife, Eula, who planted over 1,600 trees. Eula sold the place in 1932 to a Douglas physician, Dr. Edward Adamson, who made it a bridal gift for his wife, Anna, who raised Arabian horses. She gave it her initials, *AVA*, which was also her brand. Adamson kept his Douglas practice but improved the house and orchard, drilled an irrigation well, and built an apple washing and packing shed, as well as houses for workers. The photograph below shows the ranch buildings. (Both, Ted Troller.)

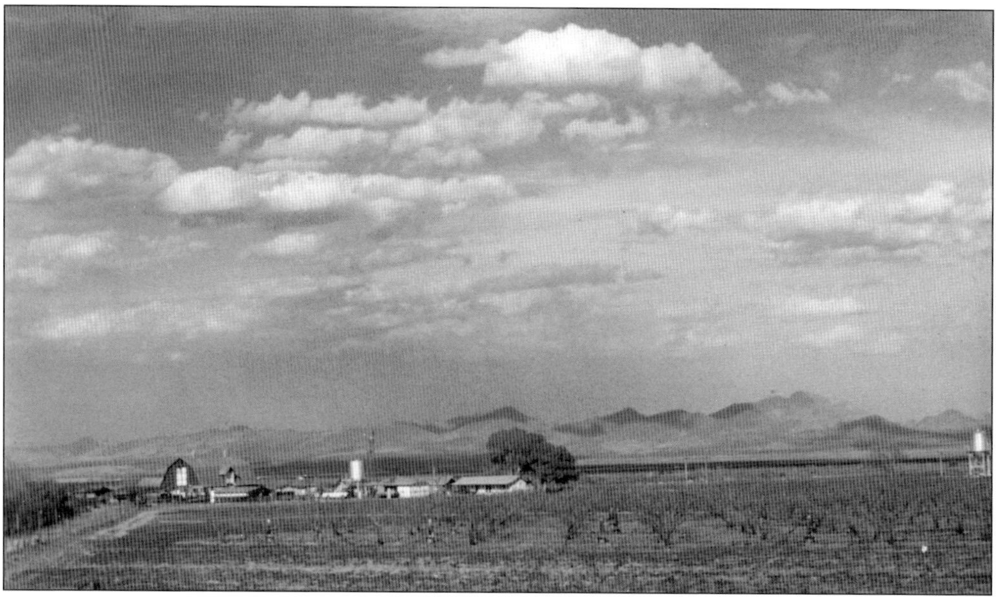

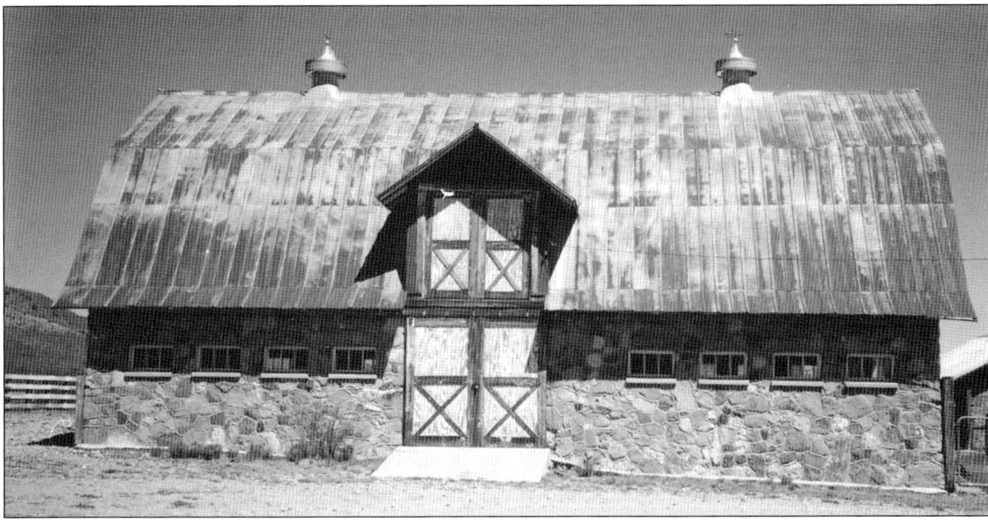

This handsome barn was built by Cristóbal Rendon, a former soldier of Pancho Villa who had helped John Schad finish the swimming pool at the Southwestern Research Station. Rendon also built a ramada at the Sierra Linda Ranch and terraces that are still solid. He probably worked with Blackie Stidham on the stone wall surrounding the house and grounds. The 1950s photograph below shows the AVA Ranch entrance and some of the orchard. (Both, Ted Troller.)

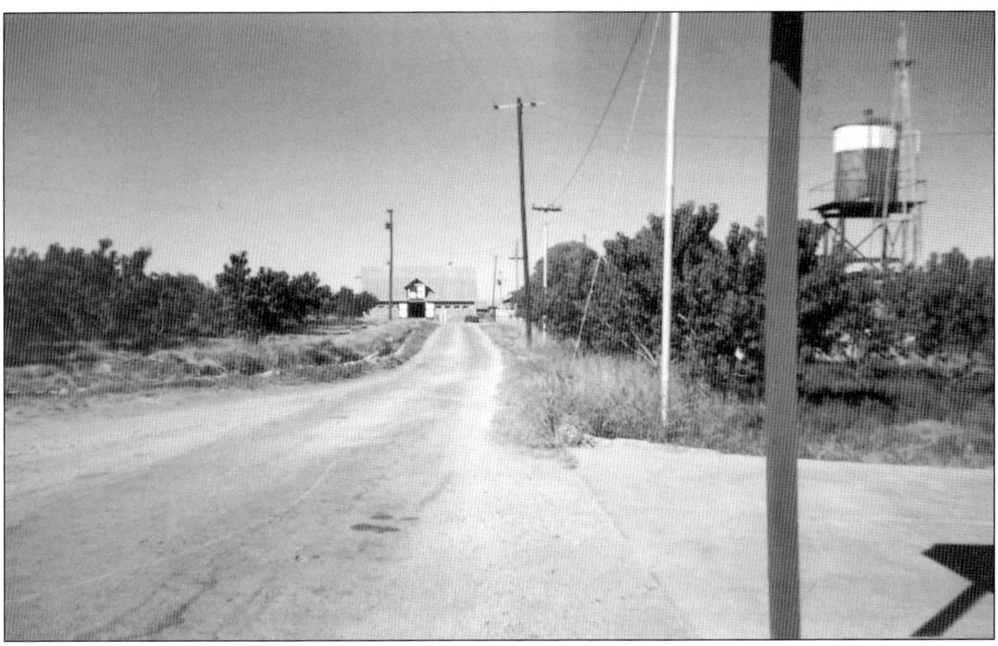

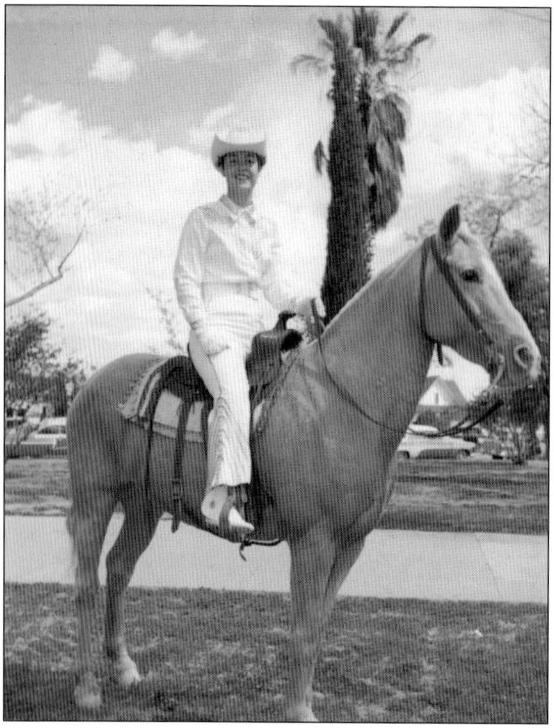

In the photograph at right, Bonnie Wallace (Catanzaro), the 1957 rodeo queen, is mounted on Goldie, the palomino mare she got from the Adamsons. They warned her that the filly was not yet well-trained. She dumped Bonnie often, but they learned together, bonding until the horse let no else ride her. The rodeo, sponsored by the Douglas Junior Chamber of Commerce, that year hosted film star John Garfield and Stan Jones, who wrote *Ghost Riders in the Sky*. In the photograph below, attendants are, from left to right, Wendy Paul (Glenn) and Mary Wallace (Winkler), the queen's sister. The three ardent horsewomen were lifelong friends. All became San Simon Valley ranchers. When the Malpais Borderlands Group began in 1994, Glenn handled public relations, and a few years later, Winkler came on the board of directors. (Both, Mary Winkler.)

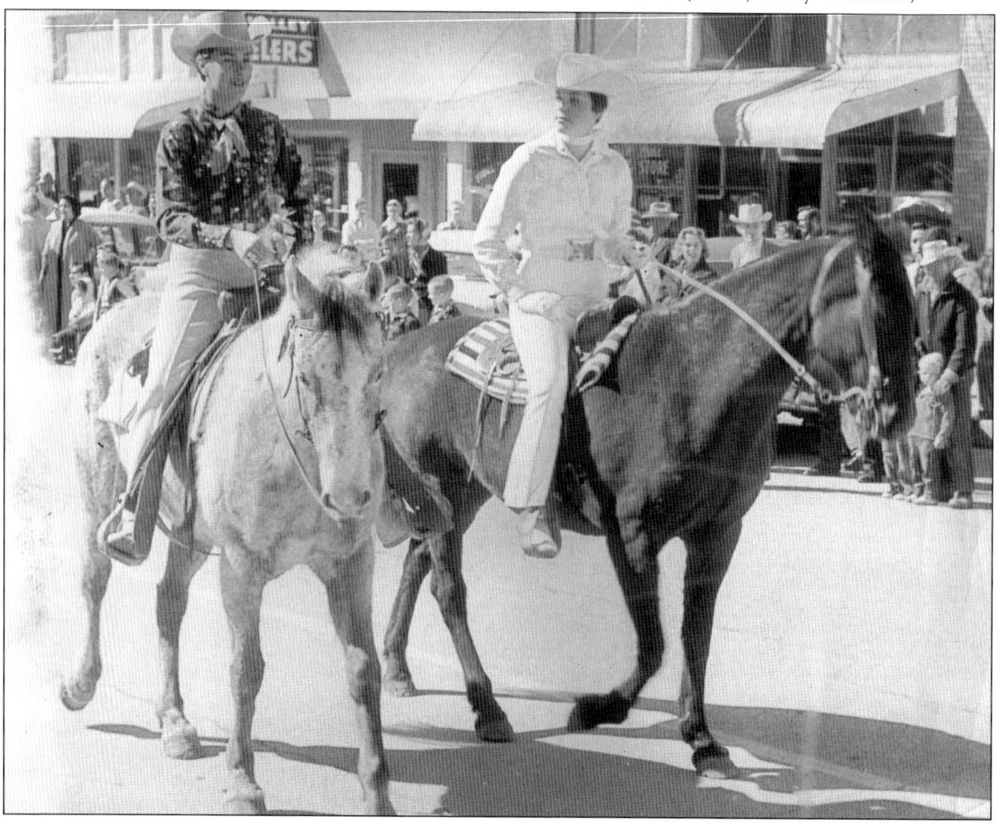

In 1932, Dr. Theodor Troller, an Austrian engineer, came to Akron, Ohio, to direct an air institute. He fell in love with the West and was so successful in business that he retired early and bought AVA in 1952. Troller processed local growers' apples and planted 10,000 peach trees. From left to right are Troller; his wife, Margaret; his sister from Vienna, Dr. Gisella Hoffman, and Theodor III. (Ted Troller.)

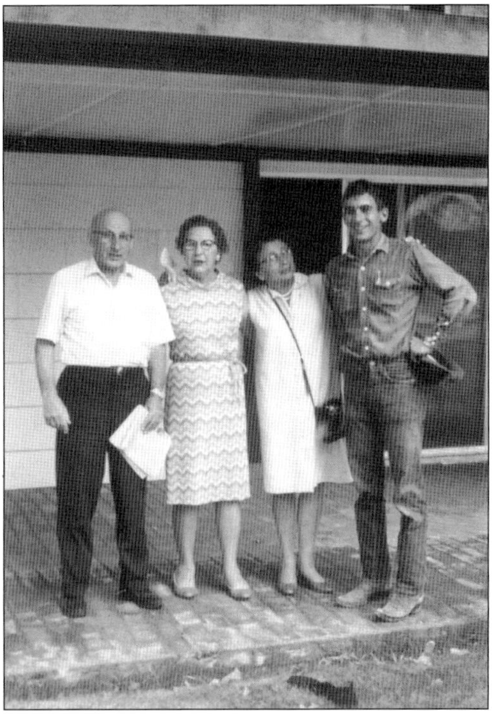

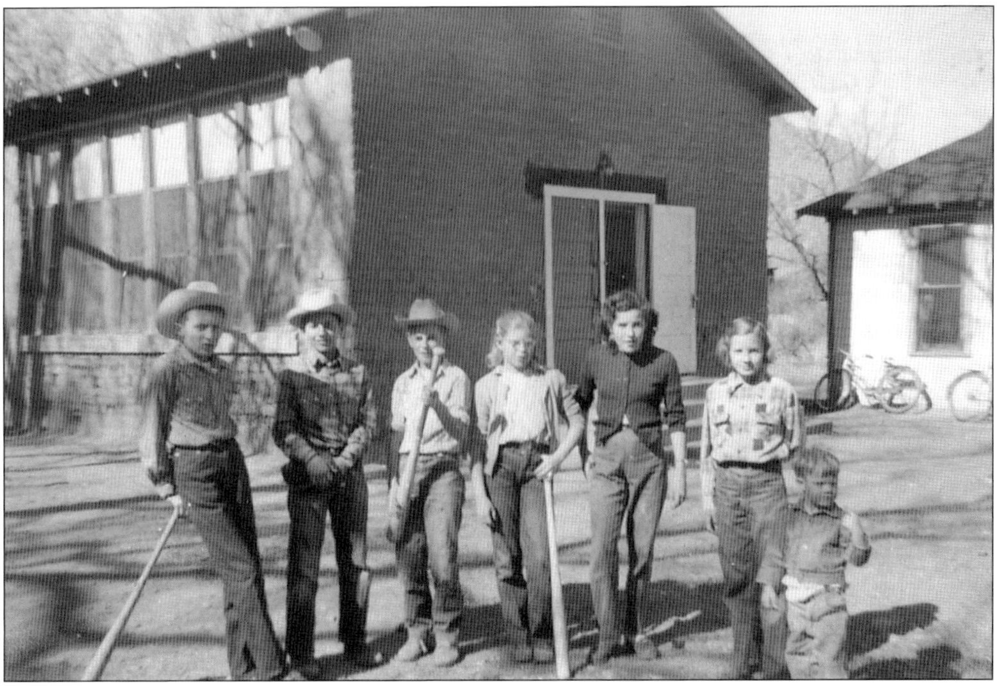

The Portal School children in this 1954 photograph are, from left to right, J.L. Hill, Ted Troller, Eric Hayes, Linda McClintock, Shirley Currier, Chris Troller, and Andy Dubois. There had been 24 pupils the year before because Hilltop Mine was operating in an intermittent way until final closure. Attendance rose later with children from AVA and the Southwestern Research Station. Eric Hayes and Ted Troller wandered far, but both returned to live in Portal. (Ted Troller.)

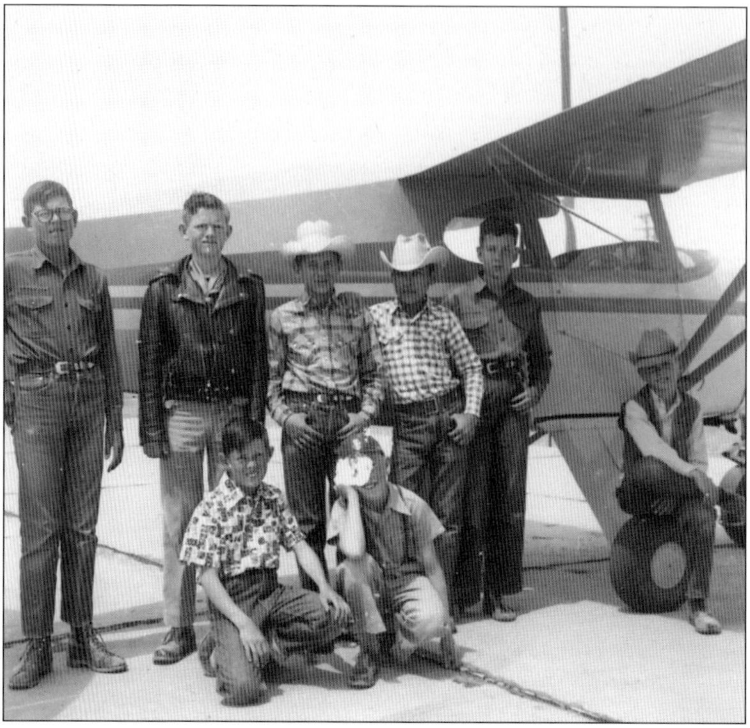

The 1954 photograph at left, taken on an outing to the Douglas airport, shows the Portal-Rodeo Boy Scouts. From left to right are (first row) Eric Hayes and Philip Dayton; (second row) Laurence Durphy, ? Dayton, Ted Troller, Izzy Dominguez, and two unidentified. Eighth-grade graduates smiling in the 1954 photograph below are, from left to right, Ted Troller, Johnnie Mae Mingus, and Zen Beecroft. (Both, Ted Troller.)

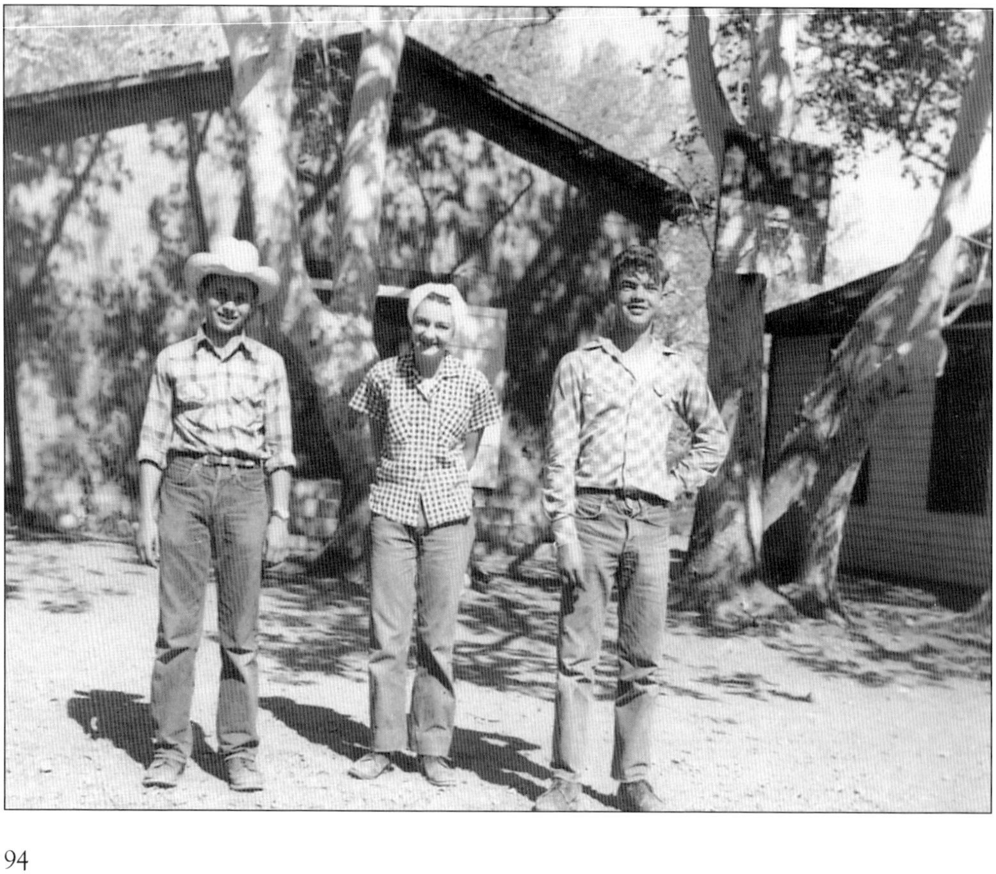

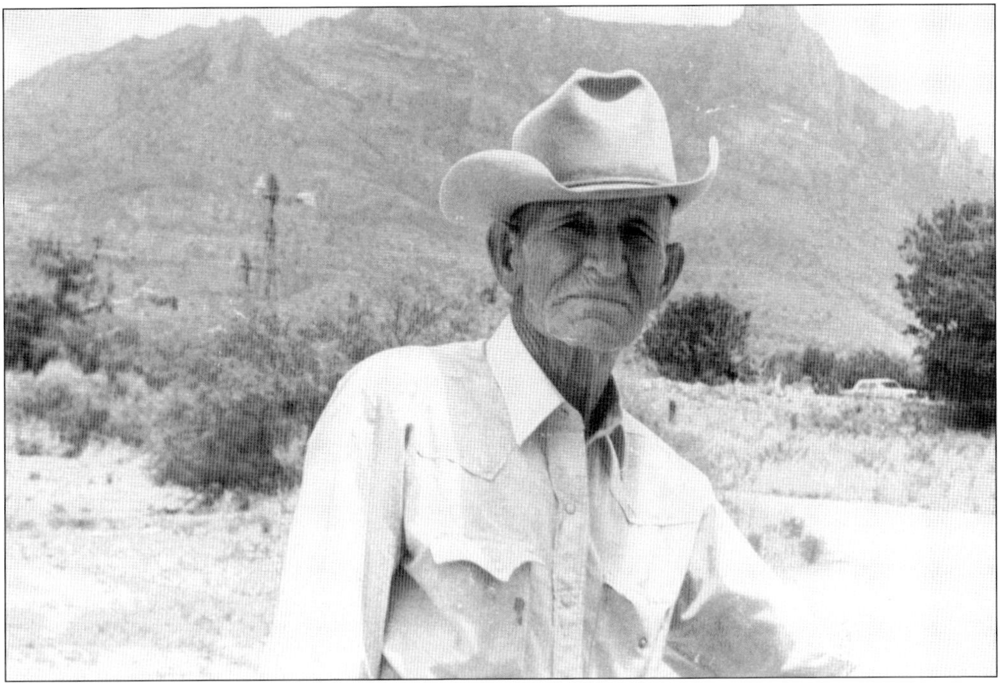

Blackie Stidham, pictured above in the 1960s, helped Ted Troller and other youngsters with their 4-H projects and always had time for them, though the former Hilltop miner kept busy with construction and masonry work as well. He worked on the first good road from the west side of the mountain over Onion Saddle down to the Portal Ranger Station. The 2016 photograph below is of the home Stidham built for his wife, Ruth. Barbara and Peter Miller bought the house in 1985, renovating and expanding it while preserving the Mexican redbrick walls, the tongue-and-groove redwood ceiling, and the welcoming fireplace inside. Barbara's magic touch with plants and flowers creates glory against adobe walls while giant sycamores form a glade near a pond where birds and wild creatures come to drink. (Both, Barbara Miller.)

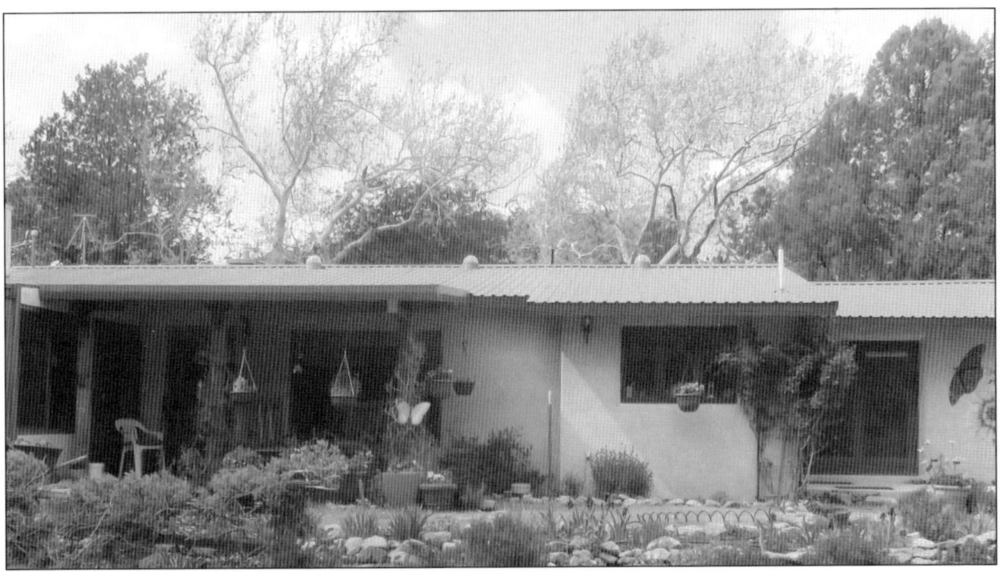

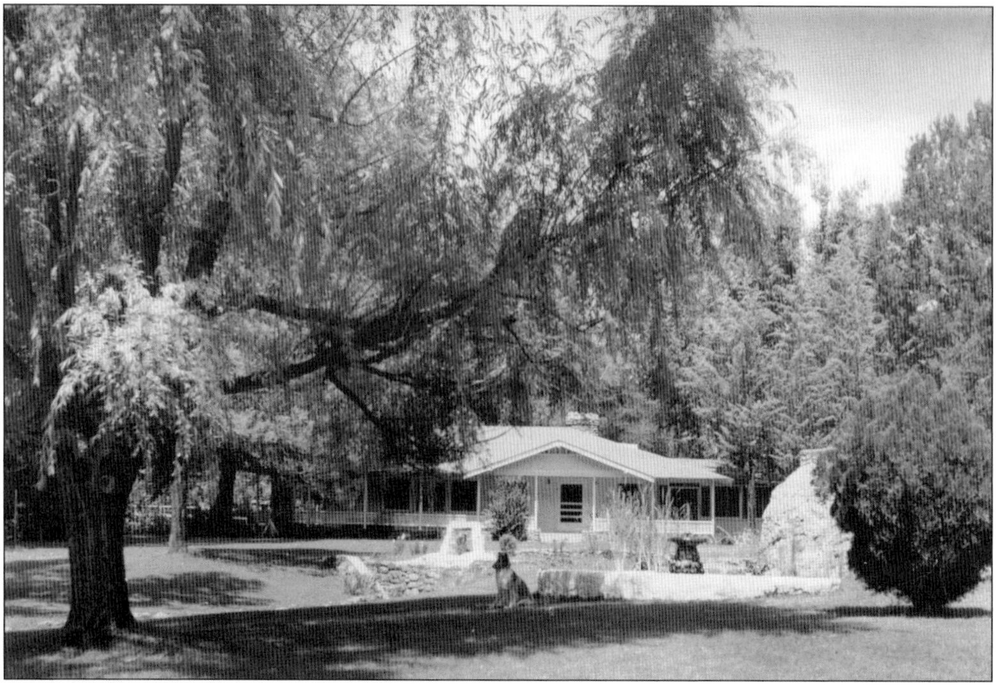

Stephen Reed's apple trees still yielded delicious fruit, but his homestead was never again farmed. John Hands bought it in 1915 to help his old friend's children. He built a few cabins, but his Bide-a-Wee Ranch attracted few visitors. Subsequent owners lacked development money. Mining executive Harry Clark bought it in 1926 for a summer home and place to entertain important guests. Caretaker John Schad finished the lodge, seen above in 1956, and completed the swimming pool, still appreciated on hot days. Jack Maloney guided Clark's hunting parties, cooked beans and venison, and entertained guests with campfire yarns. Through a shared fascination with beetles, David Rockefeller was persuaded by Dr. Mont Cazier of the American Museum of Natural History to buy the Reed holdings and establish the Southwestern Research Station. The laboratory in the 1960 photograph below is heavily used. (Both, Richard Zweifel.)

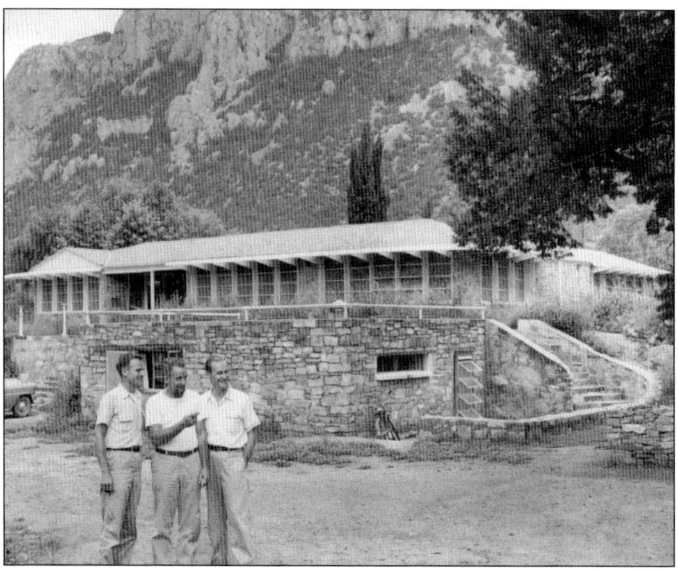

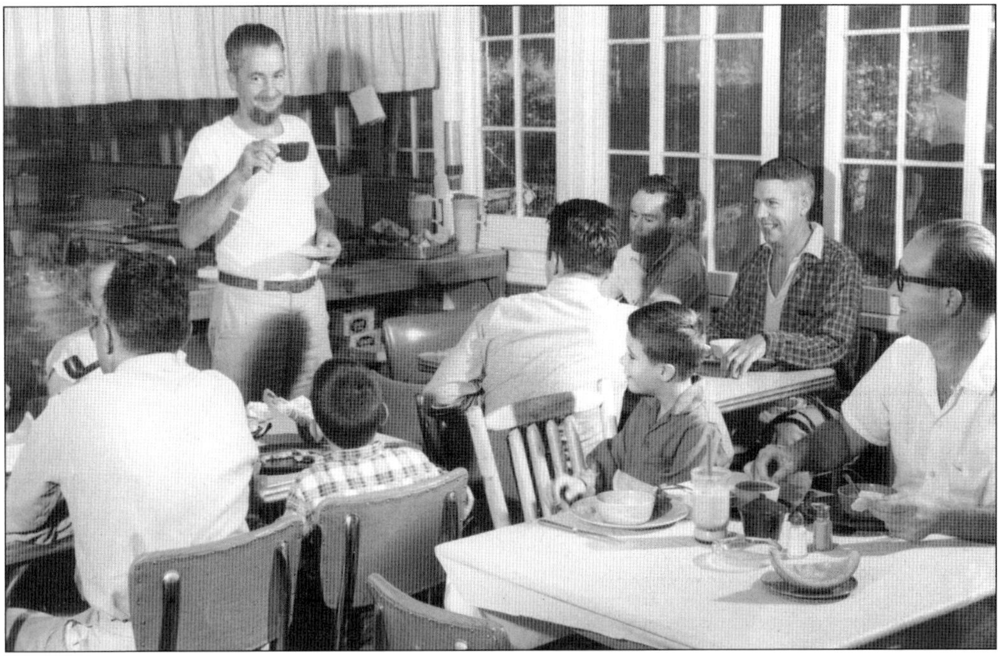

Shown giving a lecture in this 1950s photograph, Dr. Mont Cazier, as first director, welcomed biologists of all persuasions, many of them university professors who brought their families or students. There is a great diversity of species and habitats, from desert scrub to conifer forests, found within the surrounding region, which climbs from 4,000 to nearly 10,000 feet. (Richard Zweifel.)

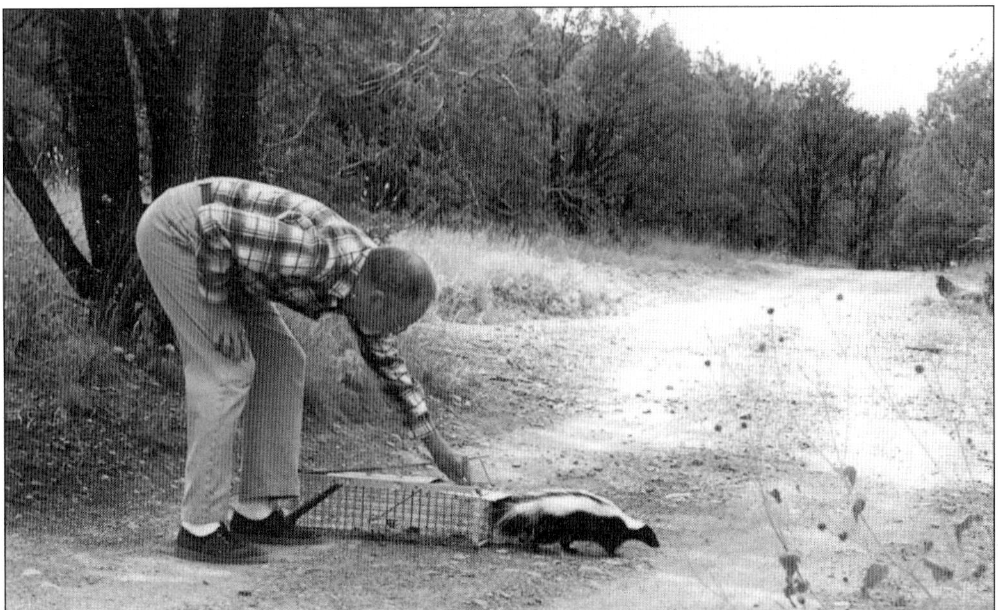

Dr. Richard "Dick" Zweifel, liberating a trapped skunk in this 1980s photograph, met Frances "Fran" Wimsatt in 1956 when she came to work as a scientific illustrator at the American Museum of Natural History. Shortly thereafter, their honeymoon tour included the first of many stays at the research station. They retired in 1989 to Paradise, where Dick, with the help of Harold Bradford, built Zweifels' two-story log house from a kit. (Richard Zweifel.)

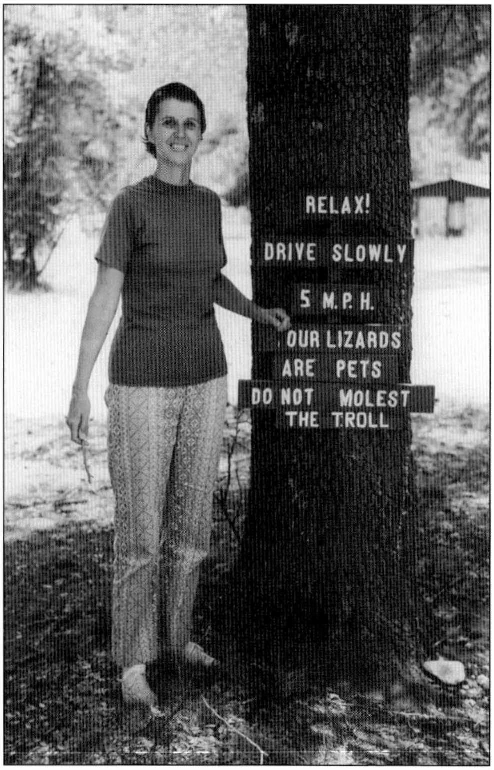

Fran Zweifel smiles in the photograph at left at the prank she and her husband, Dick, played on director Vincent K. Roth by altering his sign about molesting lizards to a troll warning. Her *Biological Illustration* was an affordable text for students for 50 years. She has written and/or illustrated acclaimed children's books, including *Animal Baby-Sitters*. Below, in 1973, daughter Ellen, age nine, removes a whipsnake from a live trap. Inheriting and adding to her parents' musical talents, she won a Celtic harp competition that allowed her to spend a year in the Hebrides. She plays for weddings and other occasions around her home in Virginia and has several times delighted Portal-area folk with her harp and beautiful voice. (Both, Richard Zweifel.)

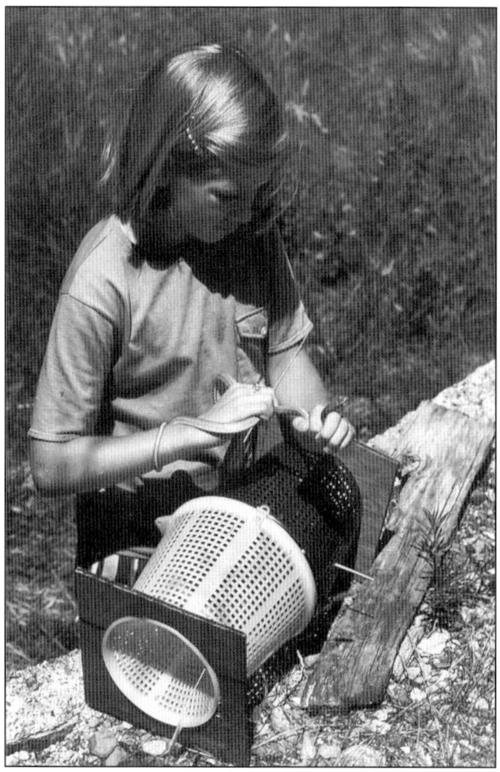

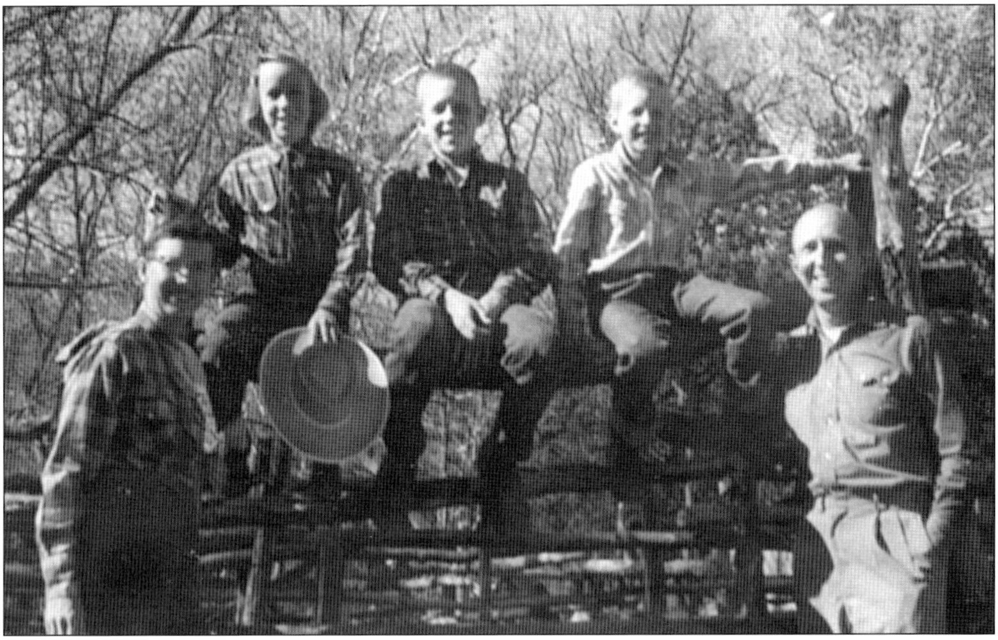

For over 50 years, ecologist Dr. Robert Chew and his science-teacher wife, Alice, studied the 24-acre plot a rancher let them fence during a sabbatical in 1958–1959 at the research station. The Chews collected and analyzed plants and soil, sleeping at the enclosure and rising early to identify, weigh, and release kangaroo rats and other creatures attracted to the live traps. Above are, from left to right, Alice, Zoe, Carl, Paul, and Robert Chew. Pictured below, Paul (left), Carl (center), and Zoe were driven with other station pupils six miles to Portal where Lillian Reed taught 23 students in eight grades. The whole family enjoyed dances on the concrete slab beside the school. The Chews retired to Portal in 1979, continuing the study that showed native grasses could not recover because creosote and brush dominated the overgrazed land. (Both, Alice Chew.)

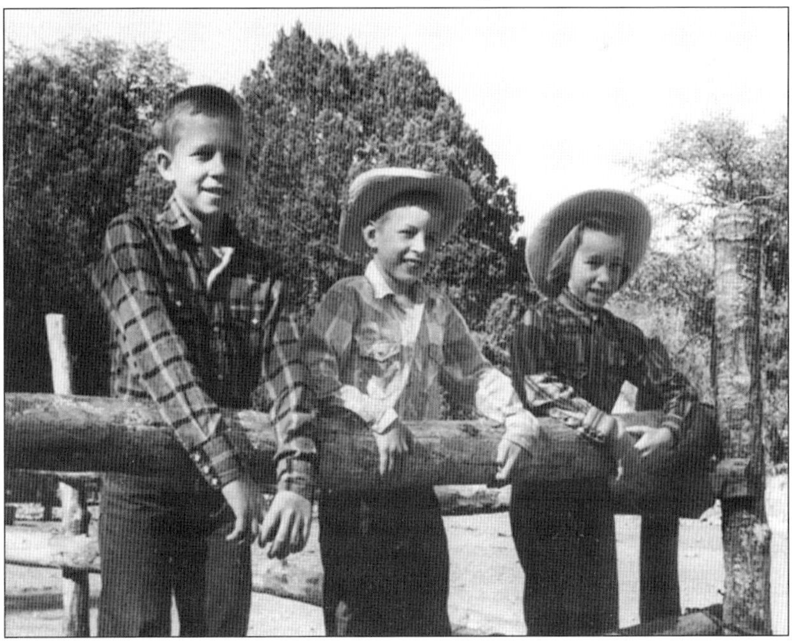

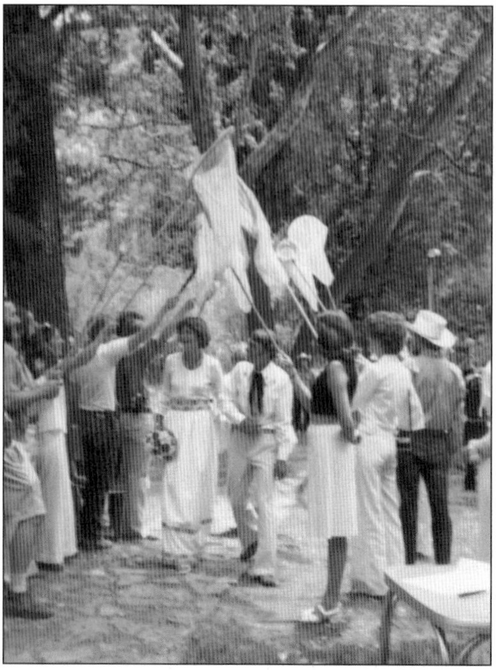

Instead of crossed sabers, butterfly nets form a wedding arch for the research station's director, spider expert Vincent Roth, and, Barbara, assistant director, on July 10, 1977. Vince Roth was director from 1962 to 1986. After retirement, the Roths adventured as far away as Madagascar, usually working at scientific outposts. Shortly before he died, Vince held their twin sons, Daniel and Taran, in his arms. (Helen Snyder.)

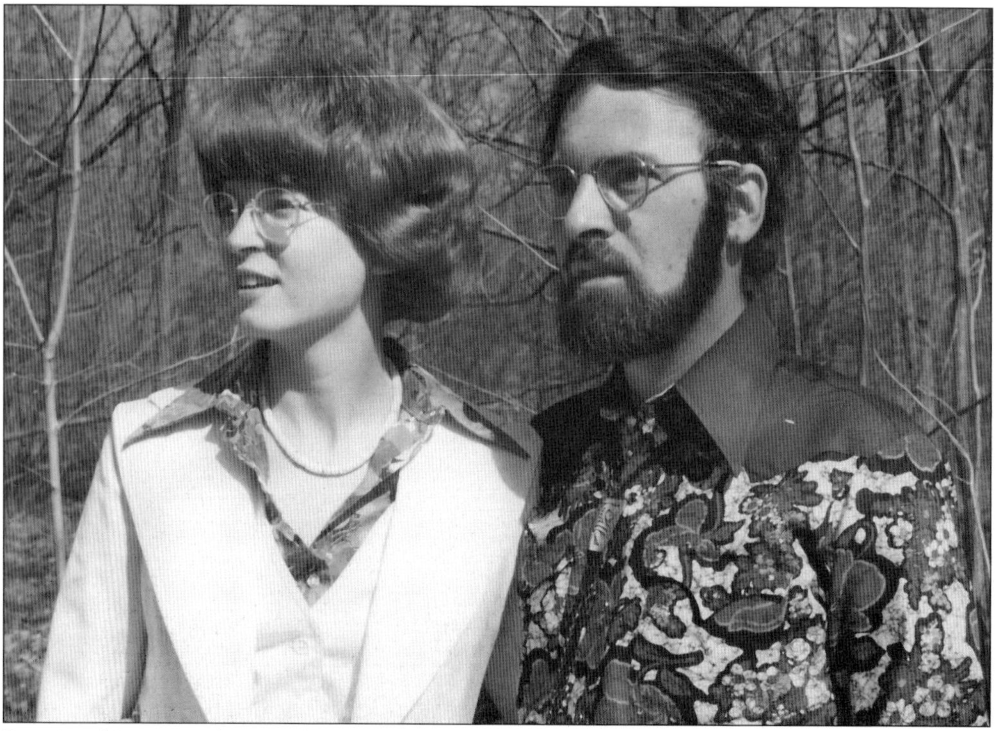

Drs. Carol Simon and Howard Topoff, shown at their 1976 wedding, met at the research station in 1964. Both taught at City University of New York and were at the American Museum of Natural History. They lecture during worldwide ecotrips. While at their Cave Creek home, Carol organizes forums and book groups and energizes hikers. Howard does school science enrichment, the local website, and creative spectacles. (Ray Mendez.)

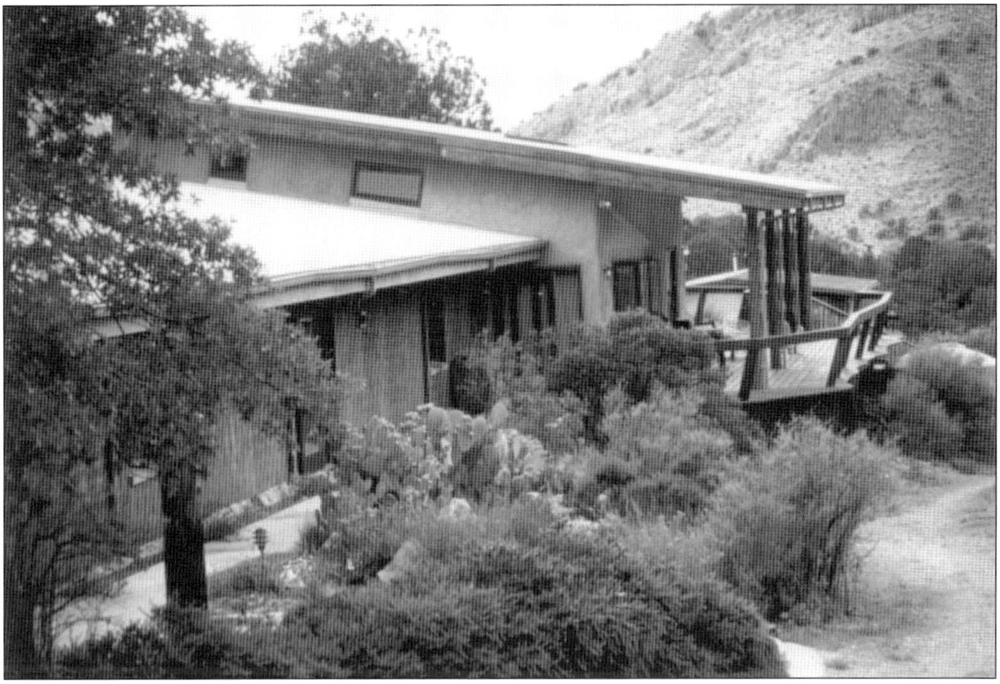

Called Post Office Canyon because rustlers left notes for each other in a hollow oak, this area is where Dr. Robert Scholes and his dietician wife, Kathryn, built the solar home pictured in this mid-1970s photograph and founded the Bioresearch Ranch. They cooperated on projects with wildlife agencies and hosted a stream of biologists. Resident wildlife biologist C.D. Littlefield studies and records observations on wildlife, birds, plants, and precipitation. Below, in the 1990s, the Scholeses' son-in-law Ed Newbold, a brilliant Seattle wildlife artist, soaks weary feet in the atrium pool after checking a circuit of water catchments. (Both, Delia Scholes.)

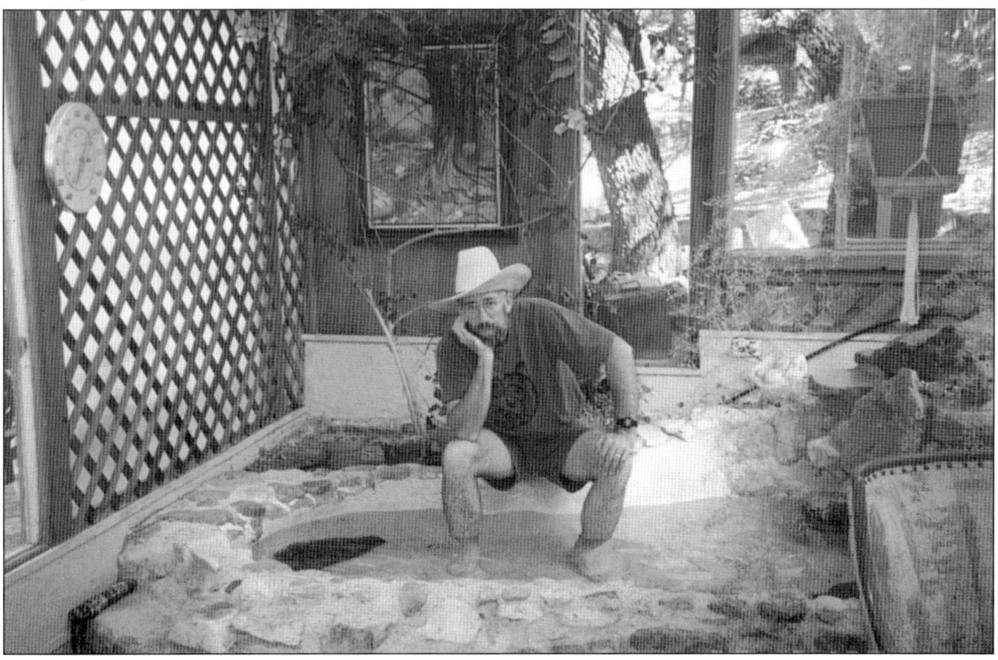

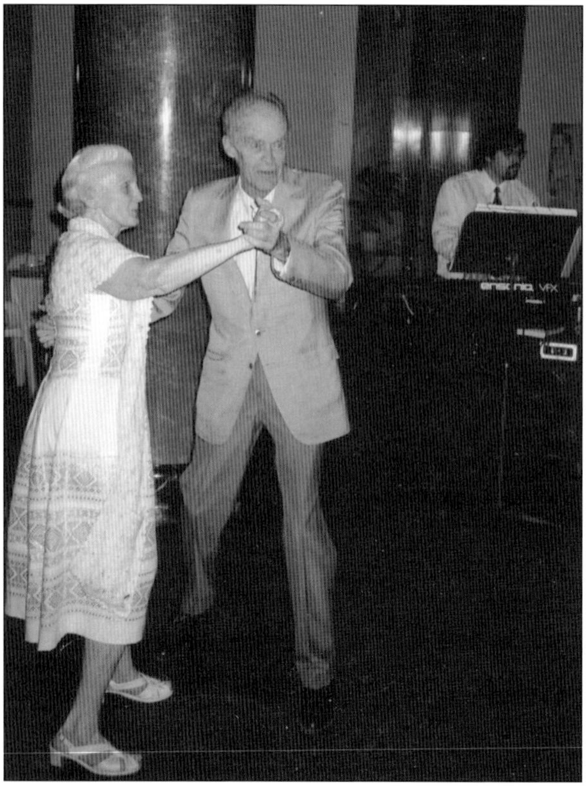

The Scholeses step out at their 1996 golden wedding celebration organized by their daughter Delia and nieces Patricia and Petie. Dozens of guests from far and near—birders, ranchers, and scientists—came to celebrate with them, including colleagues from their distinguished public health service careers in remote villages of Bolivia and Paraguay. Their experience and tenacity brought better health care and senior citizens' benefits to the San Simon Valley. Below, they stand at the foot of the Gadsden Hotel's marble staircase with daughter Dr. Delia Scholes of Seattle and her husband, Ed Newbold. The landing above them, lit by Tiffany lamps, has a stained-glass window of settlers entering Cave Creek Canyon. (Both, Delia Scholes.)

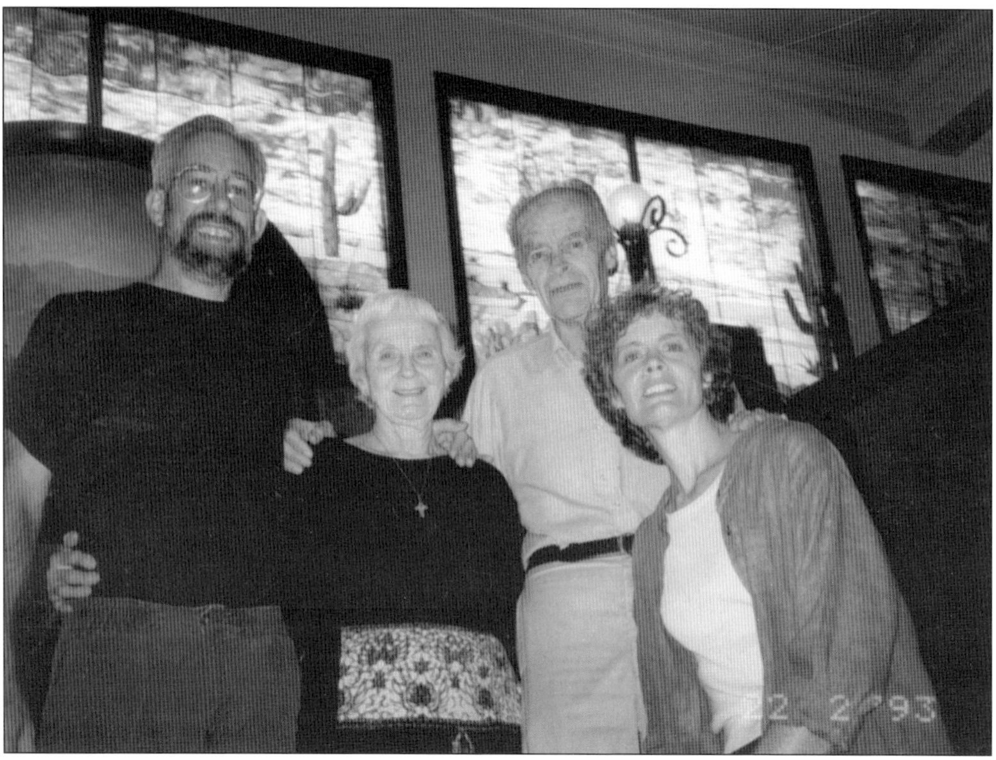

Seven

Drowsy? Not These Days!

Thick-billed parrots once feasted on pinecone seeds in the Chiricahuas but were killed out in the 1930s, filling many kettles. A different kind of bird hunter prowled the mountains, enticed by hummingbirds and Mexican exotics. Since the early 1970s, scientists retired here as did ecotour leaders, artists, writers, and, most recently, astronomers, all united by love of nature. Cattle ranching is an important part of the culture and economy.

Because of heavy seasonal tourist traffic, visitors may choose from housekeeping cabins, motels, bed-and-breakfasts, and a number of restaurants. The nonprofit Chiricahua Gallery offers works by member artists, and the Chiricahua Desert Museum has an excellent natural history shop.

Remoteness and a small permanent population are challenges to making a living, though technology facilitates working from home, as do Ray and Joy Mendez. After 14 years at the American Museum of Natural History, Ray founded Work as Play, creating exhibits for faraway zoos and museums.

Barney Tomberlin, retired from a California fire department, did surveys for New Mexico Game and Fish and began supplying educational institutions with rattlesnakes and other creatures, often working with the BBC on documentaries. Portal Rescue's fire chief for many years, Tomberlin had California contacts who donated expensive equipment and helped get a bargain price on Portal's first reliable fire engine, still in use. Dennis McAvoy used his welding torch to repair and retrofit vehicles and storage tanks he wrangled from Phelps Dodge. He installed these in strategic locations, a vast improvement from siphoning water from creeks, ponds, or the research station's pool.

Artist Dave Utterback called area denizens his tribe. Neighbors of wildly diverse backgrounds rallied in 1990 to battle the Newmont Mining Company's projected open pit mine, which would crush a mountain to leach out gold with cyanide. Assailed by protests from influential naturalists around the world, the company withdrew. In 1993, Congress passed the Cave Creek Protection Act, banning mineral extraction in the watershed. After the 2011 Horseshoe II fire, folks mourned their charred moonscapes, but one said then and after the 2014 flood, "The rocks are still there."

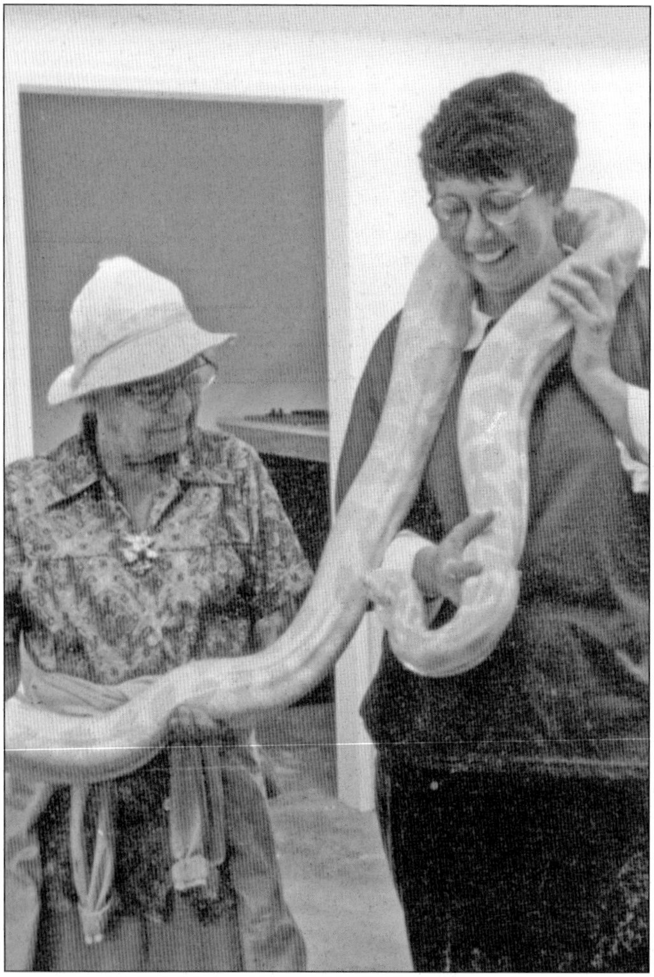

Drs. Sarah "Sally" and Walter "Spoff" Spofford retired to a home on Cave Creek in the early 1970s. Spoff, a neurologist and falconer, pursued his passion for raptors. Sally, a licensed wildlife rehabilitator, restored many owls, eagles, and other birds to the sky. The 1980s photograph at left captures her admiring Jeff Gee's albino boa with Deborah "Deby" Galloway. Deby, with Sherry Nelson, built a home downstream from the Spoffords where they held their Magic Brush seminars. Sally, former assistant to the director of Cornell's ornithology department, organized the first local Audubon Christmas Count and hosted the compilation meetings for a number of years. A huge oak in her yard presided over feeders that attracted a myriad of birds and birders from many lands. Below, in the 1990s, Sally makes sure her birds will not be disappointed. (Left, Sherry C. Nelson; below, Alice Chew.)

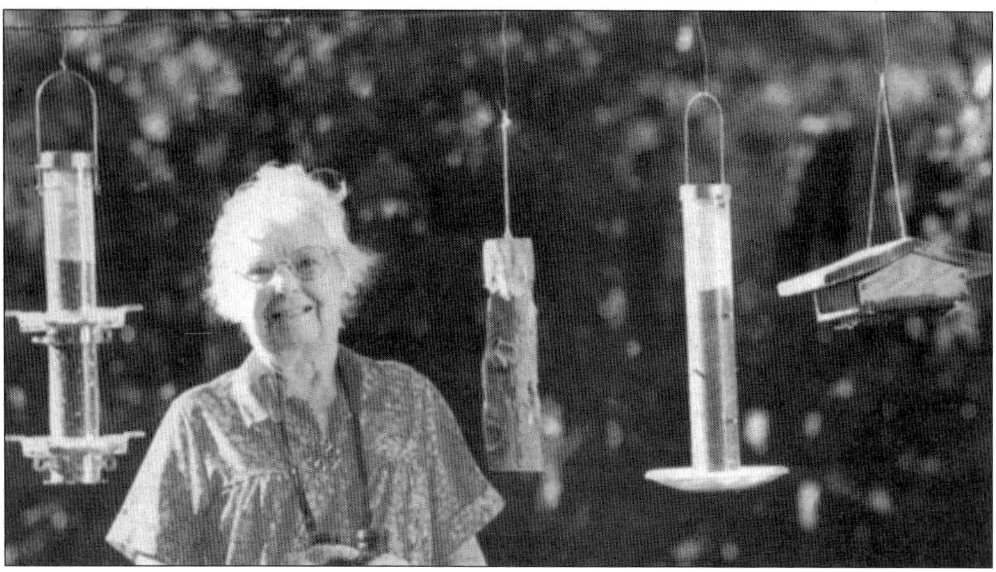

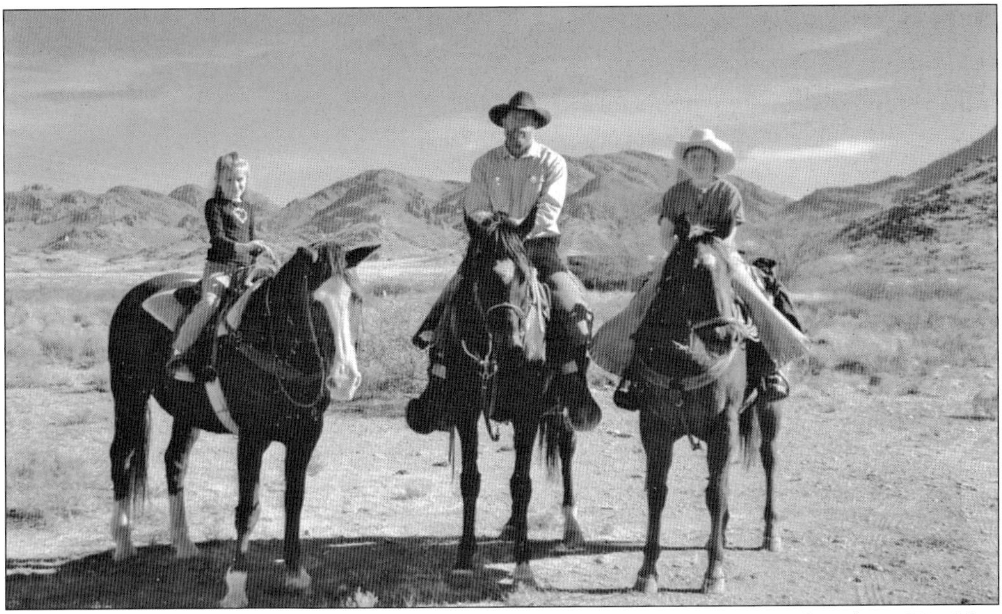

From left to right in this 2012 photograph are Parker, Richard "Rich" Jr., and Zachary Winkler, regular hands and second and third generations of the Winkler outfit in the San Simon Valley. Son of former judge Richard and Mary Winkler, Rich took his mother's place on the board of the Malpais Borderlands Group, which works with agencies and conservationists to maintain sustainable grazing with benefits for wildlife. (Mary Winkler.)

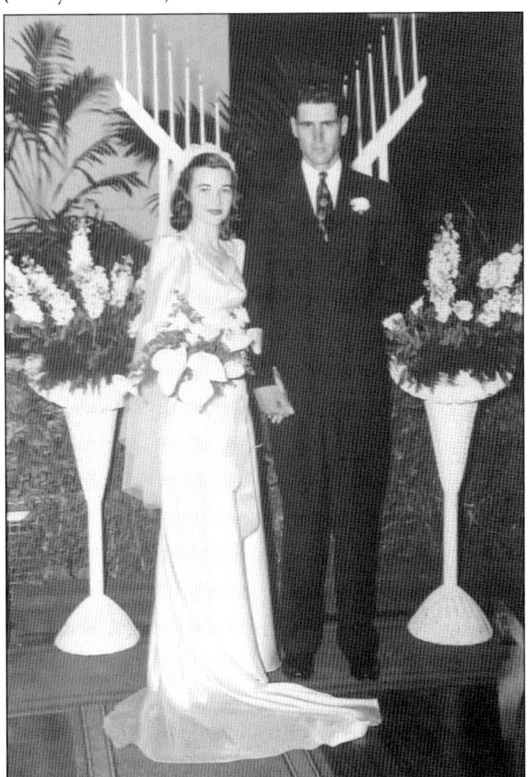

Sally Darnell married James Finley Richards, a survivor of the Bataan Death March, on February 9, 1949. They lived on their ranch, and she taught in Portal until drought caused them to move to Texas in 1958, where he worked in oil fields and she taught until they could return to their ranch. In 1965, with their three children, they moved into their beautiful and happy Portal home. (Sally Richards.)

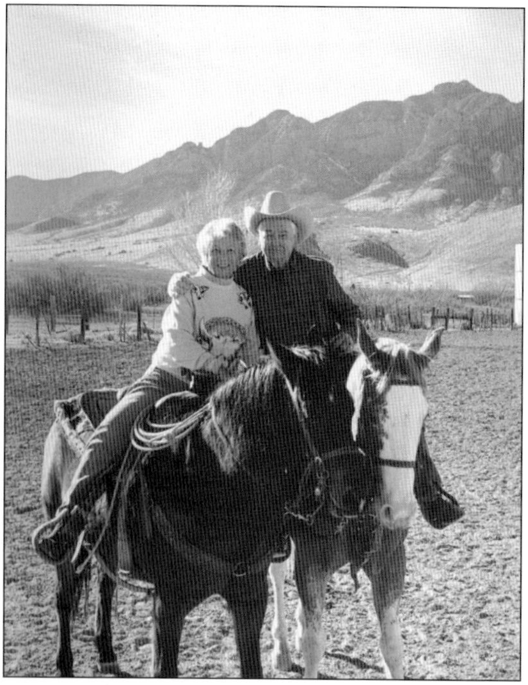

Guy and Audrey Miller rode countless miles together through many years. Guy was a cowboy for Birt Roberds until the couple acquired land and cattle. Audrey, daughter of game warden Ralph Morrow, was a successful real estate agent. Guy was an expert roper, and his arena was a popular gathering place. Their daughter Custie, known for her generosity, owned and ran the Rodeo Store with her husband, Loyd Mauzy. (Ray Mendez.)

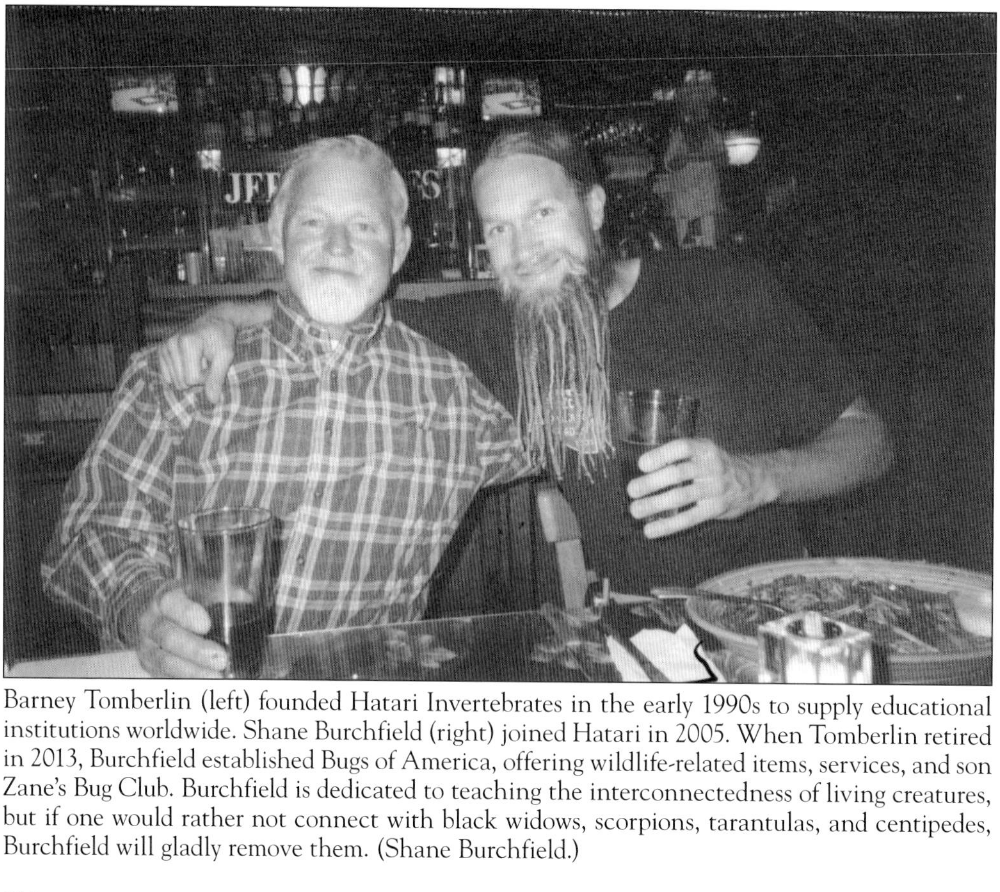

Barney Tomberlin (left) founded Hatari Invertebrates in the early 1990s to supply educational institutions worldwide. Shane Burchfield (right) joined Hatari in 2005. When Tomberlin retired in 2013, Burchfield established Bugs of America, offering wildlife-related items, services, and son Zane's Bug Club. Burchfield is dedicated to teaching the interconnectedness of living creatures, but if one would rather not connect with black widows, scorpions, tarantulas, and centipedes, Burchfield will gladly remove them. (Shane Burchfield.)

Firefighter and EMT Jeff Gee, who, with his wife, Kim, created the Captive Bred Wildlife Foundation, feeds a Galapagos tortoise in this 1989 photograph. Gee's rock climbing skills saved a woman trapped on a narrow cliff ledge for eight hours when he was lowered 250 feet to sweep her to safety. Gee, Kim, and son Cody have planned and built the innovative Sky Island Grill & Grocery between Portal and Rodeo. (Kim Gee.)

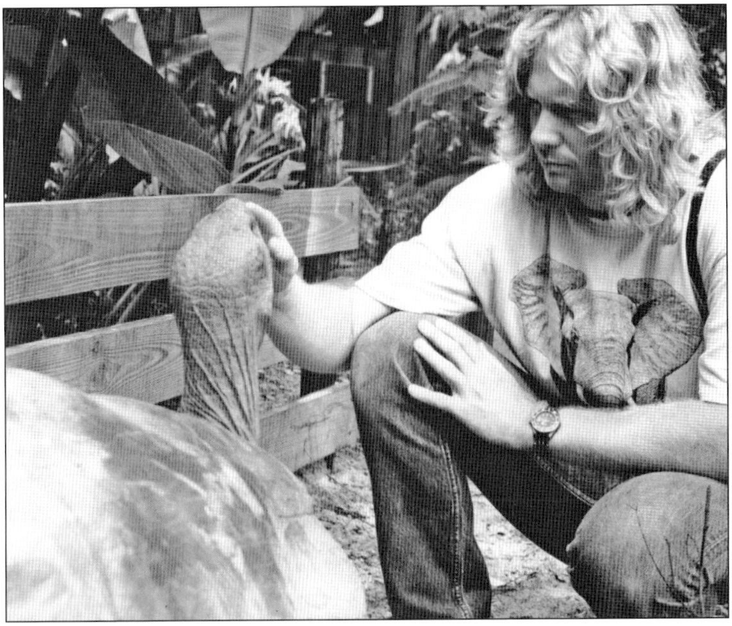

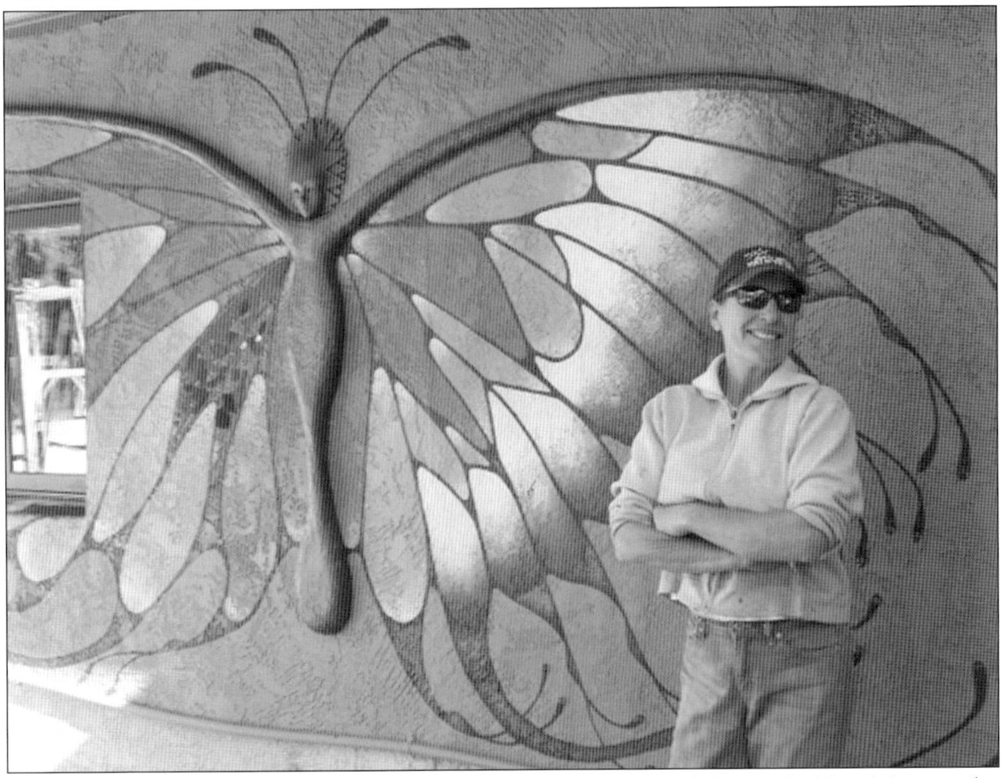

Terry Miller began selling her paintings while a teenager in California. In New Mexico, she continued to sell to galleries and revitalized Lordsburg's closed storefronts with Western murals. She supported her art with ranch work and house renovation. In this 2013 photograph, she stands by the butterfly lady that won her acclaim and many clients. Miller's haunting animal skulls shine with the spirits of deer, coyotes, and other creatures. (Alice Newton.)

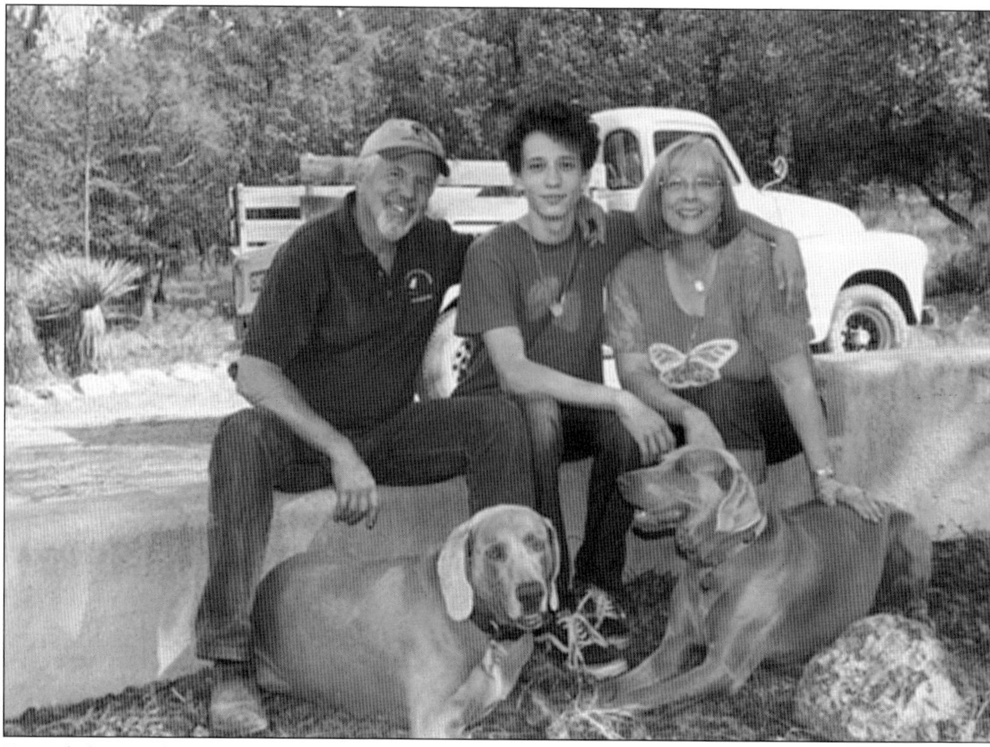

From left to right in this 2014 photograph are Ray, Wyatt, and Joy Mendez with Weimaraners Niko and Shadow—"perfect guard dogs and saddle buddies" despite starring in film and television, according to Ray. The Mendezes' company, Work as Play, cooperates with institutions such as Disney's Animal Kingdom in Florida and Australia's Melbourne Zoo to create exhibits that inspire questions and, says Ray, "are fun, visually exciting, informative, and easy to maintain." (Karen Tweedy-Holmes.)

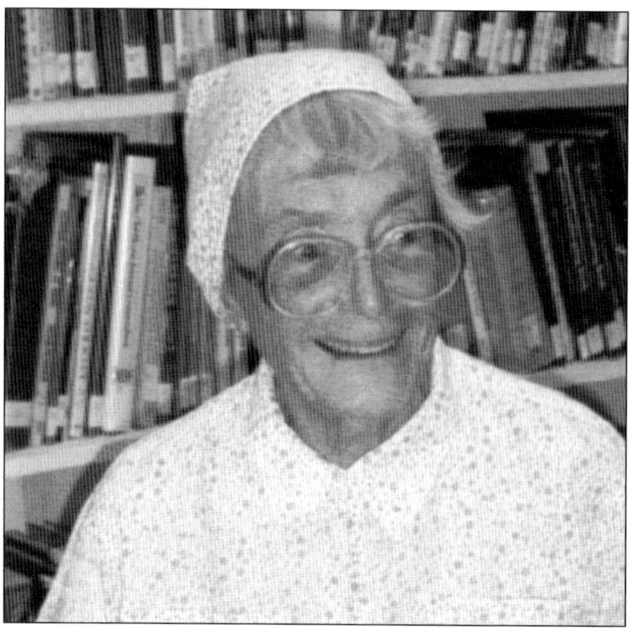

Former Eastern farmers Ginny and Herbert Appelt built their solar home and set up their looms in sight of Bear Mountain. They lived by weaving and growing most of their food, watered by captured rain. Retiring from market weaving, they volunteered almost daily at the Portal Library, where they are remembered with apple and pomegranate trees and engraved bench plaques. (Barbara Miller.)

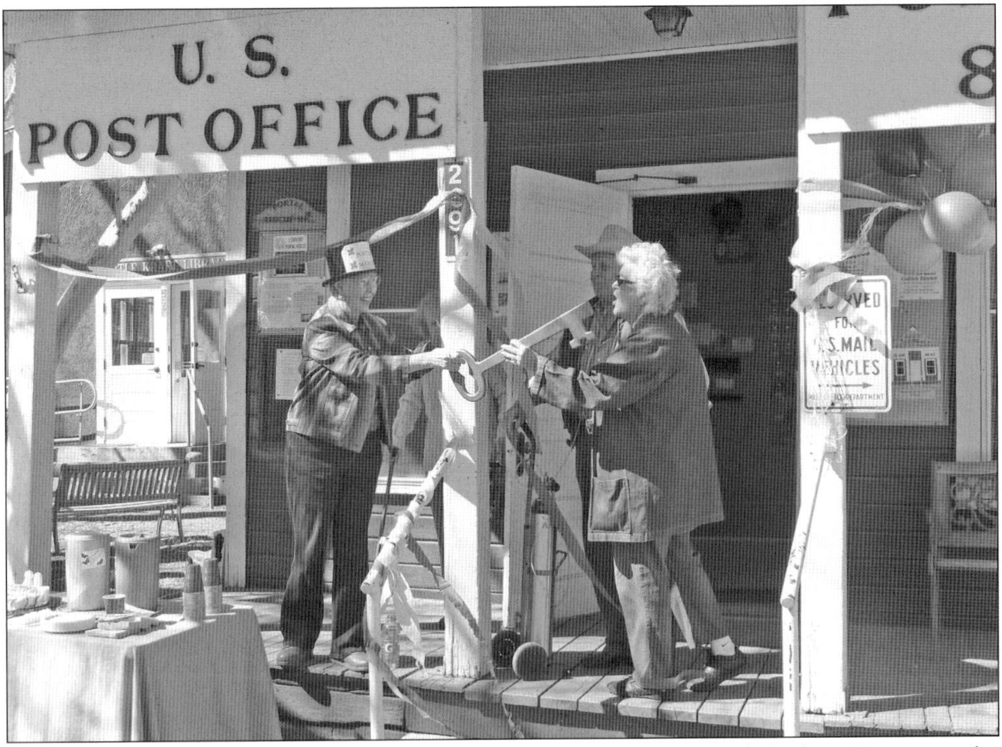

Honorary mayor Gerry Hernbrode (right) praises Joan Jensen (center) for her 30 years as the Portal postmaster, giving personal service undreamed of in cities. Husband Chuck Jensen approves in this 2012 photograph. For many years, Joan was Portal Rescue's backup dispatcher, spending hours on the radio, often accompanied by Chuck. He donated extensive wiring as well as his time to wire the Portal Rescue classroom and for 20 years drove the school bus to San Simon, where he was custodian and took care of the former Portal School/teacherage. The Jensens are shown in photograph below with daughters Loy Guzman (third from left), teacher/computer whiz, and former firefighter and I-EMT Debbie Bernard (right), past president of Portal Rescue. Advanced training enabled Debbie to give lifesaving intravenous fluids and medications. With her husband, Rob, she owns and operates the historic Rodeo Tavern. Son Macky is a Tucson paramedic. (Both, Barbara Miller.)

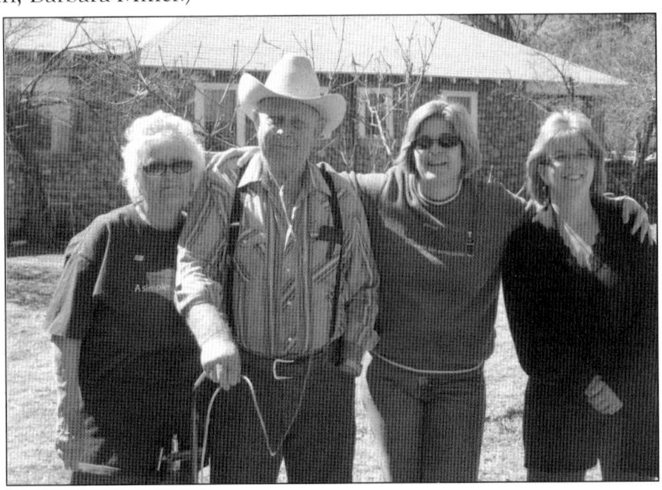

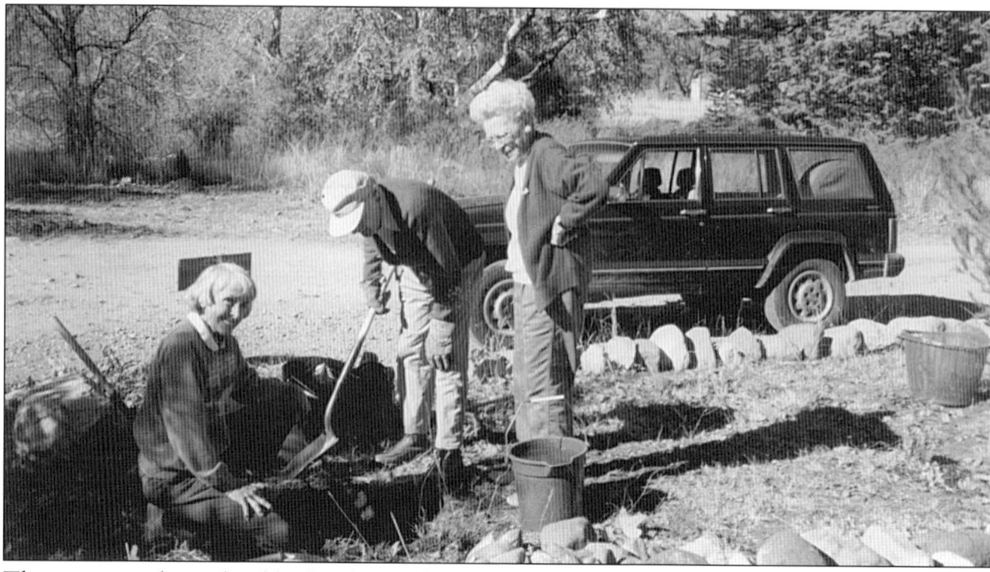

There was, and is, a boulder by the road to the post office. A workday was set to enclose this hazard with numerous sharp rocks pried from in front of the library. In this mid-1980s photograph, Penny Johnston and Robert Squier plant a Douglas fir donated by the National Forest Service while Kay Muma supervises. The park is named for lovable curmudgeon Bert Schaughency. (Sally Spofford.)

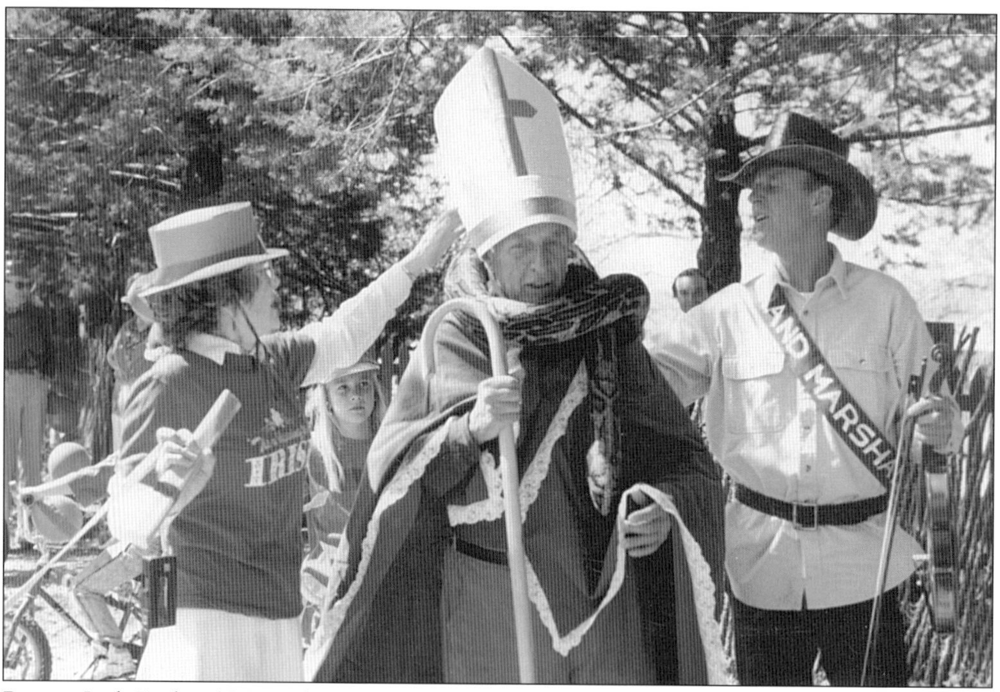

Boston Irish Evelyn (O'Leary) Squier, Penny Johnston, and Delane Blondeau organized Portal's first St. Patrick's Day parade in 1994. In this 2006 photograph, O'Leary (left) and Kim Murphy (right) help Pat Willy, born on the saint's day, adjust his outfit. Willy was also poet laureate. After the procession, his birthday cake was served in the library while Jean Wadsworth played lilting tunes on her keyboard for a sing-along. (Sally Spofford.)

These little leprechauns, in elfin wear made by Tamara Winkler (right), charmed everyone at the 1998 parade. Now, they are all in college. From left to right are Daniel Roth, Wyatt Mendez, Zachary Winkler, and Taran Roth with Joy Mendez in back at left. When they were older, these boys and their friends enjoyed annual pumpkin parties at Mendezes' mountaintop home. (Mary Winkler.)

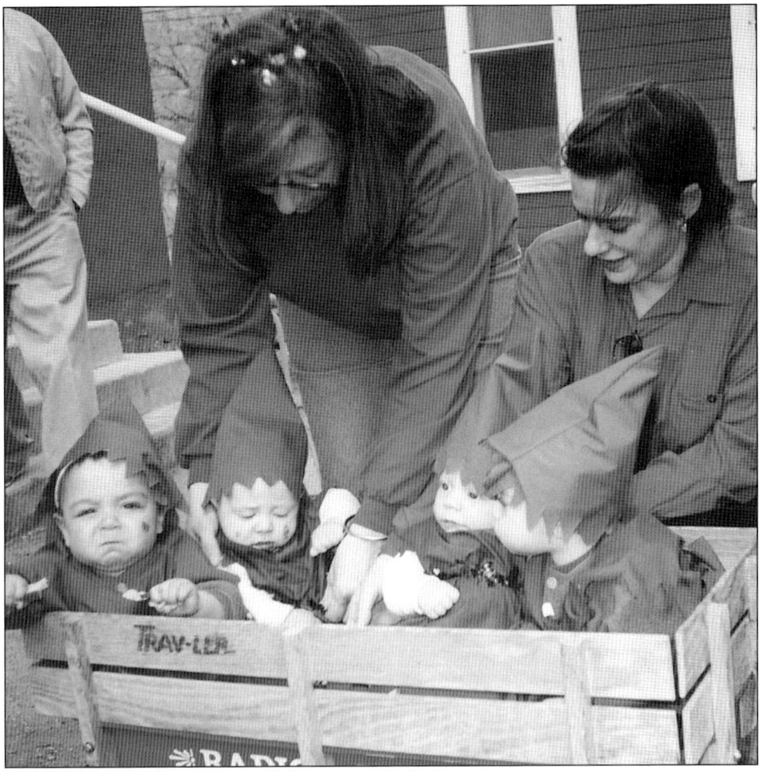

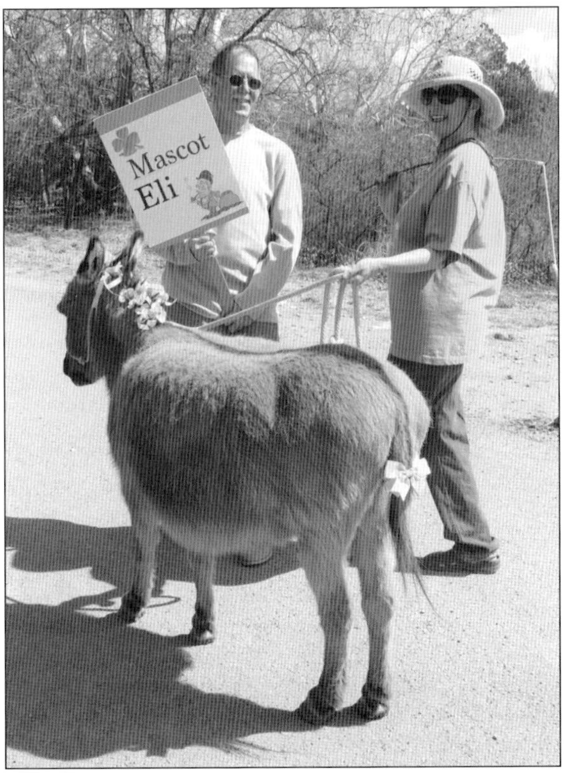

Laughing with sign-bearer David Johnson in this 2015 parade, Chris Wilbur escorts mascot donkey Eli. While dog grooming in California, Chris homed about 200 rescue dogs a year, after they were spayed or neutered, housebroken, and trained. The Wilburs' verdant oasis nurtures many animals and birds. (Howard Topoff.)

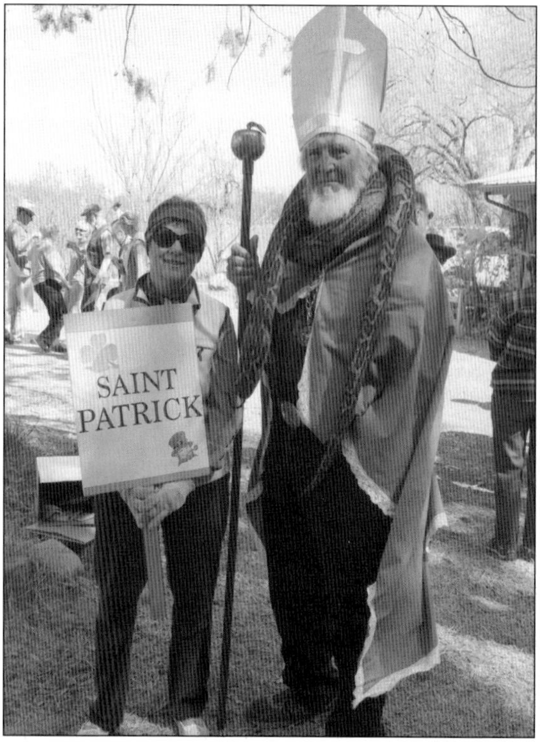

Linda Pretty heralds Bill Wilbur as St. Patrick. Raised on a California ranch, Wilbur worked on the early Mars projects as an aerospace engineer and helped put satellites in space. Both Wilburs have powered Portal Rescue—he as president, Chris as an EMT and current organizer of the soup kitchen. (Howard Topoff.)

Mary Abbott (back turned), sponsor of the 4-H Peloncillo Riders, leads a horse in a St. Patrick's Day parade. From left to right are Parker Winkler, an unidentified boy, and Catherine Racicot. Abbott loves kids and horses. Her joyous gift is to bring them together. (Mary Winkler.)

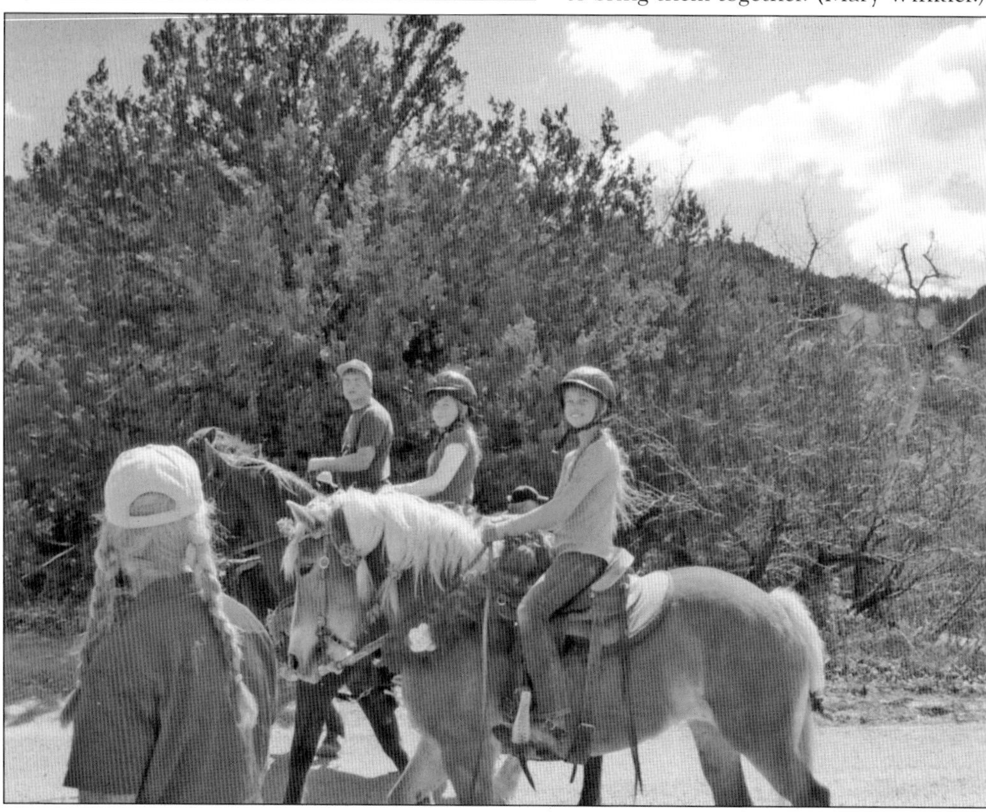

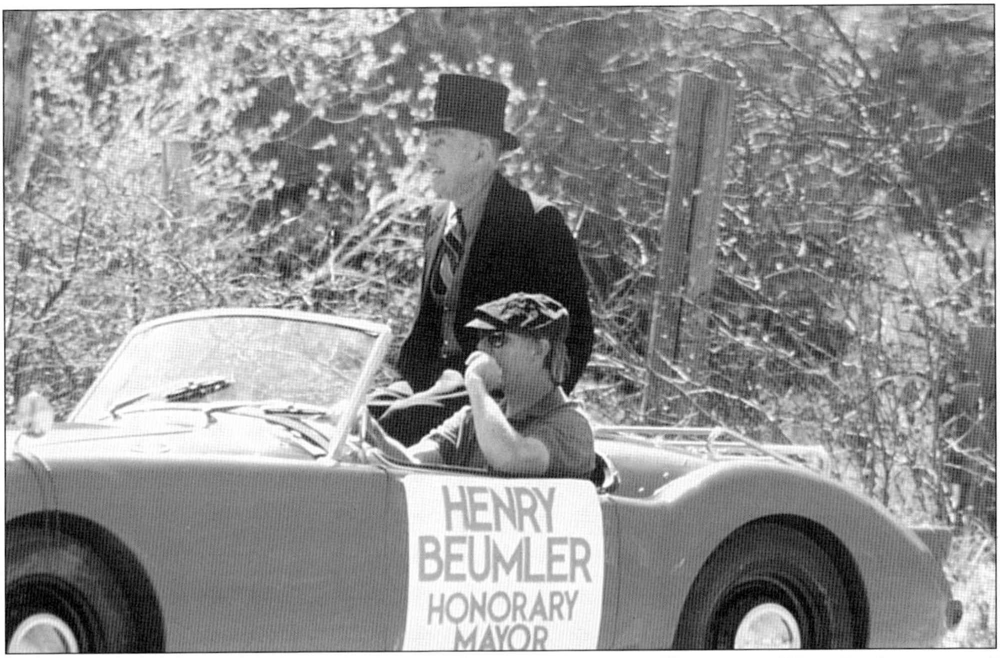

Honorary mayor Henry Beumler, driven by Alex Stone, was actually mayor of Douglas from around 1950 to 1960. He loved teaching, fitting his law practice around it. He served in the cavalry in World War II, retiring as a lieutenant colonel in the Army Reserve. Retiring to Portal in 1978 with his wife and square dance partner, Estelle, he practiced law. In his 80s, with congestive heart failure, he learned to tango. (Barbara Miller.)

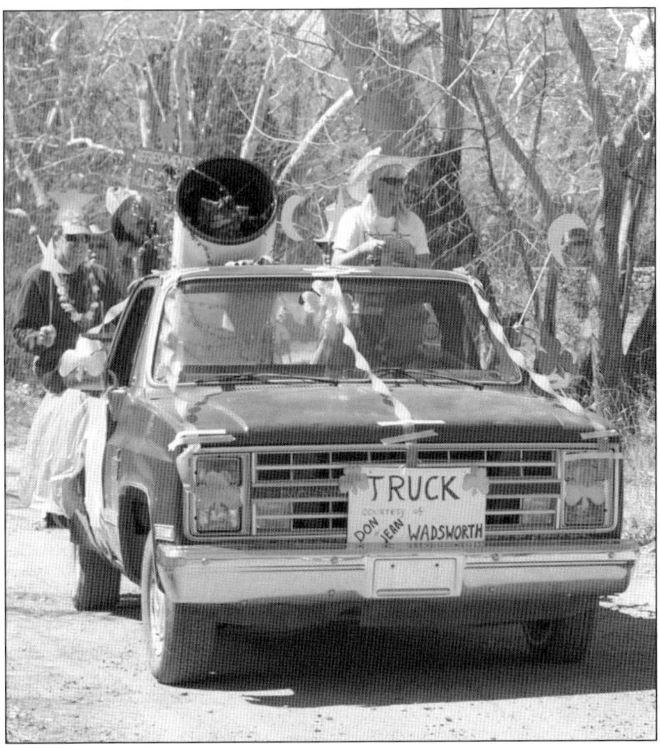

"Mr. Eclipse" Fred Espenak drives the first Sky Village float in 2012. Passengers are, from left to right, Dr. Joseph Morris, Anne Morris, Richard Schreiber, and Pat Espenak. Attracted by unpolluted dark skies, about 80 astronomers live at least part-time in the region, many having their own observatories. They enrich the community by sharing their knowledge and taking part in Portal Rescue and other endeavors. (Jack Newton.)

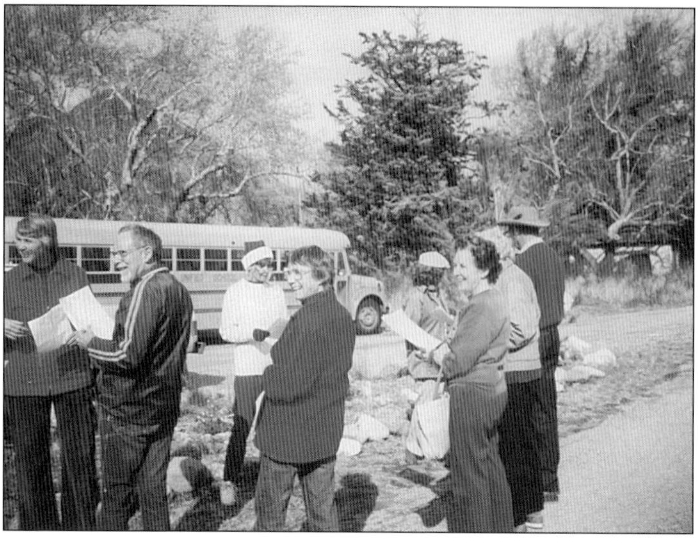

Ever since Schaughency Park was created, carolers gather when they come for their mail around noon on Christmas Eve, as in this 1991 photograph. From left to right are Fran and Dick Zweifel, unidentified, Pi Irwin, Mary Carson, Bob Squier, Bob Addison, and Jeanne Williams. Dogs may join the chorus, and visitors who stop to listen are welcomed into the circle. (Sally Spofford.)

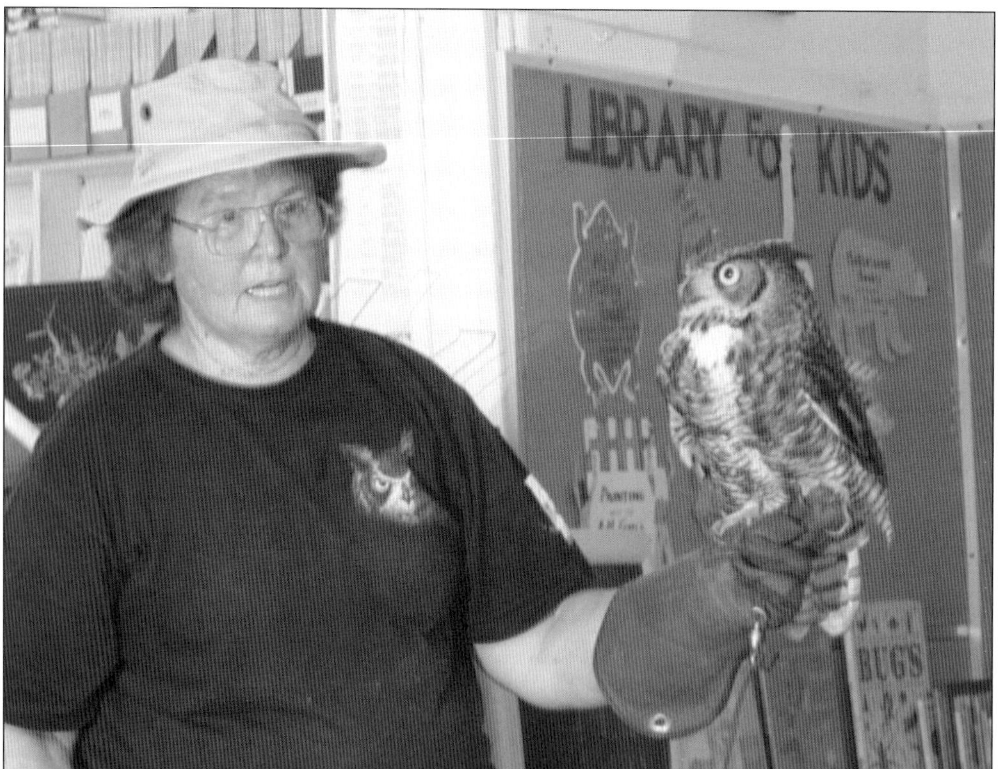

Delane Blondeau used her teaching experience to provide enthralling summer activities for children. At this 1994 Library for Kids, biologist Helen Snyder introduces McHooter, her non-releasable owl kept under government permits, who aids her goshawk research. Now a successful realtor, Snyder was a Portal Rescue EMT/firefighter. She and husband Noel have authored acclaimed books on raptors and spearheaded the battle against Newmont's mine. (Alice Chew.)

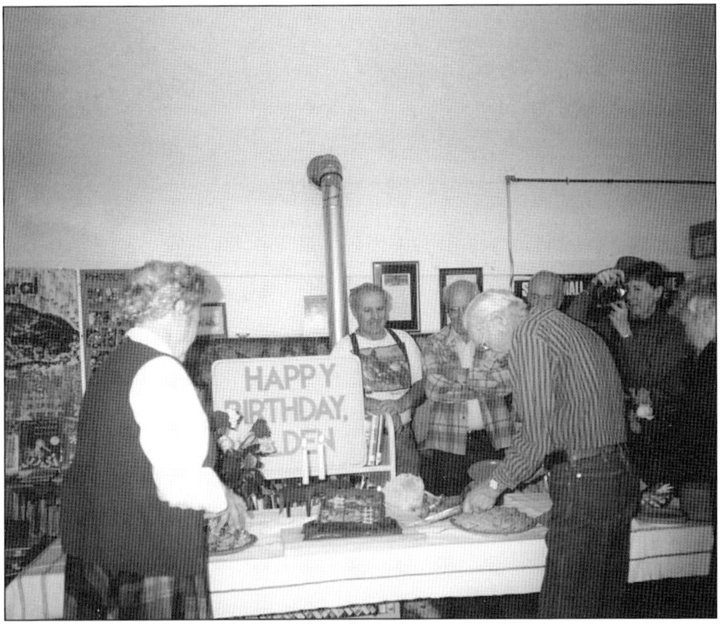

Sally Spofford's 80th birthday began the tradition of celebrating that birthday in the library when mail is ready for pickup; though, when five residents turned 90 within weeks of each other, they were honored at the Portal Rescue classroom. In this 1986 photograph, Sally Richards presides over punch while Alden Hayes inspects his cake, watched by, from left to right, Charles Travers, René Blondeau, and Karen Hayes. (Barbara Miller.)

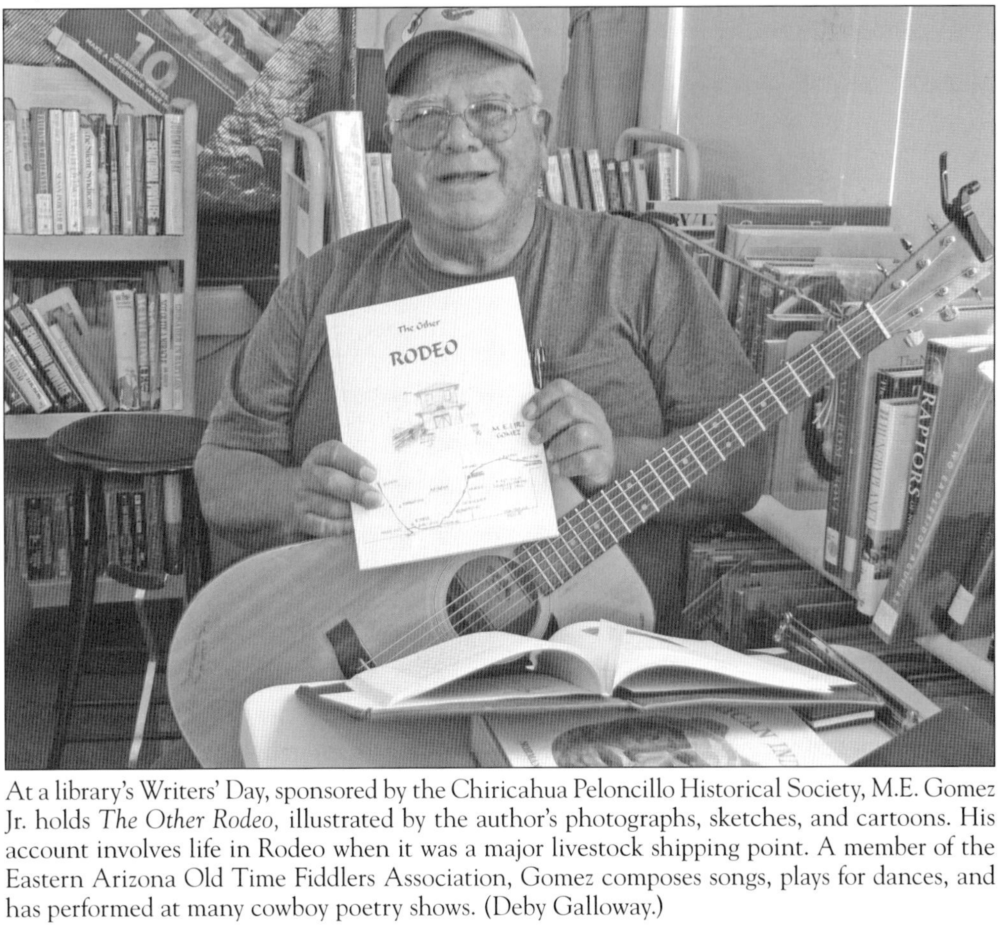

At a library's Writers' Day, sponsored by the Chiricahua Peloncillo Historical Society, M.E. Gomez Jr. holds *The Other Rodeo,* illustrated by the author's photographs, sketches, and cartoons. His account involves life in Rodeo when it was a major livestock shipping point. A member of the Eastern Arizona Old Time Fiddlers Association, Gomez composes songs, plays for dances, and has performed at many cowboy poetry shows. (Deby Galloway.)

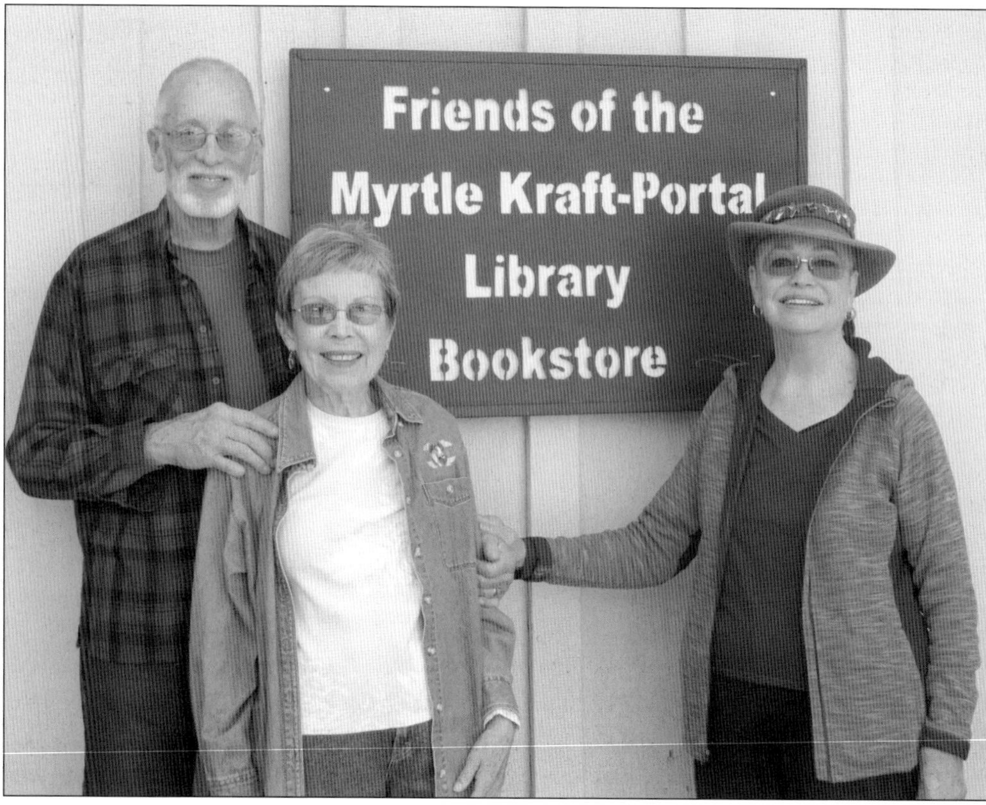

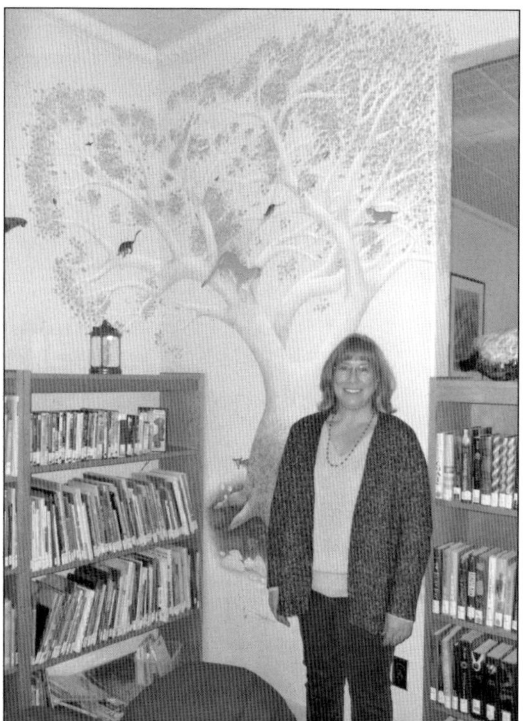

Jon and Mary Lacey, still faithful to Washington State where he was an engineer in the paper industry and she held administrative positions, discovered Portal while camping. After retirement in 2005, they bought their Portal home. Maya Decker, president of the Friends of the Myrtle Kraft Library, commends the Laceys on the attractive bookstore they created for the community. Mary also cochairs the St. Patrick's Day parade. (Deborah Galloway.)

Kathleen Talbot, a superb librarian, wrote a grant that renovated the aging building into a welcoming center with public computers and friendly assistance. In this 2015 photograph, she stands by the children's corner mural that shows a girl reading under a tree while wild creatures frolic about. Painted by Celia Reed with Pam Eberlein's help, the work is dedicated to charismatic library volunteer and community leader Penny Johnston. (Debb Johnson.)

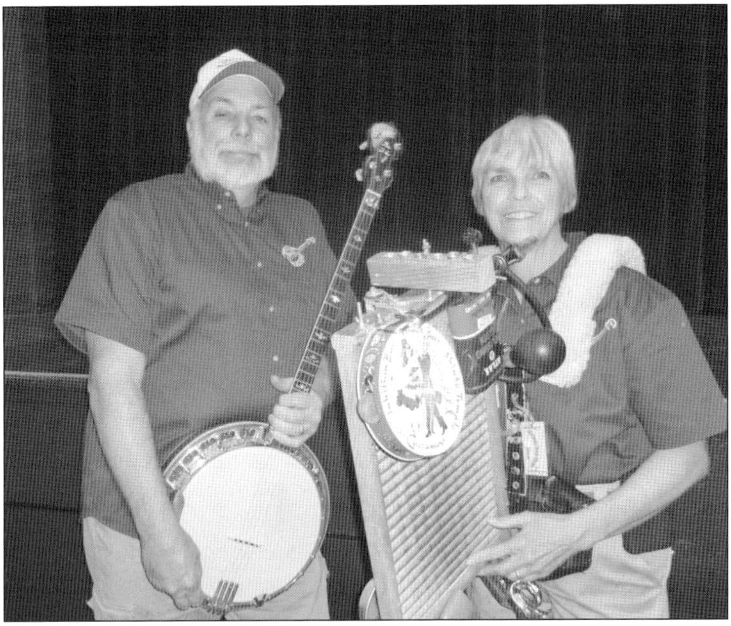

Debb and Bud Johnson play with Banjo Blasters, a nonprofit band that raises funds for good causes. Both are skilled wildlife photographers. Debb illustrated her book on Harris's hawks, inspired by volunteer work with free-flying birds at Tucson's Desert Museum. The Johnsons' community responsibilities include watering shrubs and trees at village hub. (Debb Johnson.)

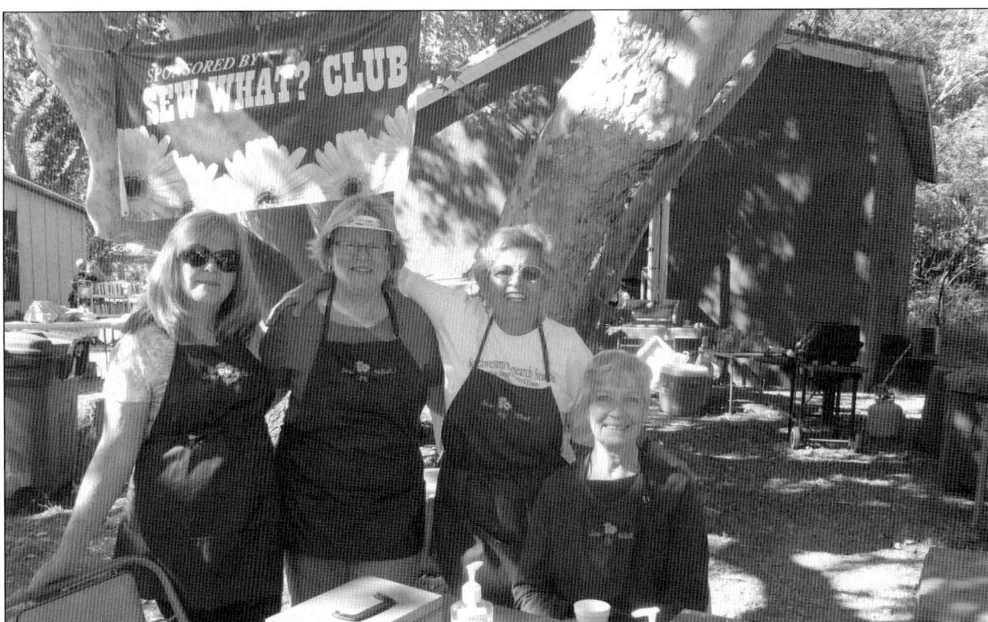

Shaded by bronze-golden sycamores, diners at Oktoberfest enjoy bratwurst with German side dishes, may browse the adjacent bookstore, and can choose desserts from homemade baked goods. Keeping tables supplied are, from left to right, Joanna Hotton, Vicki Beno (Oktoberfest chairman), Patricia Esser (bakery coordinator), and Jo Yeomans. (Debb Johnson.)

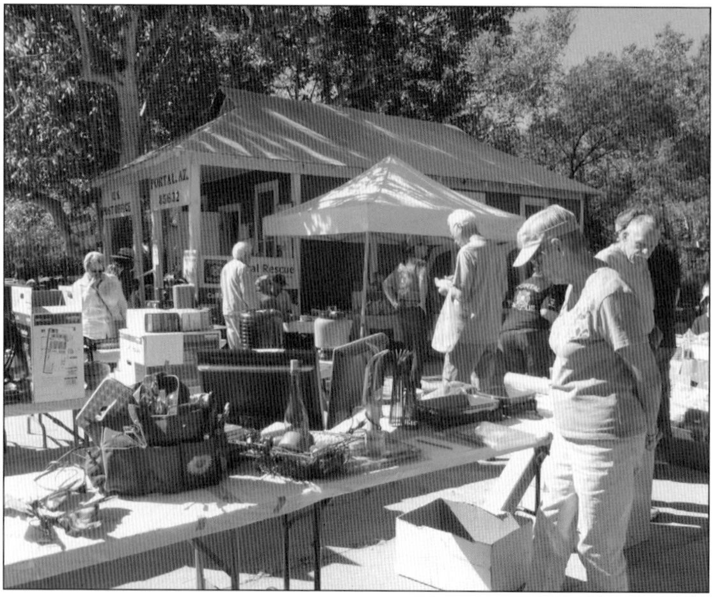

For years, Sew What funded projects with an autumn bake sale and spring rummage. After the success of a silent auction implemented by Gerry Hernbrode, JoAnn Julian organized both sales and held them during Oktoberfest. A language arts teacher for 14 years and principal for 11, JoAnn settled in Portal in 2001 with her husband, Doug Julian; both became community innovators. Here, tables and canopies cover "downtown" as the Julians examine a find. (Debb Johnson.)

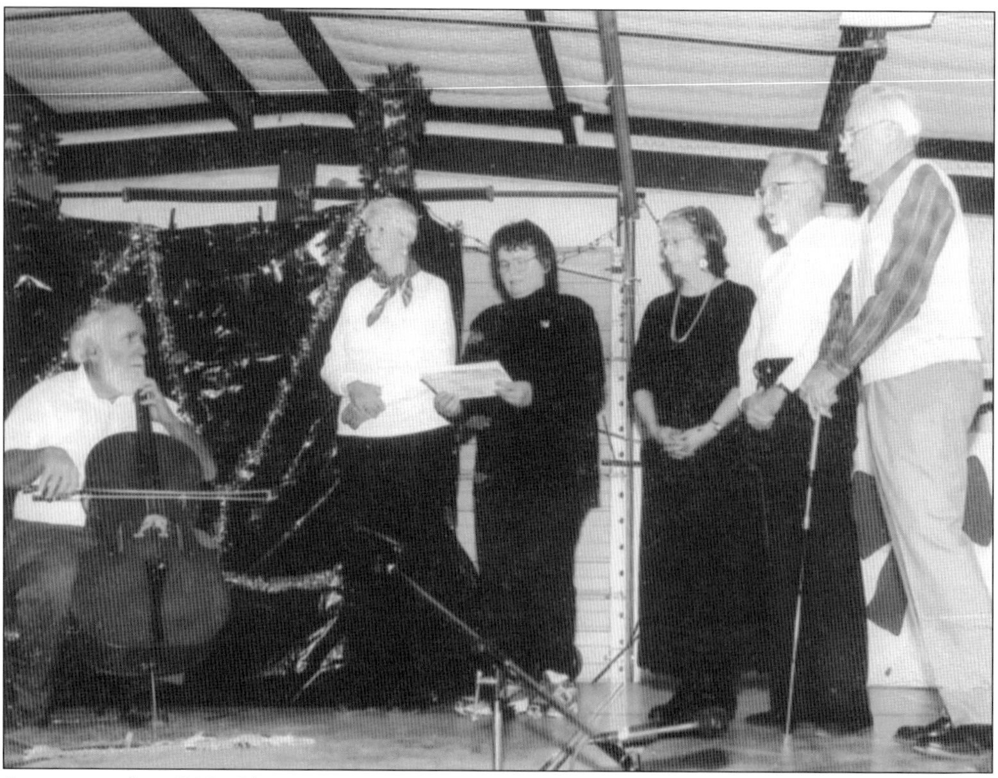

Starring in this 1990s Christmas program at the Rodeo Community Center, cellist Noel Snyder accompanies the Red Hot Chili Peppers. From left to right are Snyder, Fran Zweifel, Helen Snyder, Joy Mendez, Bob Squier, and Dick Zweifel. The large community building accommodates gatherings from Bible study to dances, weddings, funerals, public meetings, and programs. (Richard Zweifel.)

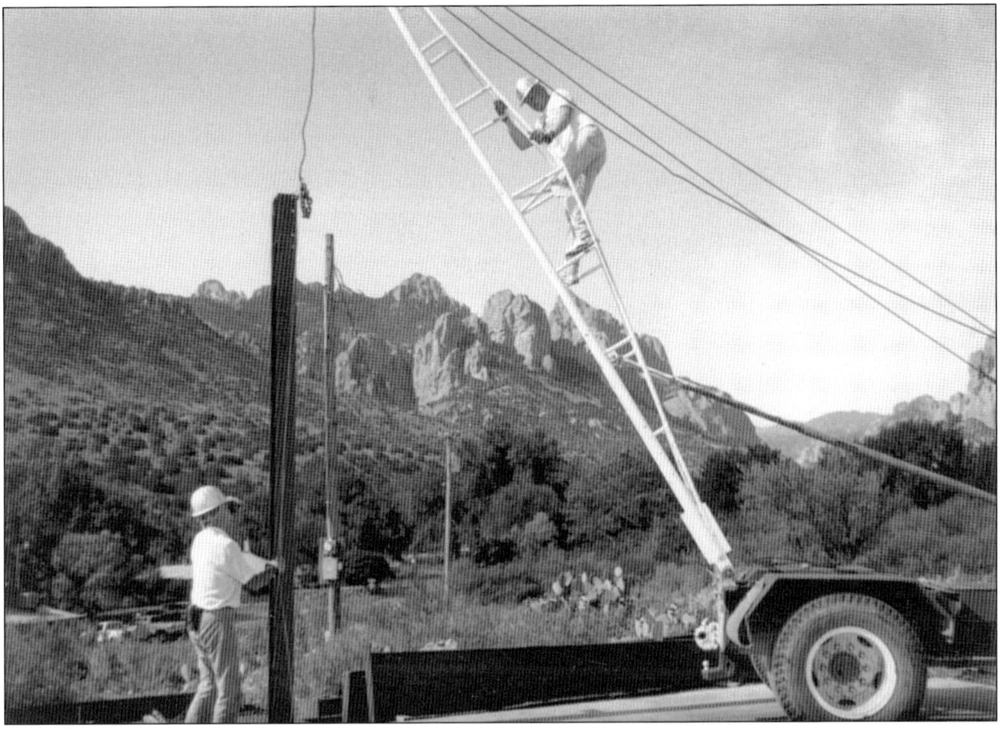

Construction of Portal Rescue's first building is under way in this August 1991 photograph. EMT Ralph Willy and his wife, Mary, donated this scenic location. The community raised the needed $19,000 in a fund drive headed by EMTs René Blondeau and Bob Morse. Penny Johnston and Kay Muma drove many backcountry miles to tell residents about Portal Rescue, suggest contributions, detail medical conditions, and record directions on how rescue vehicles could get to all dwellings in the area. (Bob Morse.)

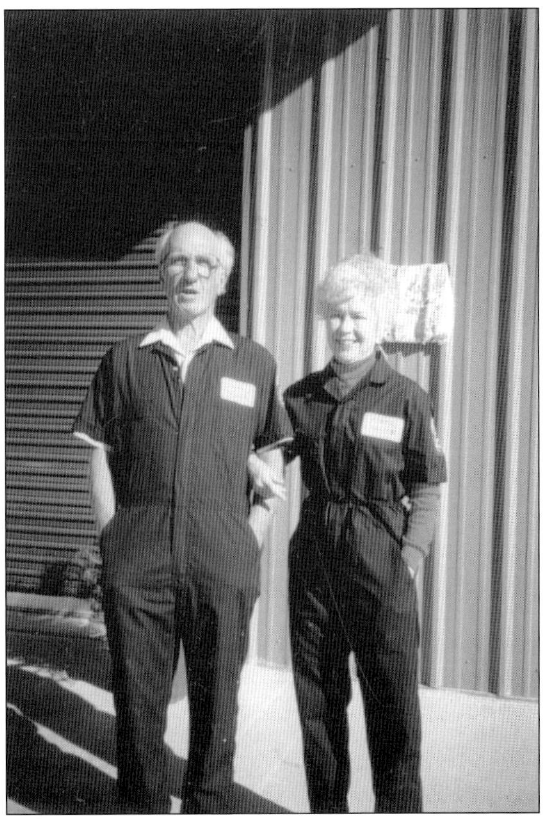

René and Delane Blondeau moved into the first solar house in Portal in 1980, after working on it four years. René, a plant biologist, retired from Shell's agricultural branch. Delane's 24-year teaching career took her to Santo Domingo Pueblo, Japan, and Germany. The Blondeaus were among 24 area people who took the 1980 EMT class in Rodeo. Four years later, they were the only active Portal members. (Bob Morse.)

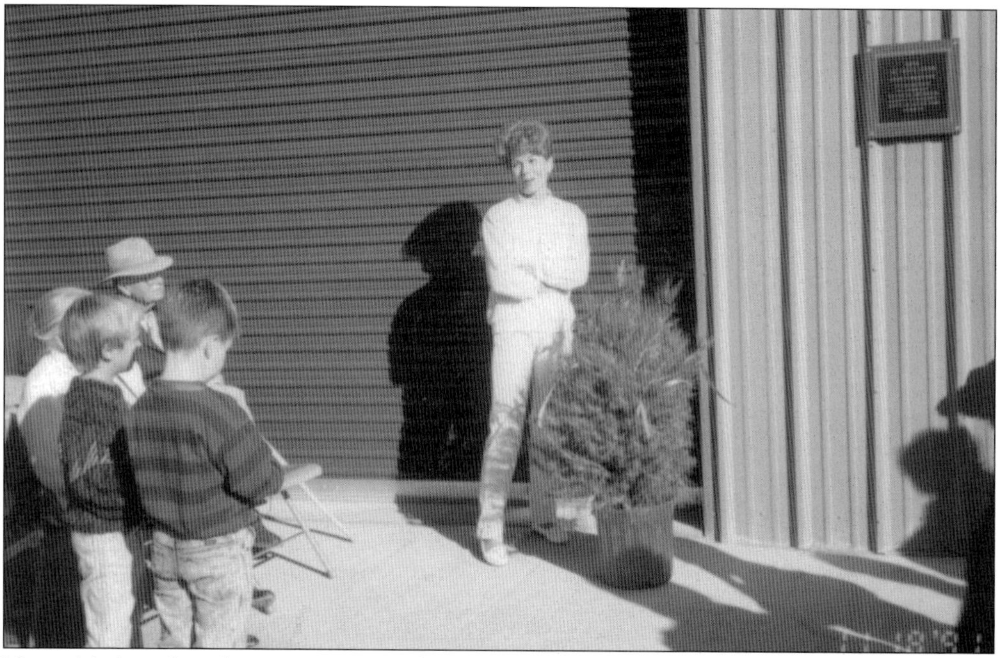

Nancy McAvoy drew from experience as former Sunnyside fire chief Dennis McAvoy's wife to raise funds for Portal Rescue by organizing spaghetti dinners. For many yeas, she has also graciously and efficiently supervised precinct elections. She speaks here at the dedication of the first Portal Rescue building in November 1991. Seated at far right is Dr. Walter Spofford. (Bob Morse.)

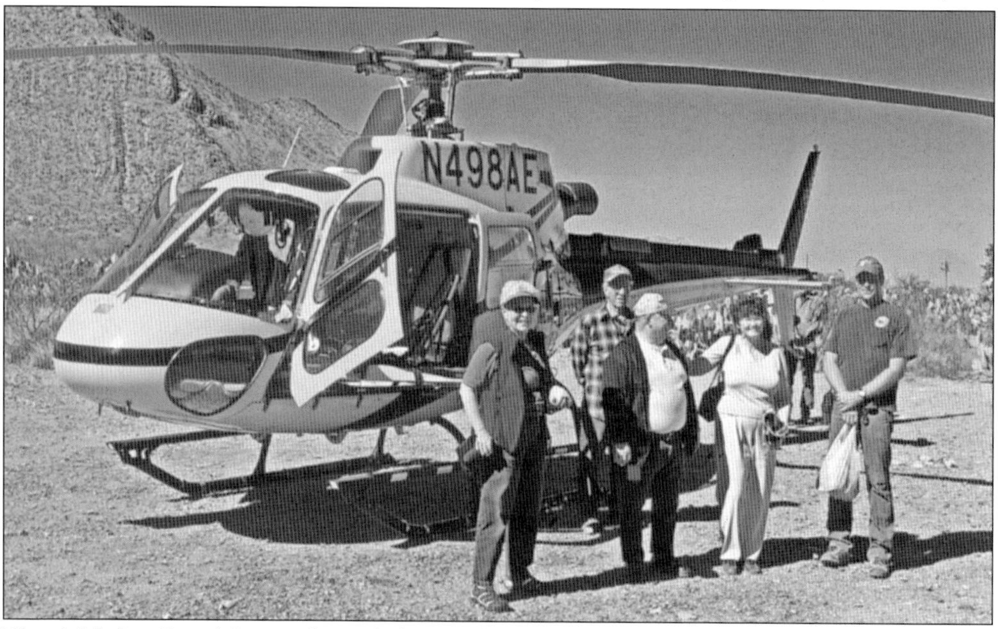

Thankful that Portal Rescue has a helispot where aircraft like this can land to whisk patients to Tucson under the care of nurses and paramedics, are, from left to right, Barbara Miller, Portal Rescue president René Blondeau, communications officer Dennis McAvoy, and two unidentified members. McAvoy customized vehicles and, with other volunteers, kept hand-me-downs running, including the sheriff's department's bullet-scarred castoff Blazer. (Bob Morse.)

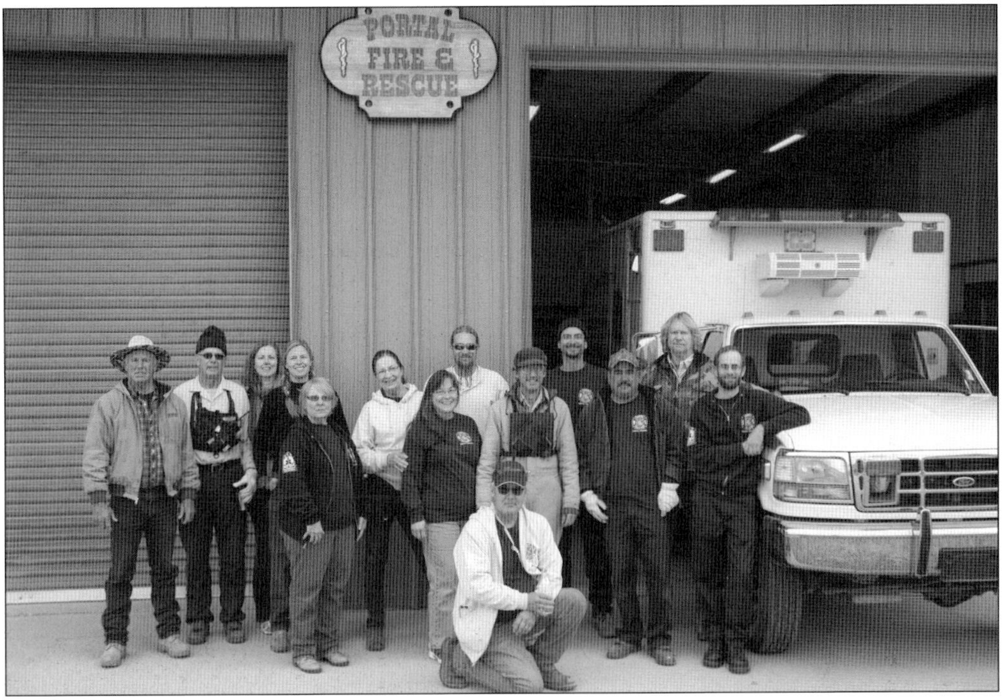

Firefighters, EMTs, and 2015 volunteers are, from left to right, (kneeling) Joe Meenach; (second row) Larry Rivers, Lee Dyal, Susanne Apitz, Jennifer Racicot, Stevie Wayman, Donna Meenach, Jackie Lewis, Shane Burchfield, David Newton (fire chief), Jerry Racicot (EMS chief), Lance Shultis, Jeff Gee, and John Yerger. Absent are treasurer Rick Beno, E.T. Collinsworth, Chris Husband, Ken Joens, David Johnson, and Bob Walton. (Tim Lawson.)

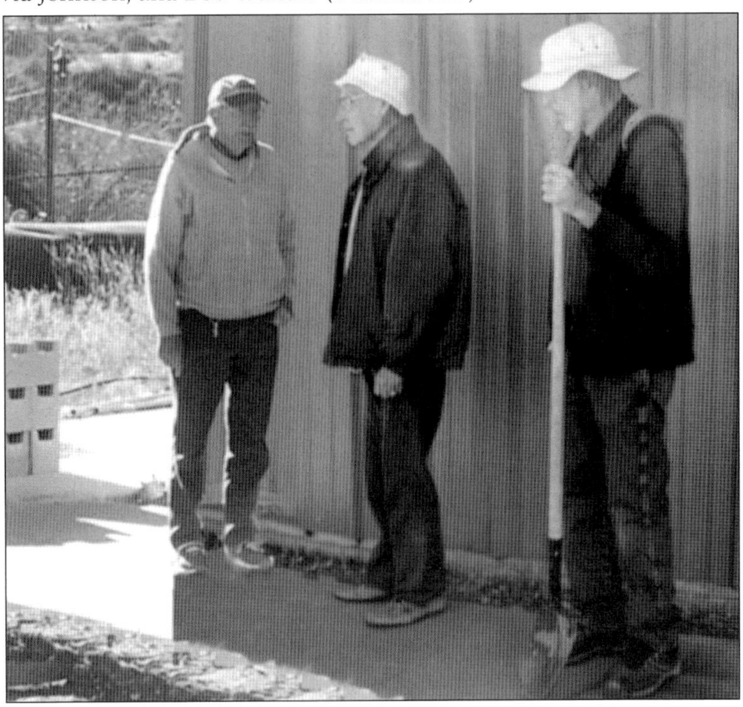

These friends led the building of the huge garage that completed Portal Rescue's complex. From left to right are Bill Reinbold, Don Wadsworth, and Bob Dearing. Reinbold custom-made wooden boats until fiberglass scuttled that. He turned full-time to carving birds and wildlife. Wadsworth, a chemist in the Army, later worked for Kodak. Dearing sculpts junk into art. He built two airplanes and seven houses, living in six of them. (Don Wadsworth.)

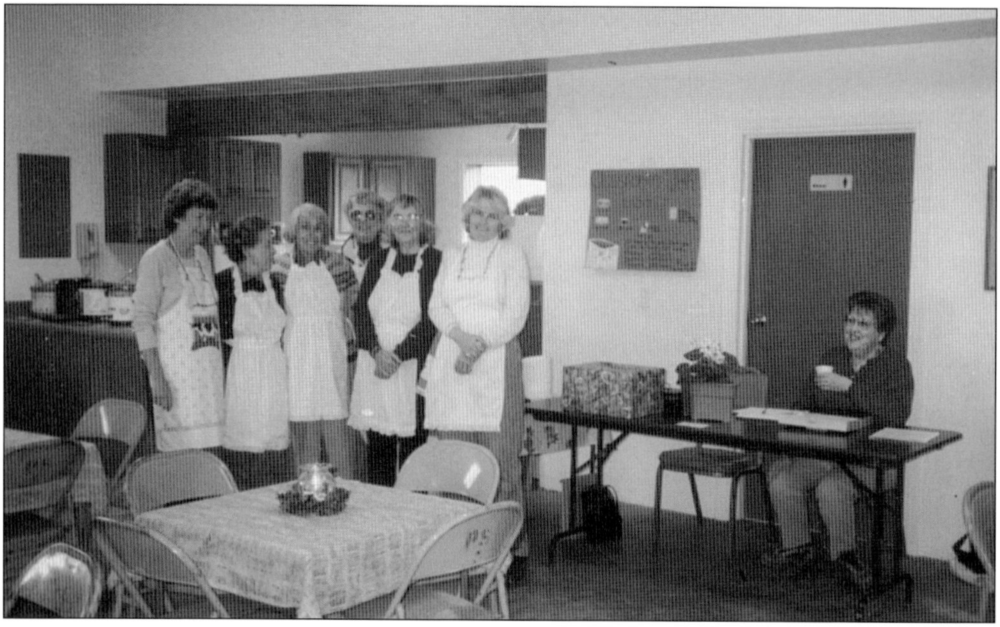

The first soup kitchen was held in the mid-1990s in the only Portal Rescue building, which had no plumbing. Bathrooms and a kitchen enhanced the spacious classroom and were added under Bruce Miller's leadership. The above February 1997 event was probably the first soup kitchen held there. From left to right are Jan Gee, Jeanne Williams, Penny Johnston, Barbara Miller, Shirley Zent, Joan Richardson, and Yvette Rehurek (seated). In its 20th year, 2016, the kitchen served about 400 meals. Ready to work in 2003 photograph below are, from left to right, Vicki Beno, Cecelia Hessler, unidentified, JoAnn Julian, Kim Gee, Lisa Bender, Patricia Esser, Barbara Miller, Jean Wadsworth, Janice Hurd, Delane Blondeau, Jackie Lewis, Marcia Troller, Pat Owens, Gerry Hernbrode, and Penny Johnston. Portal Rescue's main fundraiser, the annual affair brings together far-flung neighbors in a high-spirited reunion. (Both, Bob Morse.)

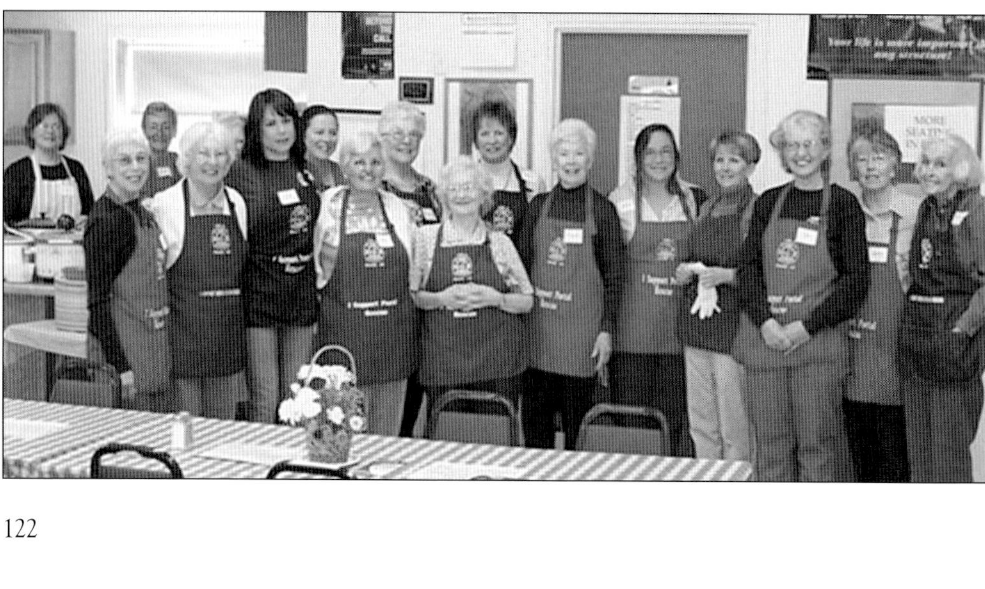

The first event held at the garage completing the Portal Rescue complex was a medieval extravaganza with sword fights, dancing, and Kim Gee on horseback as Lady Godiva. Queen O'Leary Squier confers here with impresario Wizard Howard Topoff who, in early 1990s, produced Fran Zweifel's adaptation of *The Nutcracker*. (Barbara Miller.)

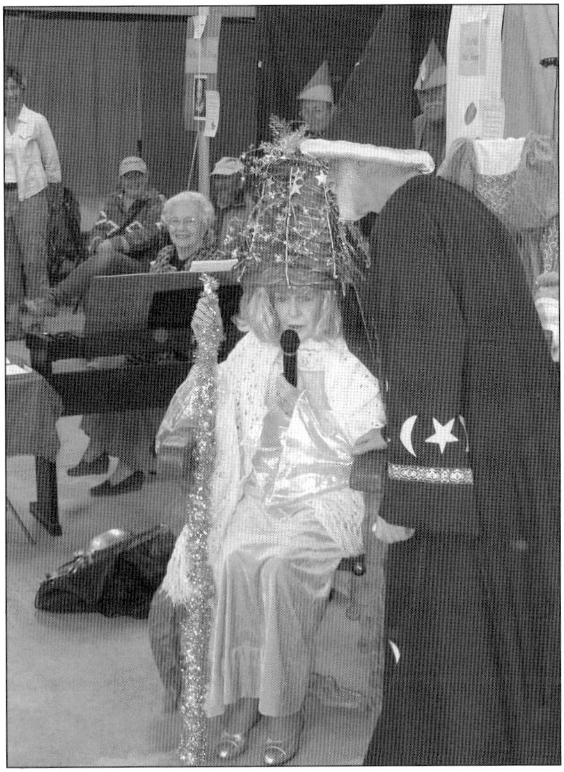

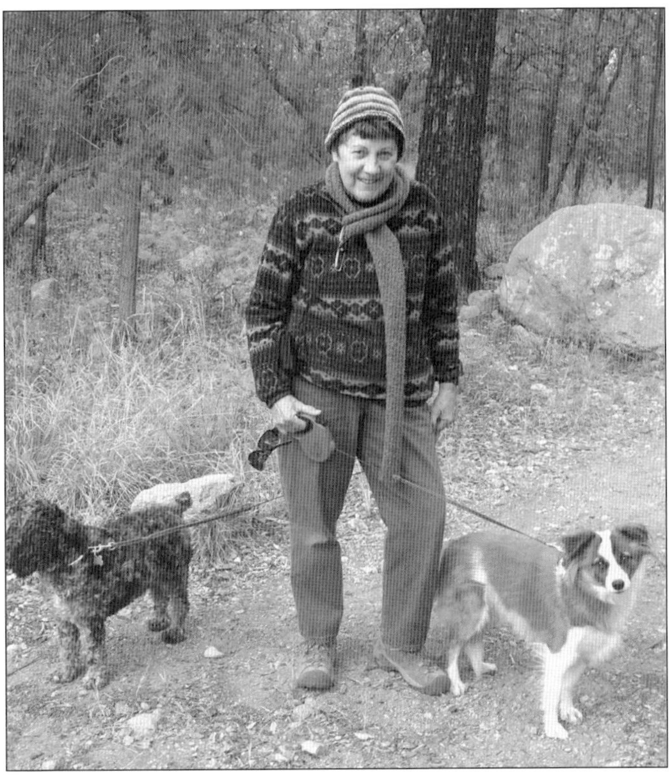

Dr. Dinah Davidson spent three decades researching in the Amazon and Borneo while teaching at the University of Utah. A Guggenheim Fellowship sent her around the world to study tropical ant/plant interaction. She has served Portal Rescue as secretary and EMT and maintains the community e-mail message service. Dogs Maddie and Pepper ski with her. Davidson, along with Barbara Miller, is doing a Friends of Cave Creek Canyon plant booklet. (Barbara Miller.)

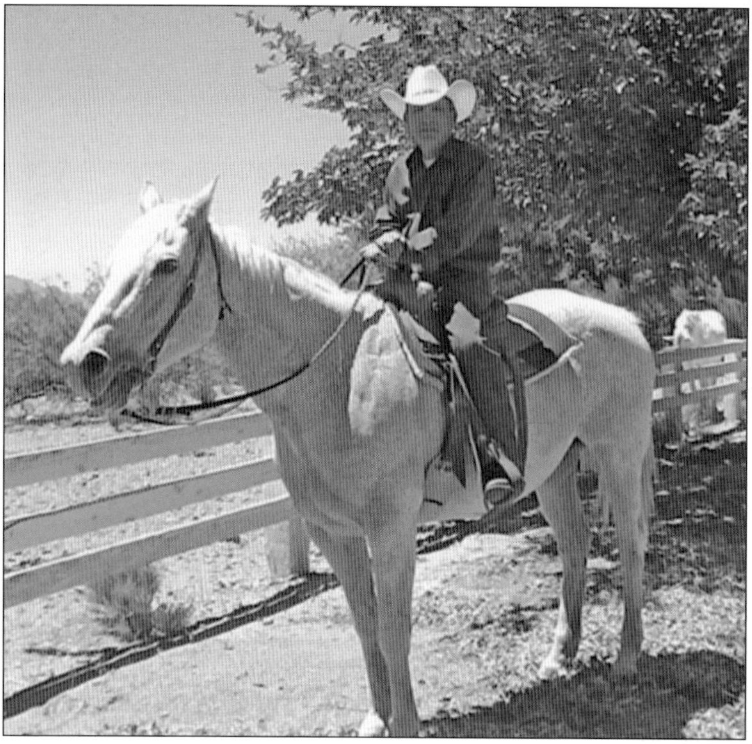

Bill Cavaliere, president of the Cochise County Historical Society and former Hidalgo County sheriff, lectures on Chiricahua Apaches at colleges and historical societies. Retired from 28 years of border law enforcement, he guides history tours, has published numerous articles, and is working on a book. Research takes him all over the Southwest and deep into Mexico. He and his wife, Jill, live on a ranch near Portal. (Tom Davidson.)

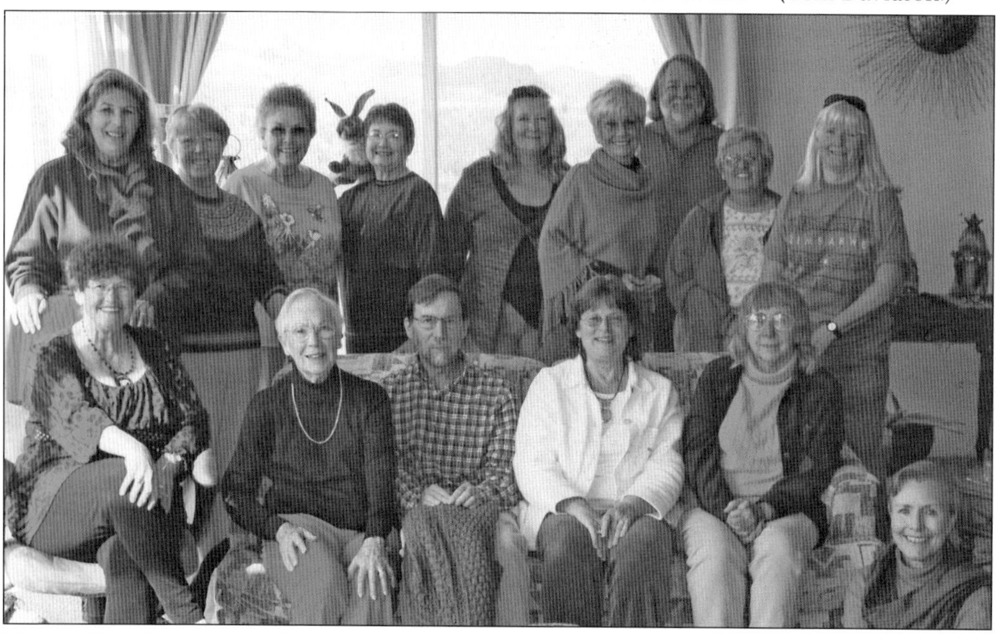

Since 1992, the Circuit Writers have met regularly to get and give feedback on each other's work. They produced four anthologies, and some members are nationally published. In this 2013 photograph are, from left to right, (first row) Alice Newton, Delane Blondeau, Harold Farmer, Vicki Beno, Nancy Farmer, and Gayle Jandrey; (second row) Jane Celaya, Gerry Hernbrode, Zola Stoltz, Carolyn Dearing, Dawn Aerts, Lynn Whiting, Roger McKasson, Pat Esser, and Pat Espenak. (Jack Newton.)

Matthew Caron celebrates his new home with good friends Peter Grill, a builder, designer, and rancher, and Frances Grill, a nurse practitioner and rancher. While earning his degree in renewable natural resources, Matthew worked for the Arizona League of Conservation Voters. He was an interpretive ranger at Saguaro National Park from 2002 until 2014. His smile, courage, and love of nature are an enduring legacy. (Frances Grill.)

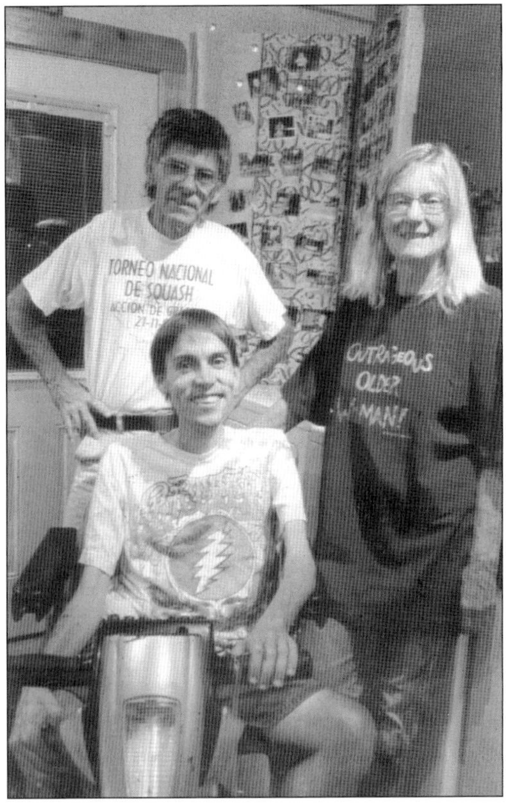

Laura Caron (left), Matthew's sister, stands beside dear friend Marge Fagan, a gifted painter who was an artist in all she did. Caron devotedly cared for her brother as his illness advanced. She gave the same loving attention to Bob and Marge Fagan as they aged, making it possible, with the help of Frances Grill, for them to pass away in their orchard home by the creek. (Barry Fagan.)

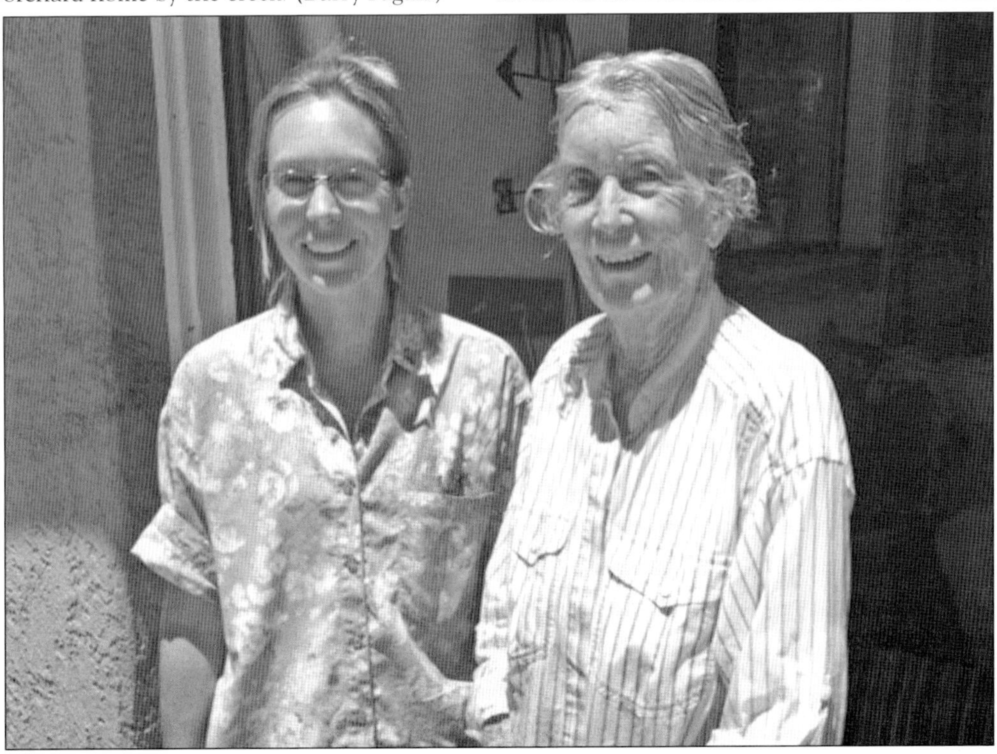

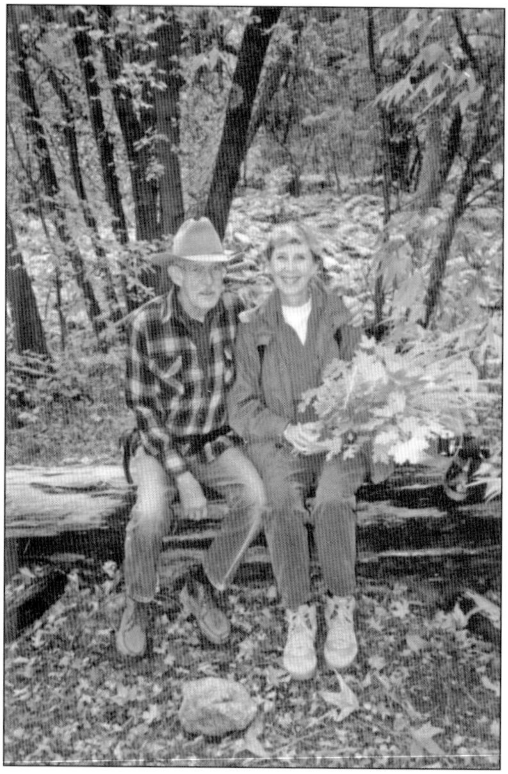

It was here at Maple Camp that, despite a 27-year difference in age, Alden and Karen Hayes decided to marry. They met on an African safari and, over their 14-year marriage, continued to travel, much of it related to Alden's previous career in archaeology. Karen was one of the founders of the Chiricahua Art Gallery in Rodeo, where she exhibited and sold her photography. (Mary Winkler.)

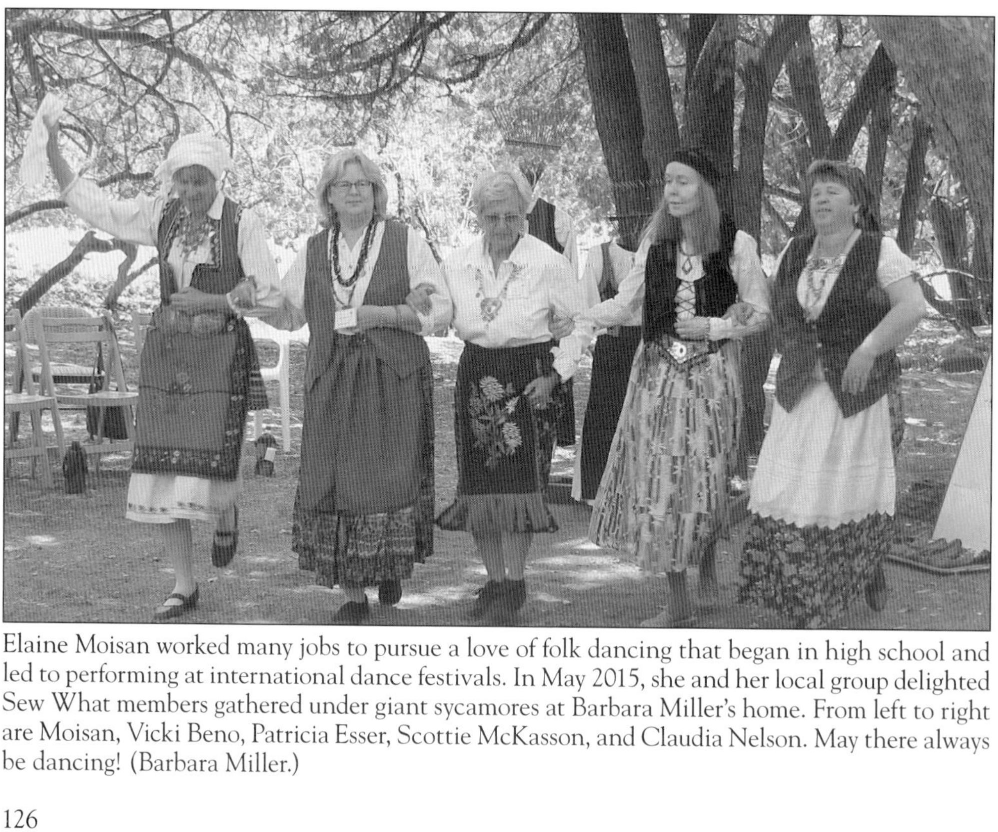

Elaine Moisan worked many jobs to pursue a love of folk dancing that began in high school and led to performing at international dance festivals. In May 2015, she and her local group delighted Sew What members gathered under giant sycamores at Barbara Miller's home. From left to right are Moisan, Vicki Beno, Patricia Esser, Scottie McKasson, and Claudia Nelson. May there always be dancing! (Barbara Miller.)

Bibliography

Blondeau, Delane. "Sew What? Club, Then and Now." *Cochise Quarterly* Vol. 26 No. 2 (Summer 1996): 3–15.

Brown, Wynne, and Reed Peters. *Cave Creek Canyon: Revealing the Heart of Arizona's Chiricahua Mountains*. Rodeo, NM: ECO Publishing, 2015.

Cavaliere, Bill. "Pioneer Greves of the Chiricahua Mountains." *Cochise County Historical Journal* Vol. 43 Issue 02 (Fall/Winter 2013): 1–24.

Chew, Alice. *Our First Year in Arizona 1958–59*. Portal, AZ: Old Goat Press, 2003.

Gomez, M.E. Jr. *The Other Rodeo*. Animas, NM: Classink Publishing, 2009.

Hayes, Alden. *A Portal to Paradise*. Tucson: University of Arizona Press, 1999.

———. *Resting in Paradise: Tales, tall and true, of the Paradise Cemetery and environs*. Portal, AZ: Paradise Cemetery Association, 1999.

——— and Jeanne Williams. "Little School in the Canyon." *Cochise County Historical Journal* Vol. 35 No. 1 (Spring/Summer 2005): 3–62.

Heald, Weldon F. *Sky Island*. New York: Van Nostrand, 1967.

McEwan, Craig. "The Last Fifteen Years of C.S. Fly." *Cochise County Historical Journal* Vol. 43 No. 2 (Fall/Winter 2013): 43–79.

Morrow, R.W. *The Chiricahua Journals*. Tucson, AZ: Chiricahua Press, 2010. Revised and annotated by Michael Morrow.

Murphy, Kimrod. *The Devil Played Hell in Paradise*. Portal, AZ: self-published, 2010.

———. *Lost Trails of an Arizona Game Ranger*. Portal, AZ: self-published, 2005.

Newton, Alice. *Paradise Revealed: Life in the Shadows of the Chiricahua Mountains*. Rodeo, NM: ECO Publishing, 2014.

Opler, Morris. *An Apache Life-Way*. Chicago: University of Chicago Press, 1941.

Otis, Alison, William D. Honey, Thomas C. Hogg, and Kimberly K. Lakin. *The Forest Service and the Civilian Conservation Corps: 1933–1942*. Washington, DC: US Department of Agriculture, Forest Service, 1986.

Patt, Jonathan. "Early Sawmillls of the Chiricahuas." *Cochise County Historical Journal* Vol. 43 No. 2 (Fall/Winter 2013): 29–42.

Stidham, Maryan. "Teacher at Hilltop." *Cochise Quarterly* Vol. 20 No. 2 (Summer 1990): 3–35.